$v = \sqrt{600} = \sqrt{6(100)} =$

THE GOLD STANDARD
DAT QR & RC

Quantitative Reasoning [Math]
and Reading Comprehension [RC]

Book III of IV

Gold Standard Contributors
• 4-Book GS DAT Set •

Brett Ferdinand BSc MD-CM
Karen Barbia BS Arch
Brigitte Bigras BSc MSc DMD
Ibrahima Diouf BSc MSc PhD
Amir Durmic BSc Eng
Adam Segal BSc MSc
Da Xiao BSc DMD
Naomi Epstein BEng
Lisa Ferdinand BA MA
Jeanne Tan Te
Kristin Finkenzeller BSc MD
Heaven Hodges BSc
Sean Pierre BSc MD
James Simenc BS (Math), BA Eng
Jeffrey Cheng BSc
Timothy Ruger MSc PhD
Petra Vernich BA
Alvin Vicente BS Arch

DMD Candidates

E. Jordan Blanche BS
[Harvard School of Dental Medicine]
Stephan Suksong Yoon BA
[Harvard School of Dental Medicine]

$ET = Ek + Ep = 1/2mv2 + mgh$

glutamate recepto
floating bridges
epithelial-mesenc
subatomic particl

Gold Standard Illustrators
• 4-Book GS DAT Set •

Daphne McCormack
Nanjing Design
· Ren Yi, Huang Bin
· Sun Chan, Li Xin
Fabiana Magnosi
Harvie Gallatiera
Rebbe Jurilla BSc MBA

ethics floating bridges
hurricanes subatomic particles
structures brain functions
receptors *Helico bacteria*

RuveneCo

The Gold Standard DAT was built for the US DAT.

 The Gold Standard DAT is identical to Canadian DAT prep except QR and ORG. Also, you must practice soap carving for the complete Canadian DAT.

 The Gold Standard DAT is identical to OAT prep except PAT, which is replaced by OAT Physics; see our Gold Standard OAT book for Physics review and OAT practice test.

Be sure to register at www.DAT-prep.com by clicking on GS DAT Owners and following the directions for Gold Standard DAT Owners. Please Note: benefits are for 1 year from the date of online registration, for the original book owner only and are not transferable; unauthorized access and use outside the Terms of Use posted on DAT-prep.com may result in account deletion; if you are not the original owner, you can purchase your virtual access card separately at DAT-prep.com.

Visit The Gold Standard's Education Center at www.gold-standard.com.

Address all inquiries, comments, or suggestions to the publisher. For Terms of Use go to: www.DAT-prep.com

RuveneCo Inc
Gold Standard Multimedia Education
559-334 Cornelia St
Plattsburgh, NY 12901
E-mail: learn@gold-standard.com
Online at www.gold-standard.com

DAT™ is a registered trademark of the American Dental Association (ADA). OAT™ is a registered trademark of the Association of Schools and Colleges of Optometry (ASCO). The Dental Aptitude Test (DAT) program is conducted by the Canadian Dental Association (CDA). Ruveneco Inc and Gold Standard Multimedia Education are neither sponsored nor endorsed by the ADA, ASCO, CDA, nor any of the degree granting institutions that the authors have attended or are attending. Printed in China.

Table of Contents

EXAM SUMMARY

The Dental Admission Test (DAT) consists of 280 multiple-choice questions distributed across quite a diversity of question types in four tests. The DAT is a computer-based test (CBT). This exam requires approximately five hours to complete - including the optional tutorial, break, and post-test survey. The following are the four subtests of the Dental Admission Test:

1. Survey of the Natural Sciences (NS) – 100 questions; 90 min.
   - General Biology (BIO): 40 questions
   - General Chemistry (CHM): 30 questions
   - Organic Chemistry (ORG): 30 questions

2. Perceptual Ability Test (PAT) - 90 questions; 6 subsections; 60 min.
   - Apertures: 15 questions
   - Orthographic or View Recognition: 15 questions
   - Angle Discrimination: 15 questions
   - Paper Folding: 15 questions
   - Cube Counting: 15 questions
   - 3-D Form Development: 15 questions

3. Reading Comprehension (RC) – 50 questions; 3 reading passages; 60 min.

4. Quantitative Reasoning (QR) – 40 questions; 45 min.
   - Mathematics Problems: 30 questions
   - Applied Mathematics/Word Problems: 10 questions

> You will get six scores from: (1) BIO (2) CHM (3) ORG (4) PAT (5) QR (6) RC.
>
> You will get two additional scores which are summaries:
> (7) Academic Average (AA) = BIO + CHM + ORG + QR + RC
> (8) Total Science (TS) = BIO + CHM + ORG

Common Formula for Acceptance:

GPA + DAT score + Interview = Dental School Admissions*

*Note: In general, Dental School Admissions Committees will only examine the DAT score if the GPA is high enough; they will only admit or interview if the GPA + DAT score is high enough. Some programs also use autobiographical materials and/or references in the admissions process. Different dental schools may emphasize different aspects of your DAT score, for example: PAT, BIO, TS, AA. The average score for any section is approximately 17/30; the average AA for admissions is usually 18-20 depending on the dental school; the AA for admissions to Harvard is around 22-23; the 100th percentile is usually 25 meaning that virtually 100% of the approximately 13 000 students who take the DAT every year have an AA less than 25. Only a handful of students score 25/30. Our two student contributors scored 27/30 (AA).

The DAT is challenging, get organized.

dat-prep.com/dat-study-schedule

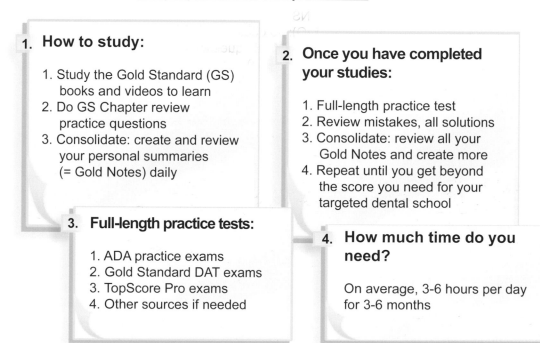

1. How to study:

1. Study the Gold Standard (GS) books and videos to learn
2. Do GS Chapter review practice questions
3. Consolidate: create and review your personal summaries (= Gold Notes) daily

2. Once you have completed your studies:

1. Full-length practice test
2. Review mistakes, all solutions
3. Consolidate: review all your Gold Notes and create more
4. Repeat until you get beyond the score you need for your targeted dental school

3. Full-length practice tests:

1. ADA practice exams
2. Gold Standard DAT exams
3. TopScore Pro exams
4. Other sources if needed

4. How much time do you need?

On average, 3-6 hours per day for 3-6 months

WARNING: Study more or study more efficiently. You choose. The Gold Standard has condensed the content that you require to excel at the DAT. We have had Ivy League dental students involved in the production of the Gold Standard series so that pre-dent students can feel that they have access to the content required to get a score satisfactory at any dental school in the country. To make the content easier to retain, you can also find aspects of the Gold Standard program in other formats such as:

Is there something in the Gold Standard that you did not understand? Don't get frustrated, get online.

dat-prep.com/forum   dat-prep.com/QRchanges-2015

Good luck with your studies!

Gold Standard Team

GOLD STANDARD
MULTIMEDIA EDUCATION

$= P2 + \rho gh2 + 1/2\ \rho v22$

$= P2 + \rho gh2 + 1/2\ \rho v22$

$= P2 + \rho gh2 + 1/2\ \rho v22$

$Ek = 1/2$

$v = \sqrt{600} = \sqrt{6(100)} = 10\sqrt{6} = 24$ m/s

$v = \sqrt{600} = \sqrt{6(100)} = 10\sqrt{6} = 24$ m/s

$Ek = 1/2\ mv2.$

$P1 + \rho gh1 + 1/2\ \rho v12$

$P1 + \rho gh1 + 1/2\ \rho v12$

$Y = \dfrac{(F/A)}{(\Delta l/l)} = \dfrac{F \times l}{A\Delta l}$

$ET = Ek + Ep = 1/2mv2 + mgh$

$0) = \sqrt{2} = 14$m/s

$ET = Ek + Ep = 1/2mv2 + mgh$

$v = \sqrt{2(300) - 2(10}$

$= P2 + \rho gh2 + 1/2\ \rho v22$

$v = \sqrt{2(300) - 2(10)20} = \sqrt{2(100)} = \sqrt{2} = 14$m.

DAT-prep.com

QUANTITATIVE REASONING

QUANT

Memorize	Understand	Not Required
* Basic Rules and Formulas * Conversions and Numerical Relationships * Shortcuts	* Nature of Questions	* Advanced Level Mathematics

DAT-Prep.com

Introduction

Beyond the math, the DAT Quantitative Reasoning section stresses proper time management. The more you practice, the more efficient you will become at solving the problems. Knowing what the test covers and building on speed and confidence are thus crucial to your preparation.

Additional Resources

Free Online Forum

1.1 General Introduction

The DAT Quantitative Reasoning Test is a section of speed and mathematical logic. It consists of 40 multiple-choice items and has a time limit of 45 minutes. This means that you have only about one minute to read, analyze, and solve each problem. Nonetheless, the most effective way to prepare for this section is to understand the question types and the concepts that each question assesses. With constant practice, you can then decide which time-saving methods will make you efficient in completing all 40 questions on time.

In general, the DAT QR is meant to gauge your first year college level knowledge of the following math areas:

- Algebra (equations and expressions, inequalities, exponential notation, absolute value, ratios and proportions, and graphical analysis)

- Numerical Calculations (fractions and decimals, percentages, approximations, and scientific notation)

- Conversions (temperature, time, weight, and distance)

- Probability and Statistics

- Geometry

- Trigonometry

- Applied Mathematics (Word) Problems

1.2 Format of the Test

Preparing for the DAT Quantitative Reasoning should also entail familiarizing yourself with the actual set-up of this section: One question is presented at a time and a pop-up on-screen calculator is provided with a click of a button.

Quantitative Reasoning

Simplify (-4) (-8).

A. -32

B. 32

C. -12

D. 12

E. -4

Click on 'Calculator' button to display a calculator.

Click on the 'Next' button to continue.

Calculator

PREVIOUS   NEXT   END

Figure QR.1.1: The Quantitative Reasoning Test Page. The calculator button is provided on every page of the QR section.

The calculator is very basic and the only functions that will be available are addition, subtraction, division, multiplication, the positive/negative (+/-) sign, a period or point sign, the square root key, and 1/x key. These can be operated by using the mouse – not the keyboard. Upon request, you will be given a permanent marker and two laminated sheets on which you can write your calculations manually.

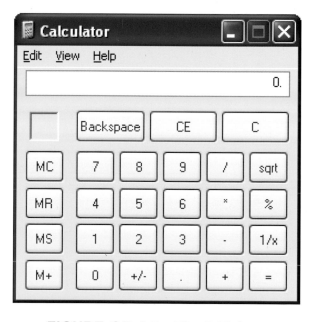

FIGURE QR.1.2: The DAT On-screen Calculator.

1.3 Pending Changes in the DAT QR

Before we delve into the important tips and strategies, you might want to note that the QR section will undergo some changes effective 2015. The following areas will be eliminated:

- Numerical Calculations
- Conversions
- Geometry
- Trigonometry

On the other hand, probability and statistics, as well as data analysis and interpretation, will be retained as critical thinking items but with the following additions:

- Data Sufficiency
- Quantitative Comparison

While the content of this book's edition focuses on the pre-2015 coverage, please take note that the new critical thinking questions will be pretested starting 2013. The results of these trial questions will not be reflected on the candidates' actual QR scores. If you have proof of having purchased this book brand new in 2015, then please email learn@gold-standard.com to access updates online for free.

1.4 How to Do Well in the QR Section

Speed and confidence in solving each problem is central in succeeding in this section. Undoubtedly, the best preparation route is to study the basics and practice with as many questions as you can under timed conditions.

Learn and review the required operations for each of the areas specified by the ADA. Thereafter, make sure that you do all of the chapter review questions plus realistic practice tests, i.e., those which reflect the actual exam.

The ADA offers the *DAT Sample Test Items* as a free download in pdf format and they offer a paid full-length practice test. Taking these tests will give you a clearer idea of the types of questions presented in the real DAT. However, for a simulation of the computer based test (CBT), the Gold Standard program at DAT-prep.com is a good alternative. Top Score Pro is another option. Regardless, you should keep three important things in mind with your QR preparation: Practice makes perfect, specific tips apply to specific topics, and logic does work with math.

1.4.1 Practice Makes Perfect

There are two main goals that you should aim to achieve as you proceed with your practice tests.

1. **Be able to instantly recognize and categorize the area of math involved in a question**

By quickly identifying the type of math problem presented, you can mentally prepare yourself for the different strategies used to solve the question. This gives you a clear direction on how to approach a problem, allowing you to be more time-efficient. When you do your practice tests, you should thus try to adopt the following techniques in order to hone your proficiency in dealing with quantitative items:

- **Ready Formulas**

If you know your squares, cubes, roots, pi, conversions between units, formulas for the area of a triangle, circle, sphere, cylinder and so forth, you would know which questions you can solve with the least amount of time. By recognizing possible relationships between numbers, you can easily determine the appropriate mathematical formula (and shortcuts!) to use.

One of the typical questions that show up in the DAT simply asks for the equivalent temperature value of Fahrenheit to Celsius. You can solve this almost instantly if you know the appropriate conversion formula!

- **Guesstimating**

This strategy is most useful if the values in the answer choices are very spread out yet the question is fairly straightforward. Most questions on the DAT QR will usually have one option that is blatantly wrong. You can then guesstimate (estimate by guesswork) or round off the numbers when doing the calculations. For example, if the question asks you to add 2,301 to 1,203, you could guesstimate and round the given numbers to 2,300 + 1,200 = 3,500. This is much easier to do mentally.

If you are unsure of your choice, the DAT allows you to mark an answer so you can come back to it later if you have spare minutes left.

- **Working Backwards**

If you find yourself stuck on a question, you can work backwards from the answer choices by plugging in an option to see if it makes sense. Starting with the middle value would help you decide quickly whether the answer choice is too small or too large.

For questions that frequently slow you down, make sure that you carefully go through the solutions in the answer key. Identify where you fall short. You might just be missing a shortcut. Repeat with more exercises until you are able to master the required manipulations. Remember that the main point of these numerous practices is for you to learn how to pace yourself so that you finish all the questions the first time through with about ten minutes left to spare. This gives you time to go back to questions you skipped earlier.

Moreover, when you practice regularly, you tend to become comfortable with the various strategies. This will also help you identify the areas on which you need further improvement.

2. Become familiar with the tools provided in the actual exam

As already mentioned, the actual DAT provides an on-screen calculator in the QR section. You are not permitted to use anything else except the laminated sheets and marker-pens at the test center.

You should be prepared to deal with possible setbacks. Because the calculator can only be operated by the mouse, this should serve only as a last resort. Using as much mental math as you can is beneficial in order to save time. Likewise, practice writing quickly and neatly as the laminated sheets may be difficult to erase.

1.4.2 Specific Tips Apply to Specific Topics

The next chapters will discuss each of the essential topics listed in the following table. However, this quick "must-know" list can serve as your constant reminder to keep you confidently on track with your QR preparation.

Math Area	Must Know Topics or Skills	Tips
Numbers and Operations	♠ Converting square roots to their exponential forms ♠ Multiplying numbers in scientific notation ♠ Converting units of time (hours to seconds), distance (mi to km, in to cm), temperature (^{0}F to ^{0}C), weight (lbs to kg)	♠ Be comfortable solving without a calculator. ♠ Be on the lookout for common terms that can be cancelled out. ♠ Pay attention to the units given in the problems and the answer choices. ♠ When comparing fractions, convert the denominators to the same value.
Algebra	♠ Solving equations ♠ Solving inequalities and differentiating between "and" or "or"	♠ Understanding the rules in solving algebraic equations is important in solving problems involving angles and triangles.
Geometry	♠ Converting between angles and radians (there are 180 degrees in 1 pi) ♠ 30-60-90 and 45-45-90 triangles ♠ Areas of circle, sphere, triangle, cylinder ♠ Volumes of cylinder, cube, sphere ♠ Identity circle ♠ Sum of interior angles in a polygon: (N-2) x 180 ♠ Graph of a line: y = mx + b (know where the line intercepts the y-axis; know how to find a line that is parallel or perpendicular to any given line) ♠ Circumference, arc length, area of a sector ♠ Distance and midpoint between two points on a coordinate plane	♠ Remember that squares can be bisected to form two 45-45-90 triangles. ♠ Certain polygons such as hexagons are actually made up of smaller triangles. ♠ In dealing with identity circle, remember that any angle over 360 is simply the same as (n-360) where *n* is the angle. ♠ A common question type relating to circumference, arc length, and area of a sector requires solving for the distance covered by a revolution of a wheel.

Trigonometry	♠ Knowing at what points the graph is undefined or 0 ♠ Trigonmetric identities ♠ Remember soh-cah-toa ♠ sin, tan, cos graphs	♠ Problems dealing with distance and angle from a flagpole or some object usually deal with sin/cos/tan. ♠ Similar polygons can be solved through ratios.
Word Problems	♠ Distance = velocity x time ♠ Average velocity = $\dfrac{\text{total distance}}{\text{total time}}$ (remember you can always re-arrange this equation to find what you need) ♠ Combined work problems: 1/time it takes one person to do the job + 1/time it takes for another person to do the same job = 1/total time it takes to do the job ♠ Simple vs. compound interest	♠ A common question type in this area involves two vehicles moving towards each other or starting at the same point. ♠ Remember that compound interest generates more interest than a simple interest given the same period of time.

1.4.3 Logic Works with Math

Do not feel intimidated when you are confronted with a seemingly unfamiliar problem. Reread the question and understand what is given and what is really asked. Sometimes, the answers are obvious and all you need is to simply use some logical reasoning. With word problems, thinking critically when solving is especially important because the answer is usually not just straight plug-and-chug values.

> **NOTE**
>
> In the succeeding pages, we will review each area specified by the ADA for the Quantitative Reasoning section, as well as techniques, for the respective topics. Each chapter comes with a set of exercises that will help reinforce your knowledge and skills.

Memorize	Understand	Importance
* Properties of Real Numbers * Order of Operations * Rules on Zero * Important Fraction-Decimal Conversions * Properties of Exponents	* Integer, Rational, and Real Numbers * Basic Operations and Definitions * Fractions, Mixed Numbers, Decimals and Percentages * Exponent Manipulations * Ratios and Proportions	**7 to 9 out of the 40 QR** questions on the DAT are based on content from this chapter (in our estimation). * This will change in 2015.

DAT-Prep.com

Introduction ▮▮▮▮

Study this chapter carefully…

Whether you notice it or not, nearly every problem you will come across in the DAT Quantitative Reasoning section will require you to perform some basic arithmetic. Becoming extremely familiar with the material and key concepts in this chapter will provide the foundation for your overall success.

Time is of the essence on the DAT, so being able to breeze through the basics is crucial, and if you put in the effort now, you will surely thank yourself later.

Let's get started!

Additional Resources

Free Online Forum

2.1 Integers, Rational Numbers, and the Number Line

2.1.1 Integers

Integers are whole numbers without any decimal or fractional portions. They can be any number from negative to positive infinity including zero.

> **EXAMPLES**   –2, –1, 0, 1, 2, 3 etc.

2.1.2 Rational Numbers

Rational numbers are numbers that can be written as fractions of integers. "Rational" even contains the word "ratio" in it, so if you like, you can simply remember that these are ratio numbers.

EXAMPLES

$$\frac{1}{2}$$

$$-5 \left(-5 = \frac{-5}{1} \right)$$

$$1.875 \left(1.875 = \frac{15}{8} \right)$$

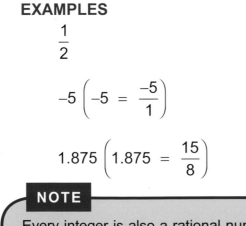

NOTE

Every integer is also a rational number, but not every rational number is an integer. You can write them as fractions simply by dividing by 1.

A large portion of the problems you will encounter on the Quantitative Reasoning section of the DAT will require you to deal only with rational numbers. Make sure you are extra careful when ratios and fractions are involved because they are notorious for causing mistakes (see section 2.4).

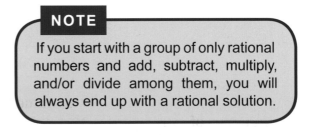

NOTE

If you start with a group of only rational numbers and add, subtract, multiply, and/or divide among them, you will always end up with a rational solution.

Irrational numbers are numbers that cannot be written as fractions of integers. Irrational numbers are normally numbers that have a decimal number that goes on forever with no repeating digits.

EXAMPLES

$$\sqrt{2} = 1.4142135623730950...$$

$$Pi = \pi = 3.14159265358979...$$

2.1.3 Real Numbers and the Number Line

Real numbers are all numbers that can be represented on the number line. These include both rational and irrational numbers.

EXAMPLES

$$0, -\frac{1}{3}, \sqrt{2}, \text{ etc.}$$

The **number line** is an infinite straight line on which every point corresponds to a real number. As you move up the line to the right, the numbers get larger, and down the line to the left, the numbers get smaller.

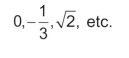

2.2 Basic Arithmetic

2.2.1 Basic Operations

An **operation** is a procedure that is applied to numbers. The fundamental operations of arithmetic are addition, subtraction, multiplication, and division.

A **sum** is the number obtained by adding numbers.

EXAMPLE

The sum of 7 and 2 is 9 since $2 + 7 = 9$.

A **difference** is the number obtained by subtracting numbers.

EXAMPLE

In the equation 7 − 2 = 5, 5 is the difference of 7 and 2.

A **product** is the number obtained by multiplying numbers.

EXAMPLE

The product of 7 and 2 is 14

since $7 \times 2 = 14$.

A **quotient** is the number obtained by dividing numbers.

EXAMPLE

In the equation 8 ÷ 2 = 4, 4 is the quotient of 8 and 2.

Unlike a sum or a product, difference and quotient can result in different numbers depending on the order of the numbers in the expression:

10 − 2 = 8 while 2 − 10 = −8
20 ÷ 5 = 4 while 5 ÷ 20 = 0.25

Now, remember that questions on the DAT Quantitative Reasoning test can involve positive and negative numbers. The sum and difference of positive numbers are obtained by simple addition and subtraction, respectively. The same is true when adding negative numbers, except that the sum takes on the negative sign.

EXAMPLES

(-3) + (-9) = -12

(-5) + (-12) + (-44) = -61

On the other hand, when adding two integers with unlike signs, you need to ignore the signs first, and then subtract the smaller number from the larger number. Then follow the sign of the larger number in the result.

EXAMPLES

(-6) + 5 = 6 − 5 = -1

7 + (-10) = 10 − 7 = - 3

When subtracting two numbers of unlike signs, start by changing the minus sign into its reciprocal, which is the plus sign. Next reverse the sign of the second number. This will make the signs of the two integers the same. Now follow the rules for adding integers with like signs.

EXAMPLES

(-6) − 5 = (-6) + (-5) = -11

7 − (-10) = 7 + 10 = 17

Multiplication and division of integers are governed by the same rules: If the numbers have like signs, the product or quotient is positive. If the numbers have unlike signs, the answer is negative.

EXAMPLES

$$5 \times 6 = 30$$
$$-5 \times -3 = 15$$
$$81 \div 9 = 9$$
$$-20 \div -4 = 5$$
$$7 \times -4 = -28$$
$$-9 \times 6 = -54$$
$$-15 \div 3 = -5$$
$$16 \div -2 = -8$$

An **expression** is a grouping of numbers and mathematical operations.

EXAMPLE

$2 + (3 \times 4) \times 5$ is a mathematical expression.

An **equation** is a mathematical sentence consisting of two expressions joined by an equals sign. When evaluated properly, the two expressions must be equivalent.

EXAMPLE

$2 \times (1+3) = \dfrac{16}{2}$ is an equation since the expressions on both sides of the equals sign are equivalent to 8.

2.2.2 Properties of the Real Numbers

Whenever you are working within the real numbers (which you always will be on the DAT), these properties hold true. It isn't necessary to memorize the name of each property, but you must be able to apply them all.

Symmetric Property of Equality: The right and left hand sides of an equation are interchangeable, so if $a = b$, then $b = a$.

Transitive Property of Equality: If $a = b$ and $b = c$, then $a = c$. This means that if you have two numbers both equal to one other number, those two numbers are also equal.

Commutative Property of Addition: When adding numbers, switching the position of the numbers will not change the outcome, so $a + b = b + a$.

Associative Property of Addition: When adding more than two numbers, it doesn't matter what order you do the addition in, so $(a + b) + c = a + (b + c)$.

Commutative Property of Multiplication: When multiplying numbers, switching the position of the numbers will not change the outcome, so $a \times b = b \times a$.

Associative Property of Multiplication: When multiplying more than two numbers, it doesn't matter what order you do the multiplication in, so $(a \times b) \times c = a \times (b \times c)$.

Identity Property of Addition: When zero is added or subtracted to any number, the answer is the number itself, so $10b - 0 = 10b$.

Identity Property of Multiplication: When a number is multiplied or divided by 1, the answer is the number itself, so $6a \times 1 = 6a$.

Distributive Property of Multiplication: When multiplying a factor on a group of numbers that are being added or subtracted, the factor may be distributed by multiplying it by each number in the group, so $a(b - c) = ab - ac$.

> Subtraction and division do not follow associative laws.

2.2.3 Order of Operations

Knowing the order of operations is fundamental to evaluating numerical expressions. If you follow it properly, you will always come up with the correct answer! Here it is in list form, to be followed from the top down:

Parentheses
Exponents (including square roots)
Multiplication
Division
Addition
Subtraction

This forms the simple acronym **PEMDAS**, which is a great way to keep the operations straight. Alternatively, some people find it easier to remember the phrase "**P**lease **E**xcuse **M**y **D**ear **A**unt **S**ally."

If you don't like either of these techniques, feel free to come up with your own. It's important to have this down because, as simple as it may seem, being able to carry out the order of operations quickly is crucial to achieving a high score in Quantitative Reasoning.

NOTE

- Multiplication and division have the same rank. It is generally recommended to do them in order from left to right as they appear in the expression, but you can also do them in whatever order that makes most sense to you.

- The same goes for addition and subtraction. Execute them from left to right, or in the order that feels most comfortable.

- When you encounter nested parentheses, evaluate the innermost ones first then work your way outward.

Using PEMDAS, let's evaluate this expression composed only of integers.

$$2^2 + [(3 + 2) \times 2 - 9]$$

First, evaluate the expression contained in the inner set of parentheses.

$$= 2^2 + [(5) \times 2 - 9]$$

You can then choose to strictly follow the PEMDAS order by evaluating the exponent next. Alternately, you can perform the operations within the square brackets, working your way outward, for a more organized procedure as follows:

First, perform the multiplication.

$$= 2^2 + (10 - 9)$$

Then, perform the subtraction.

$$= 2^2 + 1$$

Now evaluate the exponent.

$$= 4 + 1$$

Finally, evaluate the remaining expression.

$$= 5$$

2.3 Rules on Zero

2.3.1 Addition and Subtraction with Zero

Zero is a unique number, and it has special properties when it comes to operations.

Zero is known as the **additive identity** of the real numbers since whenever it is added to (or subtracted from) a number, that number does not change.

Let's examine a simple expression.

$$(3 + 2) - 4$$

We can add or subtract zero anywhere within the expression and the value will not change:

$$(3 - 0 + 2) - 4 + 0$$
$$= (3 + 2) - 4$$

The addition or subtraction of the two zeros has no effect whatsoever on the outcome.

2.3.2 Multiplication and Division with Zero

When adding zero in an expression, it is easy to come up with a practical picture of what the operation represents; you begin with a collection of things and add zero more things to them. When multiplying and dividing with zero, however, such a conceptualization is more difficult. The idea of using zero in this manner is far more abstract.

Fortunately, you don't need to wrestle with trying to picture what multiplication or division with zero looks like. You can simply remember these easy rules:

Multiplying by Zero: The result of multiplying any quantity by zero is *always* equal to zero.

Remember that by the commutative property of multiplication, $a \times b = b \times a$, so if we let $b = 0$, then we have $a \times 0 = 0 \times a$. This means that instead of trying to imagine multiplying a number by zero, you can reverse the thought and consider multiplying zero by a number instead. This second statement is more natural to visualize. You start with nothing, and then no matter how many times you duplicate that nothing, you still end up with nothing.

EXAMPLE

$$3 \times 0 = 0$$
$$123.79 \times 0 = 0$$
$$\left[1.2 + \left(37 - \sqrt{5} \right) \times 2.331 \right] \times 0 = 0$$

In the last example, there is no need to go through the order of operations and evaluate the expression inside the parentheses. Because you can see immediately that the entire parenthetical expression is being multiplied by zero, you know that the end result will be zero.

Zero Divided by a Number: The result of dividing zero by any quantity is *always* equal to zero. As with multiplication by zero, if you start with nothing and then take a portion of that nothing, you still end up with nothing.

EXAMPLE

$$0 \div 3 = 0$$
$$0 \div 123.79 = 0$$
$$0 \div \left[1.2 + \left(37 - \sqrt{5} \right) \times 2.331 \right] = 0$$

Just like with the multiplication by zero example, you do not need to evaluate the parenthetical expression in order to know that the solution is zero. Especially in the time-constrained setting of the DAT, you should avoid doing such a needless calculation.

Dividing by Zero: Dividing any nonzero quantity by zero results in a solution that is not defined and is therefore undefined.

You should never have to deal with this case on the DAT. If you end up with division by zero in a calculation, you have probably made a mistake. Similarly, you should never end up with zero divided by zero (an undefined quantity). If you do, you should go back and check your work.

2.4 Fractions, Decimals, and Percentages

2.4.1 Fractions

A **fraction** is the quotient of two numbers. It represents parts of a whole and may be seen as a proportion. The number on top is the *numerator*, and the one on the bottom is the *denominator*. Another way of understanding fractions is to consider one as the number of parts present (*numerator*) and the amount of parts it takes to make up a whole (*denominator*). These values can be divided by each other, and this fraction is the quotient.

EXAMPLE

$$\frac{2}{7}$$

In this fraction, 2 is the numerator and 7, the denominator.

Remember, all rational numbers (including integers) can be written as fractions.

2.4.2 Manipulating Fractions

A. Fraction Multiplication

To multiply fractions, simply multiply the numerators together (this will be the new numerator) and then multiply the denominators together (this will be the new denominator).

EXAMPLE

$$\frac{2}{3} \times \frac{4}{5}$$

Multiply the numerators and denominators separately.

$$= \frac{(2 \times 4)}{(3 \times 5)}$$

$$= \frac{8}{15}$$

B. Fraction Division

A **reciprocal** is the number obtained by switching the numerator with the denominator of a fraction. For example, the reciprocal of $\frac{2}{3}$ is $\frac{3}{2}$.

To divide a number by a fraction, multiply that number by the reciprocal of the fraction.

EXAMPLE

$$3 \div \frac{4}{3}$$

Switch the numerator and the denominator in the fraction and multiply. Remember that 3 is really 3 ÷ 1 so the new denominator would be the product of 1 × 4.

$$= \frac{3}{1} \times \frac{3}{4}$$

$$= \frac{9}{4}$$

C. Fraction Addition and Subtraction

With fractions, addition and subtraction are not so easy. You can only add or subtract fractions from each other if they have the same denominator. If they satisfy this condition, then to add or subtract, you do so with the numerators only and leave the denominator unchanged.

EXAMPLE

$$\frac{1}{5} + \frac{3}{5}$$

Both fractions have the same denominator, so add the numerators.

$$= \frac{1 + 3}{5}$$

$$= \frac{4}{5}$$

EXAMPLE

$$\frac{3}{5} - \frac{1}{5}$$

Both fractions have the same denominator, so subtract the numerators.

$$= \frac{3 - 1}{5}$$

$$= \frac{2}{5}$$

What if the denominators of two fractions you are adding or subtracting are not the same? In this case, you must find the Lowest Common Denominator (LCD), the smallest number that is divisible by both of the original denominators.

Ideally, you would like to find the smallest common denominator because smaller numbers in fractions are always easier to work with. But this is not always easy to do, and usually it isn't worth the extra time it will take to do the necessary calculation. The simplest way to find a common denominator is to multiply each fraction by a new fraction in which the numerator and denominator are both the same as the denominator of the other fraction.

EXAMPLE

$$\frac{2}{3} + \frac{2}{7}$$

Don't be confused by the fact that the numerators are the same. We still need to find a common denominator because the denominators are different.

$$= \left(\frac{2}{3} \times \frac{7}{7}\right) + \left(\frac{2}{7} \times \frac{3}{3}\right)$$

$$= \frac{14}{21} + \frac{6}{21}$$

Now that we have the same denominator, we can add the numerators.

$$= \frac{20}{21}$$

This method of finding common denominators utilizes the fact that any number multiplied by 1 is still the same number. The new fractions we introduce are always made of equivalent numerators and denominators, which make the fraction equal to 1, so the values of the original fractions do not change.

D. Comparing Fractions

Another method with which you should be familiar when manipulating fractions is comparing their values (i.e., which of the given fractions is greater than or lesser than the other) when they have different denominators. We will show you three ways to do this.

When you are confronted with only two fractions, finding their common denominator makes the task of evaluating the values easier.

1. Similar to the preceding discussion on adding or subtracting fractions that have different denominators, the fastest way to come up with a common denominator is to multiply both the numerator and denominator of each fraction by the other's denominator.

Let's say you are given the two fractions:

$$\frac{4}{5} \text{ and } \frac{3}{7}$$

Multiply the first fraction by 7 over 7 and the second fraction by 5 over 5. (The 7 comes from the fraction $\frac{3}{7}$ while 5 from $\frac{4}{5}$.)

$$\frac{4}{5} \times \frac{7}{7} = \frac{28}{35}$$

$$\frac{3}{7} \times \frac{5}{5} = \frac{15}{35}$$

With both fractions having 35 as the common denominator, you can now clearly see that 28 must be greater than

15. Therefore, $\dfrac{4}{5}$ is greater than $\dfrac{3}{7}$.

2. Another way to go about this is through cross-multiplication. Using the same fractions as examples, you first multiply the numerator of the first fraction by the denominator of the second fraction. The product will then serve as the new numerator of the first fraction.

$$\dfrac{4}{5} \searrow \dfrac{3}{7} \Rightarrow 4 \times 7 = 28$$

Next, multiply the denominators of the two fractions. The product will now serve as the new denominator of the first fraction.

$$\dfrac{4}{5} \rightarrow \dfrac{3}{7} \Rightarrow 5 \times 7 = 35$$

The resulting new fraction would be $\dfrac{28}{35}$.

Now, let's work on the second fraction. To get its new numerator, this time, multiply the numerator of the second fraction by the denominator of the first fraction. Then multiply the denominators of both fractions.

$$\dfrac{4}{5} \swarrow \dfrac{3}{7} \Rightarrow 3 \times 5 = 15$$

$$\dfrac{4}{5} \leftarrow \dfrac{3}{7} \Rightarrow 7 \times 5 = 35$$

The second fraction will now become $\dfrac{15}{35}$. Thus comparing the first and second fractions, we get the same result as we had in the first method.

Because $\dfrac{28}{35}$ is greater than $\dfrac{15}{35}$, therefore $\dfrac{4}{5}$ is greater than $\dfrac{3}{7}$.

Both procedures follow the same basic principles and prove to be efficient when dealing with two given fractions. But what if you were given three or four fractions?

3. A much simpler way is to convert each fraction to decimals, and then compare the decimals. All you have to do is divide the numerator of the fraction by its own denominator. For big numbers, you can use the calculator provided during the exam. For smaller ones, you could learn to do the calculations in your head or on a board. With a little practice, you can actually train your brain to work fast with arithmetic.

Now let's say a third fraction is introduced to our previous examples: $\dfrac{4}{5}$, $\dfrac{3}{7}$, $\dfrac{9}{13}$. Working on the first fraction, simply divide 4 by 5; on the second fraction, 3 by 7; and on the last, 9 by 13.

$$\frac{4}{5} = 4 \div 5 = 0.8$$

$$\frac{3}{7} = 3 \div 7 = 0.43$$

$$\frac{9}{13} = 9 \div 13 = 0.69$$

Comparing the three fractions in their decimal forms, 0.43 ($\frac{3}{7}$) is the smallest, 0.69 ($\frac{9}{13}$) is the next, and the largest is 0.8 ($\frac{4}{5}$).

E. Reduction and Cancelling

To make calculations easier, you should always avoid working with unnecessarily large numbers. To reduce fractions, you can cancel out any common factors in the numerator and denominator.

EXAMPLE

$$\frac{20}{28}$$

First, factor both the numerator and denominator.

$$= \frac{(4 \times 5)}{(4 \times 7)}$$

Since both have a factor of four, we can cancel.

$$= \frac{5}{7}$$

When multiplying fractions, it is possible to cross-cancel like factors before performing the operation. If there are any common factors between the numerator of the first fraction and the denominator of the second fraction, you can cancel them. Likewise, if there are common factors between the numerator of the second and the denominator of the first, cancel them as well.

EXAMPLE

$$\frac{5}{9} \times \frac{6}{25}$$

First, factor the numerators and denominators.

$$= \frac{5}{(3 \times 3)} \times \frac{(2 \times 3)}{(5 \times 5)}$$

Now, we see that we can cross-cancel 5s and 3s.

$$= \frac{1}{3} \times \frac{2}{5}$$

$$= \frac{2}{15}$$

F. Mixed Numbers

You may encounter numbers on the DAT that have both an integer part and a fraction part. These are called mixed numbers.

EXAMPLE

$$3\frac{1}{2}$$

Mixed numbers should be thought of as addition between the integer and the fraction.

EXAMPLE

$$3\frac{1}{2} = 3 + \frac{1}{2}$$

Now in order to convert a mixed number back to a fraction, all you have to do is consider the integer to be the fraction of itself over 1 and perform fraction addition.

EXAMPLE

$$3\frac{1}{2}$$

$$= \frac{3}{1} + \frac{1}{2}$$

Obtain a common denominator.

$$= \left(\frac{3}{1}\right)\left(\frac{2}{2}\right) + \frac{1}{2}$$

$$= \frac{6}{2} + \frac{1}{2}$$

$$= \frac{7}{2}$$

To add or subtract mixed numbers, you can deal with the integer and fraction portions separately.

EXAMPLE

$$3\frac{1}{2} - 2\frac{1}{2}$$

$$= (3-2) + \left(\frac{1}{2} - \frac{1}{2}\right)$$

$$= 1$$

NOTE

To convert a mixed number to a fraction, keep the denominator of the fraction while multiplying the integer part of the mixed number by the denominator. Then add to the numerator of the mixed number.

EXAMPLE

$$6\frac{2}{5} = (6 \times 5) + \frac{2}{5} = 30 + \frac{2}{5} = \frac{32}{5}$$

2.4.3 Decimals and Percentages

There are two other ways to represent non-integer numbers that you will encounter on the DAT: As decimals and as percentages.

A. Decimals

Decimal numbers can be recognized by the decimal point (a period) that they contain. Whatever digits are to the left of the decimal point represent a whole number, the integer portion of the number. The digits to the right of the decimal point are the decimal portion.

EXAMPLE

12.34

The integer portion of the number is 12, and .34 is the fractional portion.

The value of the decimal portion of a number operates on a place-value system just like the integer portion. The first digit to the right of the decimal point is the number of tenths (1/10 is one tenth), two digits over is the number of hundredths (1/100 is one hundredth), three digits over is the number of thousandths, then ten-thousandths, etc.

For example, in the decimal 0.56789:
- the 5 is in the tenths position;
- the 6 is in the hundredths position;
- the 7 is in the thousandths position;
- the 8 is in the ten thousandths position;
- the 9 is in the one hundred thousandths position.

Thus, to convert a decimal into a fraction, just drop the decimal point and divide by the power of ten of the last decimal digit. To convert a fraction to a decimal, simply perform the long division of the numerator divided by the denominator.

EXAMPLE

$$0.34 = \frac{34}{100}$$

B. Operations with Decimals

Addition and Subtraction: Adding and subtracting decimals is the same as with integers. The only difference is that you need to take care to line up the decimal point properly. Just like with integers, you should only add or subtract digits in the same place with each other.

EXAMPLE

Add 3.33 to 23.6.

$$\begin{array}{r} 23.60 \\ + 03.33 \\ \hline \end{array}$$

Notice how we have carried the decimal point down in the same place. Also, to illustrate the addition more clearly, we have added zeros to hold the empty places. Now perform the addition as if there were no decimal points.

$$
\begin{array}{r}
23.60 \\
+\ 03.33 \\
\hline
26.93
\end{array}
$$

Multiplication: You can multiply numbers with decimals just as you would with integers, but placing the decimal point in the solution is a little tricky. To decide where the decimal point goes, first count the number of significant digits after the decimal points in each of the numbers being multiplied. Add these numbers together to obtain the total number of decimal digits. Now, count that number of digits in from the right of the solution and place the decimal point in front of the number at which you end.

EXAMPLE

Multiply 3.03 by 1.2.

$$
\begin{array}{r}
3.03 \\
\times\ 1.20 \\
\hline
\end{array}
$$

We have written in a zero as a placeholder at the end of the second number, but be careful not to include it in your decimal count. Only count up to the final nonzero digit in each number (the 0 in the first number counts because it comes before the 3). Thus our decimal digit count is $2 + 1 = 3$, and we will place our decimal point in the solution 3 digits in from the right; but first, perform the multiplication while ignoring the decimal.

$$
\begin{array}{r}
3.03 \\
\times\ 1.20 \\
\hline
606 \\
+\ 3030 \\
\hline
3636
\end{array}
$$

Now, insert the decimal point to obtain the final solution.

$$
= 3.636
$$

When counting significant digits, remember to consider the following:

1. all zeros between nonzero digits

   EXAMPLE

   $0.45078 \rightarrow 5$ significant figures

2. all zeros in front of a nonzero number

   EXAMPLE

   $0.0056 \rightarrow 4$ significant figures

3. ignore all zeros after a nonzero digit

   EXAMPLE

   $0.2500 \rightarrow 2$ significant figures

> **NOTE**
>
> In DAT Chemistry this last rule is not so simple because in science labs, significant figures (= significant digits = sig figs) represent the accuracy of measurement. This is further discussed in the Appendix to QR A.4 and General Chemistry Chapter 12 in the Gold Standard DAT.

Division: We can use our knowledge of the equivalence of fractions to change a decimal division problem into a more familiar integer division problem. Simply multiply each number by the power of ten corresponding to the smallest significant digit out of the two decimal numbers being divided, and then, perform the division with the integers obtained. {For more information regarding significant digits, see the QR Appendix or General Chemistry Chapter 12.}

This operation is acceptable because it amounts to multiplying a fraction by 1.

EXAMPLE

Divide 4.4 by 1.6

$$\frac{4.4}{1.6}$$

Since the smallest decimal digit in either number is in the tenth place, we multiply the top and bottom by 10.

$$= \frac{4.4}{1.6} \times \frac{10}{10}$$

$$= \frac{44}{16}$$

$$= \frac{11}{4}$$

If you like, you can convert this back to a decimal.

$$= 2.75$$

Rounding Decimals: Rounding decimals to the nearest place value is just like rounding an integer. Look at the digit one place further to the right of the place to which you are rounding. If that digit is 5 or greater, add 1 to the previous digit and drop all the subsequent digits. If it is 4 or less, leave the previous digit alone and simply drop the subsequent digits.

Consider the number 5.3618:

(a) Round to the nearest tenth.

$$= 5.4$$

Since the digit after the tenth place is a 6, we add 1 tenth and drop every digit after the tenth place.

(b) Round to the nearest hundredth.

$$= 5.36$$

Since the digit after the hundredth place is a 1, we do not change any digits. Just drop every digit after the hundredth place.

Fraction-Decimal Conversions to Know: Having these common conversions between fractions and decimals memorized will help you save valuable time on the test.

Fraction	Decimal
1/2	.5
1/3	~ .33
1/4	.25
1/5	.2
1/6	~.167
1/8	.125
1/10	.1

C. Percentages

Percentages are used to describe fractions of other numbers. One percent (written 1%) simply means 1 hundredth. This is easy to remember since "percent" can literally be broken down into "per" and "cent", and we all know that one cent is a hundredth of a dollar.

We can use this conversion to hundredths when evaluating expressions containing percents of numbers, but a percentage has no real meaning until it is used to modify another value. For example, if you see 67% in a problem you should always ask "67% of what?"

EXAMPLE

What is 25% of 40?

$$= .25 \times 40$$
$$= 10$$

To find what percentage a certain part of a value is of the whole value, you can use what is known as the **percentage formula**:

$$\text{Percent} = (\text{Part/Whole}) \times 100$$

EXAMPLE

What percentage of 50 is 23?

$$\text{Percentage} = (23/50) \times 100$$
$$= (46/100) \times 100$$
$$= 46\%$$

2.5 Roots and Exponents

2.5.1 Properties of Exponents

To multiply exponential values with the same base, keep the base the same and add the exponents.

EXAMPLE

$$a^2 \times a^3 = a^{2+3} = a^5$$

To divide exponential values with the same base, keep the base the same and subtract the exponent of the denominator from the exponent of the numerator.

EXAMPLE

$$\frac{x^5}{x^3} = x^{5-3} = x^2$$

To multiply exponential values with different bases but the same exponent, keep the exponent the same and multiply the bases.

EXAMPLE

$$2^x \times 3^x = (2 \times 3)^x = 6^x$$

To divide exponential values with different bases but the same exponent, keep the exponent the same and divide the bases.

EXAMPLE

$$\frac{6^x}{2^x} = \left(\frac{6}{2}\right)^x = 3^x$$

To raise an exponential value to an- other power, keep the base the same and multiply the exponents.

EXAMPLE

$$(x^3)^4 = x^{(3\times4)} = x^{12}$$

Even though all of the preceding examples use only positive integer exponents, these properties hold true for all three of the types described in section 2.5.3.

2.5.2 Scientific Notation

Scientific notation, also called exponential notation, is a convenient method of writing very large (or very small) numbers. Instead of writing too many zeroes on either side of a decimal, you can express a number as a product of a power of ten and a number between 1 and 10. For example, the number 8,765,000,000 can be expressed as 8.765×10^9.

The first number 8.765 is called the coefficient. The second number should always have a base of ten with an exponent equal to the number of zeroes in the original numbers. Moving the decimal point to the left makes a positive exponent while moving to the right makes a negative exponent.

Questions involving scientific notation on the DAT basically boil down to multi- plying and dividing the numbers. These problems can pose a challenge in the exam since you cannot input 10^x on the on-screen calculator. The only way to do it is by hand.

In multiplying numbers in scientific notation, the general rule is as follows:

$$(a \times 10^x)(b \times 10^y) = ab \times 10^{x+y}$$

EXAMPLE

To multiply 2.0×10^4 and 10×10^2

(i)   Find the product of the coefficients first.

$2.0 \times 10 = 20$

(ii) Add the exponents.

$$4 + 2 = 6$$

(iii) Construct the result.

$$20 \times 10^6$$

(iv) Make sure that the coefficient has only one digit to the left of the decimal point. This will also adjust the number of the exponent depending on the number of places moved.

$$2.0 \times 10^7$$

Dividing numbers in scientific notation follows this general rule:

$$\frac{\left(a \times 10^x\right)}{\left(b \times 10^y\right)} = \frac{a}{b} \times 10^{x-y}$$

Going back to our preceding example, let's divide 2.0×10^4 and 10×10^2 this time:

(i) Divide the coefficients.

$$2.0 \div 10 = 0.2$$

(ii) Subtract the exponents.

$$4 - 2 = 2$$

(iii) Construct the result and adjust the values to their simplest forms.

$$0.2 \times 10^2 = 2 \times 10 = 20$$

In adding and subtracting numbers written in scientific notation, you need to ensure that all exponents are identical. You would need to adjust the decimal place of one of the numbers so that its exponent becomes equivalent to the other number.

EXAMPLE

Add 34.5×10^{-5} and 6.7×10^{-4}

(i) Choose the number that you want to adjust so that its exponent is equivalent to the other number. Let's pick 34.5 and change it into a number with 10^{-4} as its base-exponent term.

$$3.45 \times 10^{-4} + 6.7 \times 10^{-4}$$

(ii) Add the coefficients together:

$$3.45 + 6.7 = 10.15$$

(iii) The exponents are now the same, in this case 10^{-4}, so all you have to do is plug it in:

$$10.15 \times 10^{-4}$$

(iv) Adjust the end result so that the coefficient is a number between 1 and 10:

$$1.015 \times 10^{-3}$$

The same procedure basically applies to subtraction.

2.5.3 Types of Exponents

Positive Integer Exponents: This is the type of exponent you will encounter most often. Raising a base number b to a positive integer exponent x is equivalent to making x copies of b and multiplying them together.

EXAMPLE

$$2^4 = 2 \times 2 \times 2 \times 2 = 16$$

Fractional Exponents: Fractional exponents are also known as roots. Let x be the fraction. To raise a base number b to the x power we make use of the fifth property of exponents in section 2.5.1.

We can write $b^{\frac{n}{d}}$ as $\left(b^{\frac{1}{d}}\right)^n$. The value $b^{\frac{1}{d}}$ is known as the d-th root of x. So the base b raised to the x power is the same as the d-th root of b raised to the n power.

EXAMPLE

$$8^{\frac{2}{3}}$$

$$= \left(8^{\frac{1}{3}}\right)^2$$

The expression inside the parentheses is the cube root of 8. Since $2 \times 2 \times 2 = 8$, the cube root of 8 is 2.

$$= 2^2$$
$$= 4$$

Negative Exponents: The value of a base raised to a negative power is equal to the reciprocal of the base, raised to a positive exponent of the same value. For any exponential value b^{-x}, b^{-x} is equivalent to $\dfrac{1}{\left(b^x\right)}$.

EXAMPLE

$$3^{-2}$$

Take the reciprocal and invert the sign of the exponent.

$$= \frac{1}{\left(3^2\right)}$$

$$= \frac{1}{\left(3 \times 3\right)}$$

$$= \frac{1}{9}$$

2.5.4 Zero and Exponents

Raising a Number to the Zero: Any number raised to the zero power is equal to 1.

We can see that this follows the rules of exponents (see section 2.5), because $a^0 = a^1 \times a^{-1} = a/a = 1$.

> **NOTE**
>
> The quantity 0^0 (read as zero to the zero power) is 1.

EXAMPLES

$$3^0 = 1$$
$$123.79^0 = 1$$
$$\left[1.2 + \left(37 - \sqrt{5}\right) \times 2.331\right]^0 = 1$$

As with multiplication and division, you should not waste time evaluating the parenthetical expression.

2.6 Ratio and Proportion

2.6.1 What is a Ratio?

A **ratio** is the relation between two numbers. There are multiple ways they can be written, but ratios can always be denoted as fractions.

These are all ways to represent the same ratio:

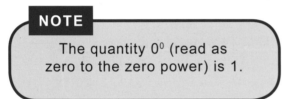

$$3 \text{ to } 4 \ = \ 3:4 \ = \ \frac{3}{4}$$

If a ratio is written out in words, the first quantity stated should generally be placed in the numerator of the equivalent fraction and the second quantity in the denominator. Just make sure you keep track of which value corresponds to which category.

2.6.2 Solving Proportions

A **proportion** is a statement of equality between two or more ratios.

Solving for an unknown variable is the most common type of proportion problem. If you have just a ratio on either side of an equation, you can rewrite the equation as the numerator of the first times the denominator of the second equal to the denominator of the first times the numerator of the second. This allows you to find the missing information more easily.

EXAMPLE

Solve for x in the following equation.

$$\frac{2}{3} = \frac{5}{x}$$

Cross multiply to eliminate fractions.

$$2 \times x = 3 \times 5$$
$$2x = 15$$
$$x = \frac{15}{2} = 7\frac{1}{2}$$

This means that the ratio 2 to 3 is equivalent to the ratio 5 to $7\frac{1}{2}$.

Unless it is stated, a proportion does not describe a specific number of things. It can only give you information about quantities in terms of other quantities. But if it is explicitly stated what one of the two quantities is, the other quantity can be determined using the proportion.

A lot of the proportions on the DAT are related to converting units to another type of unit.

EXAMPLE

1ft = 12 inches

How many ft are in 100 inches?

> **NOTE**
>
> We will be doing many examples like this in Chapter 3.

GOLD STANDARD WARM-UP EXERCISES

CHAPTER 2: Numbers and Operations

> **NOTE**
>
> We suggest that you use the default calculator on your PC or Mac computer for all QR Warm-up Exercises. Use only the features described in QR section 1.2. This will help you become accustomed to another element of the DAT QR. It is a good habit to aim to complete practice questions in under 1 minute per question. You will have a bit more time on the real DAT (i.e., 1.1 min./question) but ideally you would leave some time at the end of the exam to review your work.

1. What is the approximate value of

   $$0.125 + \sqrt{\frac{1}{9}} \, ?$$

   A. 0.40

   B. 0.46

   C. 0.50

   D. 0.45

   E. 0.30

2. 0.8 is to 0.9 as 80 is to:

   A. 9

   B. 100

   C. 8

   D. 10

   E. 90

3. If you invest in Bank A, you will receive 19% interest on the amount you invest. If you invest in Bank B, you will receive 21% interest. The maximum amount you can invest in Bank A is $6,430, and the maximum amount you can invest in Bank B is $5,897. How much more interest will you earn if you invest the maximum amount in Bank B than if you invest the maximum amount in Bank A?

   A. $16.67

   B. $16.30

   C. $101.27

   D. $111.93

   E. $533.00

4. Board C is 3/4 as long as Board B. Board B is 4/5 as long as Board A. What is the sum of the lengths of all three Boards if Board A is 100 m long?

   A. 255 m

   B. 225 m

   C. 240 m

   D. 235 m

   E. 250 m

5. The proportion of the yellow marbles in a jar of yellow and green jars is 7 out of 9. If there are 999 marbles in the jar, how many of these are yellow?

A. 111
B. 777
C. 2
D. 222
E. 0

6. If 0.25 months is equal to one week, what fraction of a month is equal to one day?

A. 1/7
B. 4/7
C. 7/4
D. 1/30
E. 1/28

7. Which of the following is 6.4% of 1,000?

A. $64^{\frac{3}{4}}$
B. $256^{\frac{3}{4}}$
C. $\left(\dfrac{64}{100}\right)^2$
D. 0.8^2
E. $6.4/100$

8. $2+\left[71-8\left(\dfrac{6}{2}\right)^2\right]$ is what percent of $\sqrt{2500}$?

A. 50%
B. 1%
C. 44%
D. 2%
E. 6%

9. Which is the largest?

A. 0.636
B. 0.136
C. 0.46
D. 0.163
E. 0.3

10. Determine the sum of 9, -5, and 6.

A. 20
B. −20
C. −10
D. 10
E. −6

11. Determine the value of 1.5×10^7 divided by 3.0×10^4.

A. 5.0×10^3
B. 0.5×10^3
C. 5.0×10^{-2}
D. 0.5×10^{-3}
E. 0.5×10^2

Go online to DAT-prep.com for additional chapter review Q&A and forum.

GS ANSWER KEY

CHAPTER 2

		Cross-Reference				Cross-Reference
1.	B	QR 2.2.3, 2.4.3		7.	B	QR 2.2.3, 2.4.3, 2.5.2
2.	E	QR 2.6.2		8.	D	QR 2.2.3, 2.4.3
3.	A	QR 2.4.3		9.	A	QR 2.4.3
4.	C	QR 2.4.2		10.	D	QR 2.2.1
5.	B	QR 2.6.2		11.	B	QR 2.5.2
6.	E	QR 2.6.1				

* Explanations can be found at the back of the book.

GOLD NOTES

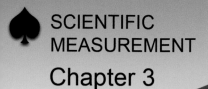
Memorize	Understand	Importance
* Conversions between units in the same system (whenever applicable) * Conversions between certain units in different systems	* Metric prefixes * How to convert between units	**2 to 4 out of the 40 QR** questions on the DAT are based on content from this chapter (in our estimation). * This will change in 2015.

DAT-Prep.com

Introduction

While scientific measurement is not a primary focus of the Quantitative Reasoning test, the DAT does use problems involving specific measurements. In order to solve these problems effectively, you must be familiar with British, Metric, and SI units, and some of the relationships between them.

Additional Resources

Free Online Forum

Special Guest

3.1 Systems of Measurement

3.1.1 British Units (Imperial System of Measurement)

You are probably already familiar with several of these units of measurement, but we recommend reviewing them at least once. If you don't know the following information backwards and forwards, you risk losing time on the test.

A. Length: These units are used to describe things like the length of physical objects, the displacement of a physical object, the distance something has traveled or will travel, etc. Area and volume are also measured as the square and cube (respectively) of these units.

Inches	The *inch* is the smallest measurement of length in the British System.
Feet	There are 12 inches in every foot. 1 ft. = 12 in.
Yards	There are 3 feet in every yard. 1 yd. = 3 ft.
Miles	The *mile* is the largest unit of length in the British System. There are 5,280 feet in every mile. 1 mi. = 5,280 ft.

B. Time: These units describe the passage of time.

Seconds	The *second* is the smallest unit of time in the British System.
Minutes	There are 60 seconds in every minute. 1 min. = 60 s.
Hours	There are 60 minutes in every hour. 1 h. = 60 min.
Days	There are 24 hours in every day. 1 day = 24 h.
Years	The *year* is the largest unit of time in the British System. There are 365 days in every year. 1 yr. = 365 days

C. Mass/Weight: Though not technically the same, we can consider mass and weight to be interchangeable for the DAT. The following units describe the amount of matter in an object.

Ounces	The *ounce* is the smallest unit of mass in the British System.

Pounds	There are 16 ounces in every pound. 1 lb. = 16 oz.
Tons	The *ton* is the largest unit of mass in the British System. There are 2,000 pounds in every ton. 1 ton = 2,000 lb.

> **NOTE**
>
> Make sure you memorize the conversions between the different units in each category. You will most likely be required to supply some of this information in order to solve problems on the test.

3.1.2 Metric Units

Measuring with Powers of 10: Unlike the British System, the Metric System has only one unit for each category of measurement. In order to describe quantities that are much larger or much smaller than one of the base units, a prefix is chosen from a variety of options and added to the front of the unit. This changes the value of the unit by some power of 10, which is determined by what the prefix is. The following are the most common of these prefixes:

Milli	One thousandth (10^{-3}) of the base unit
Centi	One hundredth (10^{-2}) of the base unit
Deci	One tenth (10^{-1}) of the base unit
Deca	Ten (10^1) times the base unit
Kilo	One thousand (10^3) times the base unit

There is a mnemonic that may be used to identify these prefixes:

King	Kilometer	Kilo
Henry	Hectometer	Hecto
Died	Decameter	Deca
Unexpectedly	Unit Base	Unit
Drinking	Decimeter	Deci
Chocolate	Centimeter	Centi
Milk	Milimeter	Milli

As you go down, you divide by 10 and as you go up, you multiply by 10 in order to convert between the units.

EXAMPLE

How many meters is 1 kilometer?

$$1 \text{ km} = 1,000 \text{ m}$$

From general knowledge, we know that kilo means one thousand. This means there are 1,000 meters in a kilometer. But just in case you get confused, you can also use the clue from the mnemonic. Now we know that **K**ilo is three slots upward from the **U**nit base. Hence we multiply 3 times by 10: 10 x 10 x 10 = 1000.

An even less confusing way to figure out how to do the metric conversions quickly and accurately, is to use a metric conversion line. This is quite handy with any of the common units such as the *meter*, *liter*, and *grams*.

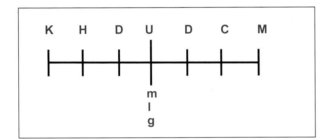

Fig QR 3.1: The Metric Conversion Line. The letters on top of the metric line stands for the "King Henry" mnemonic. On the other hand, the letters below the metric line - **m**, **l**, **g** – stand for the unit bases, **m**eter, **l**iter, or **g**ram, respectively.

To use this device, draw out the metric line as shown in Fig QR 3.1. From the centermost point **U**, the prefixes going to the left represent those that are larger than the base unit (kilo, hecto, deka). These also correspond to the decimal places that you will be moving from the numerical value of the unit to be converted. Those going to the right are for the ones smaller than the unit (deci, centi, milli).

EXAMPLE

How much is 36 liters in milliliters?

Step 1: Place your pen on the given unit, in this case L (liter). Then count the number of places it takes you to reach the unit being asked in the problem (milliliter).

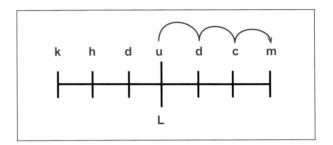

Fig QR 3.2: Converting liter to milliliter using the metric conversion line.

Step 2: Because it took you three places going to the right to move from the liter to the milliliter units, you also need to add three places from the decimal point of the number 36.0.

36 L = 36,000 ml

Now, let's try converting centimeter to kilometer: What is 6.3 cm in km?

1.   Place your pen on the **c** (centi) point in the metric line.

2.   Moving from **c** to **k** (kilo) takes five places going to the left. This also means moving five places from the decimal point of the number 6.3. 6.3 cm = .000063 km

Using this method definitely makes doing the metric conversions so much faster than the fraction method!

There are other prefixes that are often used scientifically and may be found in the DAT:

Tera	10^{12}	times the base unit
Giga	10^{9}	times the base unit
Mega	10^{6}	times the base unit
Micro	10^{-6}	of the base unit
Nano	10^{-9}	of the base unit
Pico	10^{-12}	of the base unit

A. Length: As with British length units, these are used to measure anything that has to do with length, displacement, distance, etc. Area and volume are also measured as the square and cube (respectively) of these units.

Meters	The *meter* is the basic unit of length in the Metric System.

Other Common Forms	millimeter, centimeter, kilometer

B. Time: These are units that quantify the passage of time.

Seconds	Just as in the British System, the *second* is the basic unit of time in the Metric System. Minutes, hours, and the other British units are not technically part of the Metric System, but they are often used anyway in problems involving metric units.

Other Common Forms	millisecond

C. Mass: These are units that describe the amount of matter in an object.

Grams	The *gram* is the basic metric unit of mass.

Other Common Forms	milligram, kilogram

3.1.3 SI Units

SI units is the **International System of Units** (abbreviated **SI** from the French *Le Système International d'Unités*) and is a modern form of the metric system. They are used to standardize all the scientific calcu- lations that are done anywhere in the world. The base units are meters, kilograms and seconds. These are the only SI units that may appear on the Quantitative Reasoning test:

Meters — Same as Metric meters

Seconds — Same as Metric and British seconds

Grams — Same as Metric grams (will usually appear as kilograms)

All of these SI units are duplicates from other systems of measurement. There are other distinct units in this system, but it is highly unlikely that they will appear on the QR because they are chemistry and physics units (i.e., moles, kelvin, amperes and candelas).

NOTE

The values of these SI units can be modified by powers of 10 using the same prefixes as in the metric system.

3.2 Conversions

3.2.1 Quick Conversion Formulas

In many instances, having a ready set of memorized formulas saves you time in the test. Here is a quick list of those that you should know for the DAT:

1 inch = 2.54 cm

1 meter = 1.0936 yd

1 mile = 1,760 yards

1 mile = 1.6 km

1 kg = 2.2 lbs

1 kg = 35.27396 oz

1 g = 1000 mg = 0.0353 oz

1 oz = 0.0295735 liter

1 gallon = 128 fl oz

1 hr = 60 min = 3,600 seconds

3 feet = 1 yard = 0.9144 m

12 inch = 1 foot = 0.3048 m

Formula for converting Fahrenheit to Celsius: $\dfrac{\left(°F - 32\right)}{1.8} = °C$

Celsius to Fahrenheit: $°C \times 1.8 + 32 = °F$

3.2.2 Mathematics of Conversions

While it is possible to memorize the conversions between every possible set of units, this would require much more effort than it would be worth. You do need to memorize the basic conversions but there is no point in knowing how many millimeters there are in a mile, for example. Odds are, these obscure conversions won't come up on the test; if they do, the math is simple enough to do without difficulty.

Whether you are converting units between different systems of measurement or simply within a single system, the math involved is the same.

A. The Process: In order to convert a quantity from one type of unit to another type of unit, all you have to do is set up and execute multiplication between ratios. Each conversion that you have memorized from the preceding sections is actually a ratio.

Let's look at the conversion from feet to inches.

"There are 12 inches in 1 foot."

This can be rewritten as a ratio in two ways:

"12 inches to 1 foot" or "1 foot to 12 inches."

$$= \frac{12 \text{ in}}{1 \text{ ft}} \text{ or } \frac{1 \text{ ft}}{12 \text{ in}}$$

When you are performing a conversion, you should treat the units like numbers. This means that when you have a fraction with a certain unit on top and the same unit on bottom, you can cancel out the units leaving just the numbers.

You can multiply a quantity by any of your memorized conversions, and its value will remain the same as long as all of the units, but one, cancel out.

EXAMPLE

How many inches are there in 3 feet?

First, determine which memorized conversion will help. Of course we have a conversion directly between feet and inches, so that is what we'll use.

Next, determine which of the two possible conversion ratios we should use. The goal is to be able to cancel out the original units (in this case, feet), so we want to use whichever ratio has the original units in the denominator (in this case, inches/feet).

$$3 \text{ ft} = 3 \text{ ft} \times \frac{12 \text{ in}}{1 \text{ ft}}$$

Now perform the unit cancellation.

$$= 3 \times \frac{12 \text{ in}}{1}$$
$$= 36 \text{ in}$$

In many instances, you will not have a direct conversion memorized. All you have to do in such a case is multiply by a string of ratios instead of just one.

EXAMPLE

How many inches are there in 5.08 meters?

We cannot convert meters directly into inches, but we can convert meters to centimeters and then centimeters into inches. We can set up both these conversions at the same time and evaluate.

$$5.08 \text{ m} = 5.08 \text{ m} \times \frac{100 \text{ cm}}{1 \text{ m}} \times \frac{1 \text{ in}}{2.54 \text{ cm}}$$

Next, cancel the units.

$$= 5.08 \times \frac{100}{1} \times \frac{1 \text{ in}}{2.54}$$

$$= \frac{508 \text{ in}}{2.54}$$

$$= 200 \text{ in}$$

NOTE

Make sure you check and see that all of your units cancel properly! A lot of unnecessary errors can be avoided simply by paying attention to the units. "Dimensional analysis" is the formal term given to these types of calculations that are solved while keeping an eye on the relations based on units.

GOLD STANDARD WARM-UP EXERCISES

CHAPTER 3: Scientific Measurement

1. How many millimeters are there in 75 meters?
A. 750 mm
B. 75 mm
C. 1000 mm
D. 75,000 mm
E. 7,500 mm

2. Which of the following is the shortest distance?
A. 10 m
B. 1,000 mm
C. 10 cm
D. 0.5 km
E. 0.1 km

3. A triathlon has three legs. The first leg is a 12 km run. The second leg is a 10 km swim. The third leg is a 15 km bike ride. How long is the total triathlon in meters?
A. 37,000 m
B. 3,700 m
C. 1,000 m
D. 37 m
E. 0.037 m

4. If a paperclip has a mass of one gram and a staple has a mass of 0.05 g, how many staples have a mass equivalent to the mass of one paperclip?
A. 10
B. 100
C. 20
D. 25
E. 2

5. Which of the following is the number of minutes equivalent to $17\frac{5}{6}$ hours?
A. 1,080
B. 1,056
C. 1,050
D. 1,020
E. 1,070

6. The three children in a family weigh 67 lbs., 1 oz., 93 lbs., 2 oz., and 18 lbs., 5 oz. What is the total weight of all three children?
A. 178.8 lbs.
B. 178.5 lbs.
C. 178.08 lbs.
D. 179.8 lbs.

7. A lawyer charges clients $20.50 per hour to file paperwork, $55 per hour for time in court, and $30 per hour for consultations. How much will it cost for a 90-minute consultation, $\frac{8}{6}$ hours time filing paper-work, and 1 hour in court?
    A. $110.28
    B. $100.75
    C. $88.25
    D. $127.33
    E. $95.25

8. If a car moving at a constant speed travels 20 centimeters in 1 second, approximately how many feet will it travel in 25% of a minute?
    A. 10
    B. 15
    C. 12
    D. 9
    E. 39

GS ANSWER KEY

CHAPTER 3

Cross-Reference

1. D QR 3.2.2
2. C QR 3.1.2
3. A QR 3.2
4. C QR 3.1

Cross-Reference

5. E QR 3.2.2
6. B QR 3.2.2
7. D QR 3.1.1, 3.2
8. A QR 3.2.2

* Explanations can be found at the back of the book.

Go online to DAT-prep.com for additional chapter review Q&A and forum.

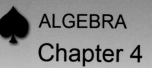

ALGEBRA
Chapter 4

Memorize

* The #1 Rule of Algebra
* Slope-Intercept Form for Linear Equations
* The Quadratic Formula

Understand

* Multiplying Polynomials
* Basic Concepts of Functions
* Manipulating Inequalities
* Basic Equations and Methods of Equation Solving
* Simplifying Equations
* Solving One or More Linear Equations
* Graphing Linear Equations in Cartesian Coordinates
* Factoring and Completing the Square

Importance

7 to 9 out of the 40 QR

questions on the DAT are based on content from this chapter (in our estimation).

* This will change in 2015.

DAT-Prep.com

Introduction ▌▌▌

Becoming comfortable with manipulating and solving algebraic equations is perhaps the single most important skill to have when tackling the Quantitative Reasoning test. This section covers a breadth of important information that will help you deal with any algebraic problem that is thrown at you on the DAT. Almost every problem requires some form of algebra and consequently, you should make it your goal to be confident in all of these concepts.

Additional Resources

Free Online Forum

4.1 Equation Solving and Functions

4.1.1 Algebraic Equations

Before we jump into more complicated algebra, let's review the basics.

A. Terms

Variable: A variable is a symbol - usually in the form of a small letter - that represents a number. It can take on any range of values.

Most problems that are strictly algebraic in nature will provide you with an equation (or equations) containing one or more unknown variables. Based on the information given, the values of the variables will most likely be fixed. Your job is to solve for those values.

Constant: A constant is an expression that contains only numbers and never changes because it has no variables.

Polynomial: A polynomial is an expression (usually part of a function or an equation) that is composed of the sum or difference of some number of terms. Please note that some of the terms can be negative. The **order** of a polynomial is equal to the largest exponent to which a variable is raised in one of the terms.

EXAMPLE $3x^2 + x + 5$

This expression is a polynomial. The variable here is x, and the order of the polynomial is 2 because that is the largest exponent to which x is raised.

B. Preserving Equality

The #1 Rule of Algebra: Whatever you do to one side of an equation, you *must* do to the other side also!

The equals sign implies equality between two different expressions. When you are given an equation, the equality established must be considered to be always true for that problem (unless you are told otherwise). So if you change one side of the equation and you do not also change the other side in the same way, you fundamentally alter the terms of the equation. The equation will no longer be true.

EXAMPLE

Consider this equation:

$$2x + 3 = 5$$

The following manipulation violates the above rule:

$$(2x + 3) - 3 = 5$$

Here, we have subtracted three from one side but not the other, so the equality no longer holds.

This manipulation, however, does not violate the rule:

$$(2x + 3) - 3 = 5 - 3$$

Here, we have subtracted three from both sides, so the equality still holds true.

NOTE

If two sides of an equation are equal, you can add or subtract the same amount to both sides, and they will still be equal.

EXAMPLE

$a = b$

$a + c = b + c$

$a - c = b - c$

The same rule applies to multiplication and division.

EXAMPLE

$a = b$

$ac = bc$

$a \div c = b \div c$

C. Solving Basic Equations

We can use the rule of algebra described in Part B to help solve algebraic equations for an unknown variable. Keep in mind that addition and subtraction, along with multiplication and division, are inverse operations: They undo each other. First decide the operation that has been applied and then use the inverse operation to undo this (make sure to apply the operation to both sides of the equation). The idea is to isolate the variable on one side of the equation. Then, whatever is left on the other side of the equation is the value of the variable.

EXAMPLE

Solve: $2x + 3 = 5$

$2x + 3 - 3 = 5 - 3$

$2x = 2$

Subtracting 3, however, has not isolated the variable x. Hence, we need to continue undoing by dividing 2 on both sides.

$2x \div 2 = 2 \div 2$

$x = 1$

Here's a little more complicated equation to solve: $2x + 2/3 = 3x - 2$

When you have an equation with the variable on both sides, choose whichever you think will be easier to focus on. In this case, we will isolate x on the right. First, subtract $2x$ from both sides.

$$(2x + 2/3) - 2x = (3x - 2) - 2x$$

$$\Rightarrow 2/3 = x - 2$$

Next, add 2 to both sides to isolate x.

$$(2/3) + 2 = (x - 2) + 2$$
$$\Rightarrow 8/3 = x$$

4.1.2 Addition and Subtraction of Polynomials

When adding or subtracting polynomials, the general rules for exponents are applied and like terms are grouped together. You can think of it as similar to collecting the same things together.

EXAMPLE

$$4x^3y + 5z^2 + 5xy^4 + 3z^2$$

$$= 4x^3y + 5xy^4 + (5+3)z^2$$
$$= 4x^3y + 5xy^4 + 8z^2$$

By grouping the similar terms, seeing which terms may be added or subtracted becomes easier.

4.1.3 Multiplying Polynomials

When multiplying two polynomials, you must multiply every term of the first polynomial with every term of the second. The order of this multiplication doesn't matter, but most people find it easiest to keep track by starting with the first term of the first polynomial, multiplying it by every term in the second from left to right, then taking the second term of the first polynomial and doing the same, and so on until all terms have been used. Following this pattern will ensure that every combination of multiplication is done.

EXAMPLE

Evaluate the following expression:

$$(2x + 1)(x^2 - 3x + 2)$$

Begin with the term $2x$ and multiply it by every term of the second polynomial, then do the same with the term 1. To make this clearer, we can even rewrite the expression as follows:

$$(2x)(x^2 - 3x + 2) + (1)(x^2 - 3x + 2)$$
$$= (2x^3 - 6x^2 + 4x) + (x^2 - 3x + 2)$$

Combining like terms, we get the following:

$$= 2x^3 - 5x^2 + x + 2$$

4.1.4 Function Basics

Before we can start working with functions, here are some basic definitions, terminology and examples with which you should be familiar.

Function: At its most basic, a function is a mathematical relation that outputs a unique number for every input.

EXAMPLE $f(x) = 2x$

In this case, the function is f; the input variable is x; and the output is $2x$. The notation used here is standard for functions. The denotation of the function (f) comes first, followed by a set of parentheses containing the input variable.

(a) Evaluate f for $x = 2$.

We need to solve for $f(2)$ (pronounced "f of two").

$$f(2) = 2 \times 2$$
$$= 4$$

(b) Find $f(-1/2)$.

$$f(-1/2) = 2 \times (-1/2)$$
$$= -1$$

Domain: The domain of a function is the set of possible values that the independent variable or variables (the input) of the function can have.

Range: The range of a function is the set of possible values that the output of the function can have.

EXAMPLE

(a) Find the domain and range of the function f defined by $f(x) = 2x$.

Remember, on the DAT we only need to worry about real numbers. So the largest domain or range we could possibly have is "all real numbers."

To find the domain of the function, look at its output expression (in this case "$2x$") and determine if there are any real number values of the variable (x) for which the expression is not defined. In this case, there are none. For any number x, we can always multiply it by 2 and obtain a new real number value.

Domain = All Real Numbers

To find the range of the function, you also need to look at its output expression. Are there any numbers the output cannot equal? In this case, no; because for any number you can think of, simply inputting half of it will output that number.

Range = All Real Numbers

(b) Find the domain and range of the function f defined by $f(x) = x^2$.

First, find the domain. Is there any number we cannot input into this function? Since x^2 is defined for all real numbers, there are none.

Domain = All Real Numbers

Now, find the range. Are there any numbers we cannot obtain as an output from this function? Since x^2 is always positive for real numbers x, we can never obtain a negative output.

Range = All Non–negative
Real Numbers

Remember, this range does include 0. We can also write this as shown in the expression that follows.

Range = $[0 , \infty)$

The "[" bracket means that 0 is included in the set and the ")" bracket means that ∞ is not included in the set (because infinity is not actually a number). So this notation means the set of all real numbers between 0 and infinity, including 0.

4.2 Inequalities

4.2.1 Inequality Basics

An **inequality** is a statement that describes the relative size of two quantities. This is similar to an equation; except that instead of only saying that two quantities are equal, an inequality can also mean that one quantity is always larger than another.

Inequality Symbols

> is the symbol for "greater than." The quantity on the left of this symbol is always greater than the quantity on the right.

< is the symbol for "less than." The

quantity on the left of the symbol is always less than the quantity on the right.

$\geq$ is the symbol for "greater than or equal to." The quantity on the left of this symbol is always either greater than or equal to the quantity on the right.

$\leq$ is the symbol for "less than or equal to." The quantity on the left of the symbol is always either less than or equal to the quantity on the right.

$|x|$ is the symbol for absolute value. It represents the numerical value of x and disregards its sign. Therefore, the absolute value

of any real number will always be positive.

EXAMPLE $x > 3$

This inequality states that the variable x is greater than 3. So x can have any value that is larger than 3, such as 4 or 100.

EXAMPLE $3 \leq x \leq 4$

This is an example of how multiple inequalities can be used in the same statement. It states that x is both less than or equal to 4 and greater than or equal to 3. So x can have any value between (and including) 3 and 4, such as 3 or 3.5.

4.2.2 Solving Inequalities

A. One-Sided Inequalities

Solving inequalities is almost identical to solving equations. The same rule applies: You always have to do the same thing to both sides. The only difference is that the symbols of inequality are sensitive to inversions of the sign (flipping from positive to negative). Whenever you multiply or divide both sides by a negative number, the inequality symbol changes direction (remember, squaring a negative number falls into this category because you are multiplying by that same negative number). This will never happen with addition and subtraction.

Here is a quick example that might help you understand why the inequality symbol

flips for multiplication by a negative number.

EXAMPLE

Say there are two people, person A and person B. Person A has 3 dollars and person B has 2 dollars. In inequality form, we know that $3 > 2$.

Now, instead of having money, let's say for some reason person A now *owes* 3 dollars and person B *owes* 2 dollars. As you can see, we have simply multiplied both quantities by −1. Now, which person has more money and which has less? Obviously −3 dollars is less than −2 dollars; so as an inequality, this reads as $-3 < -2$.

So, simply multiplying by a negative number has caused the direction of the inequality symbol to switch.

With this principle in mind, we can now solve inequalities. Just like with equations, all we have to do is isolate the variable on one side.

EXAMPLE

Solve the following inequality for x:

$2 - 3x \leq .5x - 1$.

First, choose the side on which you want to isolate the variable. We'll use the left side.

$$(2 - 3x) - 2 \leq (.5x - 1) - 2$$
$$\Rightarrow (-3x) - .5x \leq (.5x - 3) - .5x$$
$$\Rightarrow (-7/2)x \leq -3$$
$$\Rightarrow (-2/7)(-7/2)x \geq -3 \times (-2/7)$$
$$\Rightarrow x \geq 6/7$$

B. Absolute Inequalities

In solving absolute inequalities, the inequality symbol used ($<$, $\leq$, $>$, $\geq$) is a significant consideration in writing the solution set. The following rules should apply:

- If the symbol is $>$ (or $\geq$), meaning that the absolute value is greater than the number on the other side of the inequality, the connecting word is "or."

If $a > 0$, then the solutions to $|x| > a$ are $x > a$ or $x < -a$.

EXAMPLE

Solve for the following inequality:

$|x + 2| > 7$.

In this case, the absolute value $|x + 2|$ is greater than 7. Hence,

$$\Rightarrow x + 2 > 7 \text{ or } x + 2 < -7$$
$$\Rightarrow x > 5 \text{ or } x < -9$$

You can think of "great-or" as a way of memorizing this rule.

- If the symbol is $<$ (or $\leq$), meaning that the absolute value is less than the number on the other side of the inequality, the connecting word is "and."

If $a < 0$, then the solutions to $|x| < a$ are $x < a$ and $x > -a$. This can also be written as $-a < x < a$.

Similarly, in the inequality $|x + 2| < 7$, the side containing the absolute value is less than 7 and should thus indicate the connective "and" in the solution.

EXAMPLE

Solve: $|x + 2| < 7$.

$$\Rightarrow x + 2 < 7 \text{ and } x + 2 > -7$$
$$\Rightarrow x < 5 \text{ and } x > -9$$
$$\Rightarrow -9 < x < 5$$

This time, you can think of "less th-and" to remember this rule.

C. Two-Sided Inequalities

Though it is odd to see equations with more than one equals sign, two-sided inequalities are common. You can solve them by splitting them up into two one-sided inequalities and solving these individually.

EXAMPLE

Solve the following inequality for x:

$12 > 3x > 6$.

Breaking this inequality into two, we obtain $12 > 3x$ and $3x > 6$. We must solve these:

(i) $(12)/3 > (3x)/3$
$$\Rightarrow 4 > x$$

(ii) $(3x)/3 > (6)/3$
$$\Rightarrow x > 2$$

These two inequalities can be recombined to form the new two-sided inequality $4 > x > 2$.

4.3 Simplifying Equations

In order to make solving algebraic equations easy and quick, you should simplify terms whenever possible. The following are the most common and important ways of doing so.

4.3.1 Combining Terms

This is the most basic thing you can do to simplify an equation. If there are multiple terms being added or subtracted in your equation that contain the same variables, you can combine them.

EXAMPLE

Simplify the equation: $3x + 4xy - 2 = xy + 1$

Notice that there are two terms we can combine that contain xy and two terms we can combine that are just constants.

$(3x + 4xy - 2) - xy = (xy + 1) - xy$

$\Rightarrow 3x + 3xy - 2 = 1$

$(3x + 3xy - 2) + 2 = 1 + 2$

$\Rightarrow 3x + 3xy = 3$

$\Rightarrow \left(\dfrac{3x + 3xy}{3}\right) = \dfrac{3}{3}$

$\Rightarrow x + xy = 1$

Always make sure to look for like terms to combine when you are solving an algebra problem.

4.3.2 Variables in Denominators

When you are trying to manipulate an equation, having variables in the denominators of fractions can make things difficult. In order to get rid of such denominators entirely, simply multiply the entire equation by the quantity in the denominator. This will probably cause other terms to become more complicated, but you will no longer have the problem of a variable denominator.

EXAMPLE

Simplify the expression: $\dfrac{3}{2x} + 5x = 4$.

The problem denominator is $2x$, so we multiply both sides by $2x$.

$$\left(\dfrac{3}{2x} + 5x\right)2x = (4)2x$$

$$\Rightarrow 3 + 10x^2 = 8x$$

When there are different denominators containing variables, cross multiply the denominator to cancel out.

EXAMPLE

$$\dfrac{5}{(x+3)} = \dfrac{2}{x} - \dfrac{1}{3x}$$

Multiply $3x$ on both sides:

$$\dfrac{5}{(x+3)}(3x) = \dfrac{2}{x} - \dfrac{1}{3x}(3x)$$

$$\dfrac{15x}{(x+3)} = 6 - 1$$

Multiply $(x+3)$ on both sides:

$$\dfrac{15x}{(x+3)}(x+3) = 5(x+3)$$

$$15x = 5x + 15$$

$$15x - 5x = 5x + 15 - 5x$$

$$10x = 15$$

$$x = \dfrac{15}{10} = \dfrac{3}{2}$$

4.3.3 Factoring

If every term of a polynomial is divisible by the same quantity, that quantity can be factored out. This means that we can express the polynomial as the product of that quantity times a new, smaller polynomial.

EXAMPLE

Factor the following expression:

$$2x^3 - 4x^2 + 4x$$

Every term in this polynomial is divisible by $2x$, so we can factor it out of each term. The simplified expression, then, is

$$2x(x^2 - 2x + 2).$$

To verify that you have properly factored an expression, multiply out your solution. If you get back to where you started, you've done it correctly.

4.4 Linear Equations

4.4.1 Linearity

Linear equation is an equation that describes relationships between variables in which every term is a scalar or a scalar multiple of a variable. In a linear equation, there can neither be variables raised to exponents nor variables multiplied together.

(a) $3x + 2y = z + 5$

This equation is linear.

(b) $3x^2 - 2xy = 1$

This equation is not linear. The terms $3x^2$ and $2xy$ cannot appear in a linear equation.

The reason such equations are called "linear" is that they can be represented on a Cartesian graph as a straight line (see section 4.5).

4.4.2 Solving Linear Equations with Multiple Variables

In the previous sections we have only considered equations, inequalities, and functions with single variables. In many cases though, Quantitative Reasoning problems will require you to deal with a second variable.

> **NOTE**
>
> Everything in this section applies to inequalities as well as equations. Just remember to be wary of multiplication and division by negative numbers!

A. Isolating a Variable

When you have a single equation with two variables, you will not be able to solve for specific values. What you can do is solve for one variable in terms of the other. To do this, pick a variable to isolate on one side of the equation and move all other terms to the other side.

EXAMPLE

Solve the following for y: $4y - 3x = 2y + x - 6$.

Let's isolate y on the left side:

$$(4y - 3x) + 3x - 2y = (2y + x - 6) + 3x - 2y$$

$$\frac{(2y)}{2} = \frac{(4x - 6)}{2}$$

$$y = 2x - 3$$

Now we know the value of y, but only in relation to the value of x. If we are now given some value for x, we can simply plug it in to our solution and obtain y. For example, if $x = 1$ then $y = 2 - 3 = -1$.

B. Solving Systems of Equations

How do you know if you will be able to solve for specific values in an equation or not? The general rule is that if you have the same number of unique equations as variables (or more equations), you will be able find a specific value for every variable. So for the example in Part A, since we have two variables and only one equation, in order to solve for the variables, we would need one more unique equation.

In order for an equation to be unique, it must not be algebraically derived from another equation.

EXAMPLE

$$300 = 30x - 10y$$
$$30 = 3x - y$$

From the above example, the two equations describe the same line and therefore are not unique since they are scalar multiples of each other.

There are two strategies you should know for solving a system of equations:

I. **Substitution.** This strategy can be used every time, although, it will not always be the fastest way to come up with a solution. You begin with one equation and isolate a variable as in Part A. Next, wherever the isolated variable appears in the second equation, replace it with the expression this variable is equal to. This effectively eliminates that variable from the second equation.

If you only have two equations, all you need are two steps. Once you have followed the procedure above, you can solve for the second variable in the second equation and substitute that value back into the first equation to find the value of the first variable. If you have more than two variables and equations, you will need to continue this process of isolation and substitution until you reach the last equation.

EXAMPLE

Solve the following system of equations for x and y.

$$4y - 3x = 2y + x - 6$$
$$3x + y = 12$$

We have already isolated y in the first equation, so the first step is done. The new system is as follows:

$$y = 2x - 3$$
$$3x + y = 12$$

Next, we substitute $2x - 3$ for y in the second equation.

$$3x + (2x - 3) = 12$$
$$\Rightarrow 5x - 3 = 12$$
$$\Rightarrow 5x = 15$$
$$\Rightarrow x = 3$$

Now, we have a value for x, but we still need a value for y. Substitute 3 for x in the y-isolated equation.

$$y = 2(3) - 3$$
$$y = 3$$

So our solution to this system of equations is $x = 3$, $y = 3$.

II. **Equation Addition or Subtraction.** You will not always be able to apply this strategy, but in some cases, it will save you from having to do all of the time-consuming substitutions of Strategy I. The basic idea of equation addition or subtraction is exactly what you would expect: Addition or subtraction of equations directly to each other.

Say you have two equations, A and B. Because both sides of any equation are by definition equal, you can add, say, the left side of equation A to the left side of equation B and the right side of equation A to the right side of equation B without changing anything. In performing this addition, you are doing the same thing to both sides of equation B.

The purpose of performing such an

addition is to try and get a variable to cancel out completely. If you can accomplish this, you can solve for the other variable easily (assuming you only have two variables, of course). Before adding the equations together, you can manipulate either of them however you like (as long as you maintain equality) in order to set up the cancellation of a variable.

If the only way to cancel out a variable is by subtracting the equation, this may be done as well.

EXAMPLE

Use equation addition or subtraction to solve the following for x and y.

$$2x - 2y = 1$$
$$4x + 5y = 11$$

If we multiply the first equation by two, we will have $4x$ present in each equation. Then if we subtract, the $4x$ in each equation will cancel.

$$\begin{array}{r} 4x - 4y = 2 \\ -(4x + 5y = 11) \\ \hline 0x - 9y = -9 \end{array}$$
$$\Rightarrow y = 1$$

Now, we can substitute this value of y into whichever equation looks simpler to solve for x (either one will work though).

$$2x - 2(1) = 1$$
$$\Rightarrow 2x = 3$$
$$\Rightarrow x = \frac{3}{2}$$

So our solution to this system of equations is $y = 1$, $x = \frac{3}{2}$.

4.5 Graphing Linear Functions

4.5.1 Linear Equations and Functions

Every linear equation can be rewritten as a linear function. To do so, simply isolate one of the variables as in Section 4.4.2A. This variable is now a function of the variables on the other side of the equation.

EXAMPLE

Rewrite the equation $3y - 2x = 6$ as a function of x.

$$3y - 2x = 6$$
$$\Rightarrow 3y = 2x + 6$$
$$\Rightarrow y = \frac{2}{3}x + 2$$

Now that we have isolated y, it is actually a function of x. For every input of x, we get a unique output of y. If you like, you can rewrite y as $f(x)$.

$$f(x) = \frac{2}{3}x + 2$$

4.5.2 Cartesian Coordinates in 2D

The Cartesian coordinate system is the most commonly used system for graphing. A Cartesian graph in two dimensions has two axes: The x-axis is the horizontal one, and the y-axis is the vertical one. The independent variable is always along the x-axis and the dependent variable is along the y-axis. The independent variable is controlled and the output depends on the independent variable. The further right you go on the x-axis, the larger the numbers get; and on the y-axis, the numbers get larger the further up you go. A point on the graph is specified as an ordered pair of an x value and a y value like this: (x, y). This point exists x units from the origin (the point $(0, 0)$ where the axes cross) along the x-axis, and y units from the origin along the y-axis.

EXAMPLE

Find the point $(3, -1)$ on the Cartesian graph shown.

To plot this point, simply count three units to the right along the x-axis and one unit down along the y-axis.

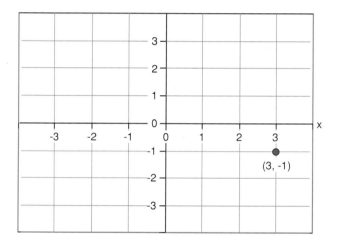

4.5.3 Graphing Linear Equations

In order to graph a straight line in Cartesian coordinates, all you need to know is two points. Every set of two points has only one unique line that passes through both of them.

To find two points from a linear equation, simply choose two values to plug in for one of the variables. It is best to pick values that will make your calculations easier, such as 0 and 1. Plugging in each of these values, we can solve for y and obtain two points.

EXAMPLE

Graph the line defined by $2x + y = 3$.

First, let's plug in $x = 0$ and $x = 1$ to find two points on the line.

$$2(0) + y = 3$$
$$\Rightarrow y = 3$$
$$2(1) + y = 3$$
$$\Rightarrow y = 1$$

Now, we have two points: (0, 3) and (1, 1). To graph the line, all we have to do is plot these points on a graph and draw a straight line between them.

4.5.4 Slope-Intercept Form

There are two pieces of information that are very useful in the graphing of a linear equation: The slope of the line and its *y*-intercept.

Slope refers to the steepness of a line. It is the ratio (Slope = rise/run) of the number of units along the y-axis to the number of units along the x-axis between two points.

EXAMPLE

$$y = 5x + 3 \text{ and } y = 5x + 10$$

These two equations would be parallel to each other since both slopes (m)=5.

$$y = 3x + 6 \text{ and } y = -\frac{1}{3x} + 3$$

These two equations are perpendicular. The line of the first equation has a positive slope and the perpendicular line has a decreasing slope and therefore allows both equations to have opposite signs.

The *y*-**intercept** of a line is the *y*-coordinate of the point at which the line crosses the *y*-axis. The value of *x* where the line intersects, is always zero and its coordinates will be (0, *y*).

One of the standard forms of a linear equation is the slope-intercept form, from which the slope and the *y*-intercept of the line are immediately obvious. This form resembles $y = mx + b$. Here *m* and *b* are constants such that *m* is the slope of the line and *b* is the *y*-intercept.

EXAMPLE

Rewrite the following equation in slope-intercept form: $2y + 5x = 8$.

$$\Rightarrow 2y = -5x + 8$$
$$\Rightarrow y = -\frac{5}{2}x + 4$$

This is now in slope-intercept form. In this case, the slope *m* is $-\frac{5}{2}$ and the *y*-intercept is 4.

Slope-intercept form is also useful for constructing the equation of a line from other information. If you are given the slope and the intercept, obviously you can simply plug them in to $y = mx + b$ to get the equation. It is also very simple to obtain the slope and intercept if you know two points on the line, (x_1, y_1) and (x_2, y_2). The slope can be obtained directly from this information:

Slope = rise/run = $(y_2 - y_1)/(x_2 - x_1)$

Once the slope m is obtained, you only need to solve for b. To do so, plug in one of the points as well as m into the slope-intercept equation. You can then solve for b.

EXAMPLE

Find the equation for the line passing through (1, 1) and (2, 3).

First, determine the slope.

$$m = \frac{(3-1)}{(2-1)} = 2$$

Now plug m and a point into the slope-intercept equation to find b.

$$y = mx + b$$
$$\Rightarrow 1 = 2(1) + b$$
$$\Rightarrow -1 = b$$

Plugging in all of this information, we now have a complete equation.

$$y = 2x - 1$$

4.6 Quadratic Equations

A **quadratic equation** is an equation that can be written in the form $ax^2 + bx + c = 0$ where a, b, and c are constants. This is a second-degree polynomial set equal to zero, and it will always have two solutions, although they are not always unique. Being asked to solve a quadratic equation is a standard type of algebra problem, so you should be very familiar with the techniques listed in the following subsections.

4.6.1 Factoring and Completing the Square

A. Factoring

Factoring is the simplest and easiest way to solve a quadratic equation, but you will not always be able to use this method. Only special quadratics can be solved this way. Still, you should always try and use this method first.

The goal is to factor the quadratic into

two first-degree polynomials so you have $(ax + b)(cx + d) = 0$. Once you have obtained this form, you know that either $(ax + b) = 0$ or $(cx + d) = 0$, so the two solutions are $x = -\dfrac{b}{a}$ and $x = -\dfrac{d}{c}$.

There is no single quick way to factor a quadratic this way. Instead, you should do many sample exercises to develop the ability to think logically and come up with the solution. As a guide, think about what values must be multiplied to obtain the constants a, b, and c of your quadratic.

More specifically, for $ax^2 + bx + c$, if the value of a is 1, your two polynomials will be $(x + m)$ and $(x + n)$ where $b = m + n$ and $c = m \times n$. Therefore, try to think about what numbers multiply together to give c and add together to give b.

EXAMPLE

Solve the quadratic equation:

$$x^2 + 3x + 2 = 0$$

To factor, we need two numbers that add to 3 and multiply to 2. We know that these numbers must both be positive since a positive and a negative number would yield a negative number when multiplied, and two negative numbers would yield a negative number when added.

Also, the two numbers must be less than 3 because otherwise their sum would have to be larger than 3. After some thought, it is clear that the numbers we are looking for are 1 and 2 since $1 + 2 = 3$ and $1 \times 2 = 2$.

$$\Rightarrow (x + 1)(x + 2) = 0$$
$$\Rightarrow (x + 1) = 0 \text{ and } (x + 2) = 0$$
$$\Rightarrow x = -1 \text{ and } x = -2$$

B. Completing the Square

This method can be a little tricky. The basic idea is to manipulate the quadratic so that you can write the portion with the variables as the square of a first-order polynomial. Then you can take the square root and find the solutions. To accomplish this for a generic quadratic $ax^2 + bx + c = 0$, follow these steps:

Step 1 Move c to the other side of the equation.

$$ax^2 + bx = -c$$

Step 2 Divide through by the leading coefficient a.

$$x^2 + \left(\frac{b}{a}\right)x = -\frac{c}{a}$$

Step 3 Take half of $\left(\dfrac{b}{a}\right)$, i.e., the coefficient of x. Square it, and add it to both sides of the equation.

$$x^2 + \left(\frac{b}{a}\right)x + \left(\frac{b}{2a}\right)^2 = -\frac{c}{a} + \left(\frac{b}{2a}\right)^2$$

This allows you to write the polynomial as a square, namely $\left(x + \dfrac{b}{2a}\right)^2$.

$$\left(x + \frac{b}{2a}\right)^2 = -\frac{c}{a} + \left(\frac{b}{2a}\right)^2$$

Step 4 Take the square root of both sides and solve for x.

$$x + \frac{b}{2a} = \pm\sqrt{\left[-\frac{c}{a} + \left(\frac{b}{2a}\right)^2\right]}$$

$$x = -\frac{b}{2a} \pm \sqrt{\left[-\frac{c}{a} + \left(\frac{b}{2a}\right)^2\right]}$$

Following the variables in this general version can be difficult, so let's look at an example.

EXAMPLE

Solve the following quadratic by completing the square:

$$2x^2 + 4x - 8 = 0$$

Step 1 $2x^2 + 4x = 8$

Step 2 $x^2 + 2x = 4$

Step 3 $x^2 + 2x + 1 = 4 + 1 = 5$

$$\Rightarrow \sqrt{(x+1)^2} = \sqrt{5}$$

Step 4 $x + 1 = \pm\sqrt{5}$

$$\Rightarrow x = -1 \pm \sqrt{5}$$

4.6.2 The Quadratic Formula

If you do not want to or cannot use one of the methods in Part 4.6.1 to solve your quadratic equation, you can simply plug numbers into the quadratic formula to come up with a solution (CHM 6.6.1).

For a generic quadratic equation $ax^2 + bx + c = 0$, these are the solutions:

$$x = \frac{-b \pm \sqrt{b^2 - 4ac}}{2a}$$

Sometimes, doing the arithmetic necessary to compute this formula can take a lot of time, so factoring and completing the square are usually better options if you feel comfortable with them. They will save you time on the test.

When there is no first degree term $ax^2 + c = 0$, we can solve the equation by isolating x^2. Such that,

$$x^2 = -\frac{c}{a}.$$

Therefore, $x = \pm\sqrt{-\dfrac{c}{a}}$.

GOLD STANDARD WARM-UP EXERCISES

CHAPTER 4: Algebra

1. If $\dfrac{x}{2} - 1 < x$, then which must be true?

    A. $\quad 2 > x$

    B. $\quad -\dfrac{1}{2} < x$

    C. $\quad -2 < x$

    D. $\quad -2 > x$

    E. $\quad 2 < x$

2. If $f(x) = \dfrac{12}{4x^3 - 6x + 5}$, then $f(2)$ equals:

    A. 12/17

    B. 12/49

    C. 12/9

    D. 12/15

    E. 12/25

3. $13xy^2z$ is to $39y$ as $9xyz^6$ is to:

    A. $3z^5$

    B. $27z$

    C. $9y$

    D. $27z^5$

    E. $9z^6$

4. At what point do the lines $y = 2x - 1$ and $6x - 5y = -3$ intersect?

    A. (2, 3)

    B. (0.5, 0)

    C. (−1,−3)

    D. (−0.5, −2)

    E. (1/4,-3/4)

5. Loubha has a total of $.85. If she has two less dimes than nickels, how many dimes and nickels does she have?

    A. 5 nickels, 7 dimes

    B. 6 nickels, 4 dimes

    C. 1 nickel, 8 dimes

    D. 4 nickels, 2 dimes

    E. 7 nickels, 5 dimes

6. If $2.5 \times 10^3 (3 \times 10^x) = 0.075$, then x equals:

    A. −3

    B. −5

    C. 0

    D. −4

    E. 2

7. If $y = 3x^2 - 5x - 7$, then which of the following represents x?

    A. $\dfrac{-5 \pm \sqrt{3y + 46}}{3}$

    B. $\dfrac{5 \pm \sqrt{12y + 109}}{6}$

    C. $\dfrac{-5 \pm \sqrt{12y + 109}}{6}$

    D. $\dfrac{5 \pm \sqrt{12y + 109}}{36}$

    E. $\dfrac{5 \pm \sqrt{3y + 46}}{3}$

8. A plank of wood is leaning against the left side of a house with vertical walls. Both are on level ground. If the plank touches the ground 7 feet away from the base of the house, and touches the house at a point 5 feet above the ground, at what slope is the plank lying?

    A. −5/7

    B. 7/5

    C. −7/5

    D. 5/7

    E. 2

9. If $n + n = k + k + k$ and $n + k = 5$, then $n = ?$

    A. 9

    B. 6

    C. 5

    D. 3

    E. 2

Go online to DAT-prep.com for additional chapter review Q&A and forum.

GS ANSWER KEY

CHAPTER 4

		Cross-Reference				Cross-Reference
1.	C	QR 4.2.2A		6.	B	QR 4.3.1
2.	E	QR 4.1.4		7.	B	QR 4.6.2
3.	D	QR 4.3.2, 4.3.3		8.	D	QR 4.5.4
4.	A	QR 4.42A, 4.4.2B		9.	D	QR 4.3.1, 4.4.2A, 4.4.2B
5.	E	QR 4.2B				

* Explanations can be found at the back of the book.

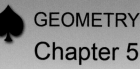
Memorize	Understand	Importance
* The Pythagorean Theorem * Perimeter, Area, and Volume Formulas * Properties of Triangles	* Points in Cartesian Coordinates * Parallel and Perpendicular Lines * Similar Polygons * Types of Triangles and Angles * Problems with Figures and Solids	**3 to 5 out of the 40 QR** questions on the DAT are based on content from this chapter (in our estimation). * This will change in 2015.

DAT-Prep.com

Introduction ▐▐▐▐

Geometry is a very visual branch of mathematics dealing with lines and shapes and relations in space, so drawing and labeling pictures can be extremely helpful when you are confronted with geometric problems. But don't forget about algebra! More often than not, these problems are simply algebraic equations in disguise.

Additional Resources

Free Online Forum

5.1 Points, Lines and Angles

5.1.1 Points and Distance

Knowing your way around the Cartesian coordinate systems begins with understanding the relationships between simple points. As discussed in section 4.5, points on a graph are represented as an ordered pair of an x and y coordinate, (x, y).

A. Addition and Subtraction of Points

To add or subtract two points, simply add or subtract the two x values to obtain the new x value and add or subtract the two y values to obtain the new y value.

EXAMPLE

Add the points (2, 3) and (1, –5).

$$(2, 3) + (1, –5)$$
$$= (2 + 1, 3 – 5)$$
$$= (3, –2)$$

Graphically, addition of points is easy to visualize. All you are doing when you add two points is treating the first point as the new origin. You then plot the second point in terms of this new origin to find the sum of the two points.

You can add more than two points in the same way. Just add all of the x values together, and then add all of the y values together.

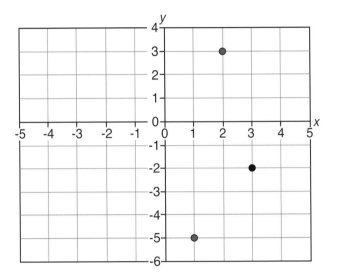

B. Distance between Points

Finding the distance between two points requires the use of the Pythagorean Theorem. This theorem is probably the most important tool you have for solving geometric problems.

> **Pythagorean Theorem:** $x^2 + y^2 = z^2$

This theorem describes the relationship between the lengths of the sides of a right triangle. The lengths x and y correspond to the two legs of the triangle adjacent to the right angle, and the length z corresponds to the hypotenuse of the triangle. For a further discussion of the Pythagorean Theorem and right triangles, see section 5.2.2.

In order to find the distance between two points (x_1, y_1) and (x_2, y_2), consider there to be a line segment connecting them. This line segment (with length z equivalent to the distance between the points) can be thought of as the hypotenuse of a right triangle. The other two sides extend from the points: One is parallel to the x-axis; the other, to the y-axis (with lengths x and y, respectively).

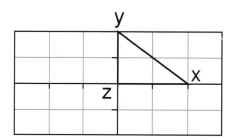

To find the distance between the two points, simply apply the Pythagorean Theorem.

$$x = (x_2 - x_1)$$
$$y = (y_2 - y_1)$$
$$z = \sqrt{(x^2 + y^2)}$$

Plugging in the point coordinates will yield z, the distance between the two points.

EXAMPLE

Find the distance between the points $(5, 0)$ and $(2, -4)$.

$$x = (2 - 5) = -3$$
$$y = (-4 - 0) = -4$$
$$z = \sqrt{(-3^2 + -4^2)}$$
$$= \sqrt{(9 + 16)} = \sqrt{25} = 5$$

So the distance between the points is $z = 5$.

5.1.2 Line Segments

A. Segmentation Problems

These problems are a kind of geometry-algebra hybrid. You are given a line segment that has been subdivided into smaller segments, and some information is provided. You are then asked to deduce some of the missing information.

In a segmentation problem, some of the information you are given may be geometric, and some may be algebraic. There is not, however, a clear algebraic equation to solve. You will need to logically determine the steps needed to reach a solution.

EXAMPLE

The line segment QT of length $4x + 6$ is shown in the figure that follows. Point

S is the midpoint of QT and segment RS has length $x - 1$. What is the length of line segment QR?

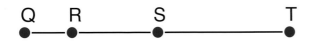

First, determine what information you know. The length of QT and RS are given. Also, since we have a midpoint for QT, the length of QS and ST are simply half of the length of QT.

Now, determine an algebraic relationship regarding the length of QR, which is what we are looking for. We can see that the length of QR is simply QS with the RS segment removed.

$$QR = QS - RS$$

Plugging in our information, we get the following:

$$QR = \frac{(4x + 6)}{2} - (x - 1)$$
$$= 2x + 3 - x + 1$$
$$= x + 4$$

Before you start working out a solution, it can be extremely helpful to list the information you are given. This will help you understand and organize the problem, both in your own mind and on the page.

B. Segments in the Plane

In segmentation problems, you only have to deal with one dimension. However, line segments can also turn up in problems dealing with a two dimensional Cartesian graph.

To determine the length of a line segment in a plane, simply find the distance between its endpoints using the Pythagorean Theorem (see section 5.1.1).

Any line segment in a plane corresponds to a single linear equation. This can be determined as in chapter 4 from any two points on the line segment. Knowing this linear equation can help you find other points on the line segment.

5.1.3 Angles

An **angle** is formed by the intersection of two lines.

In problems that are not trigonometric, angles are almost always measured in degrees. A full circle makes 360°.

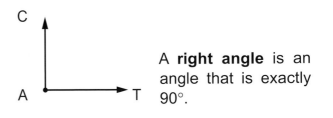

A **right angle** is an angle that is exactly 90°.

An **obtuse angle** is an angle that is greater than 90°.

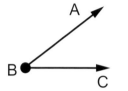

An **acute angle** is an angle that is less than 90°.

A **straight angle** is an angle that is exactly 180°.

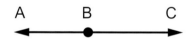

A **vertical angle** is the angle opposite of each other that is formed by two intersecting lines. The two angles across from each other are equal in measure. The following example shows that angles 1 and 3 are vertical angles and equal to each other. Same are angles 2 and 4. At the same time, adjacent vertical angles 1 and 4 or 2 and 3 are also supplementary angles and will form 180°.

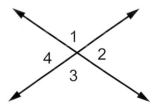

Complementary angles are two angles that add up to 90°. The example that follows shows that angles A and B add up to 90°.

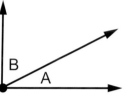

Supplementary angles are two angles that add up to 180°. This example shows that angles A and B add up to 180°.

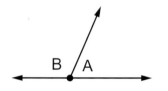

A. Angles and Lines in the Plane

If two lines are **parallel**, they have the same slope. Such lines will never intersect, and so they will never form angles with one another.

If two lines are **perpendicular**, their intersection forms only 90° angles. If the slope of a given line is a/b, then the slope of any perpendicular line is $-b/a$.

EXAMPLE

Consider the line defined by $y = 2x + 3$.

(a) Give the equation for a parallel line:

$$y = 2x + 2.$$

Any line that still has a slope of 2 will suffice. So, in slope-intercept form, any line of the form $y = 2x + a$ will be a parallel line.

(b) Give the equation for the perpendicular line that intersects the given line at the y-axis.

In this case, there is only one solution since the line can only intersect the *y*-axis once. The solution will be a line with the same *y*-intercept (which is 3) and the negative reciprocal slope (which is −½).

$$y = -\frac{1}{2}x + 3$$

The standard kind of angle-line problem deals with a setup of two parallel lines that are cut by a transversal, like the one in the following.

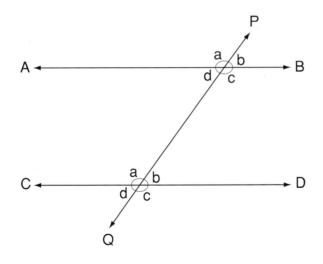

The trick with these problems is to realize that there are only ever two values for the angles.

First, think of the two areas of intersection as exact duplicates of each other. The upper left angles are equivalent, as are the upper right, the lower left, and the lower right. Using just this information, you automatically know the value of the twin of any angle that is given to you.

Also, angles that are opposite each other are equivalent. So the lower left angle is the same as the upper right and vice versa.

The other fact you can use to determine unknown angles is that the angle along a straight line is 180°. When you are given an angle *a*, you can find supplement *b* by subtracting 180° − *a*.

EXAMPLE

In the figure that follows, if angle *a* is 35°, what is the value of angle *b*?

Angle *b* is the twin of the supplement of *a*, so *b* is equal to 180° − *a*.

$$b = 180° - 35° = 145°$$

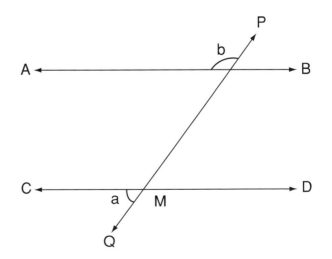

B. Properties of Parallel Line Angles

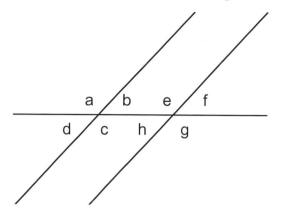

When two parallel lines are cut by a transversal line:

1. both pairs of acute angles as well as obtuse angles are equal: $a = e$, $b = f$, $d = h$, $c = g$.

2. alternate interior angles are equal in measure as well: $c = e$, $b = h$.

C. Interior Angles of a Polygon

Sometimes you may be dealing with a shape that you are not familiar with and do not know the total of all interior angles. If the polygon has x sides, the sum, S, is the total of all interior angles for that polygon. For a polygon with x sides, the sum may be calculated by the following formula:

$$S = (x - 2)(180°)$$

EXAMPLE

A triangle has 3 sides, therefore,

$$S = (3 - 2) \times 180°$$
$$S = 180°$$

A rectangle has 4 sides,

$$S = (4 - 2) \times 180°$$
$$S = 360°.$$

Given the total angles for a polygon, you can determine each interior angle of a polygon by dividing the sum of the polygon by the number of sides.

EXAMPLE

A rectangle has a sum of 360°. Given that $x = 4$, $360° \div 4 = 90°$. Therefore, each angle in a rectangle is 90°.

NOTE

The assumption here is that all angles of a given polygon have the same measure, which may not always be the case on the DAT. In order to apply this, be certain that the polygon has equal angles.

5.2 2D Figures

Make sure you know how to find the area, perimeter, side lengths, and angles of all the figures in this section. There are all kinds of ways to combine different shapes into the same problem; but if you can deal with them all individually, you'll be able to break down any problem thrown your way!

5.2.1 Rectangles and Squares

A **rectangle** is a figure with four straight sides and four right angles. In rectangles, opposite sides always have the same length, as do the two diagonals that can be drawn from corner to corner.

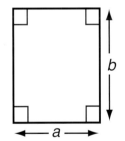

Perimeter: The perimeter of a rectangle is equal to the sum of its sides.

$$\text{Perimeter} = a + b + a + b = 2a + 2b$$

Area: The area of a rectangle is equal to the product of its length and width.

$$\text{Area} = \text{Length} \times \text{Width} = a \times b$$

A **square** is a rectangle with all four sides of the same length, so $a = b$.

The perimeter of a square is

$$P = a + a + a + a = 4a.$$

The area of a square is

$$A = a \times a = a^2.$$

5.2.2 Types of Triangles

While there are a wide variety of types of triangles, every one shares these properties:

(i) The sum of the interior angles of a triangle is always equal to 180°. In the following figure, a, b, and c are interior angles.

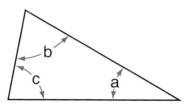

$3x - 10 = 25 + x + 15$

$2x = 10 + 25 + 15$

$2x = 50$

$x = 25$

(ii) The sum of the exterior angles of a triangle is always equal to $360°$. The following figure shows d, e, and f to be exterior angles.

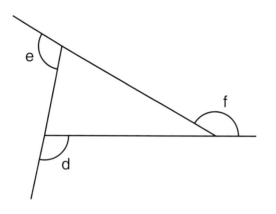

(iii) The value of an exterior angle is equal to the sum of the opposite two interior angles.

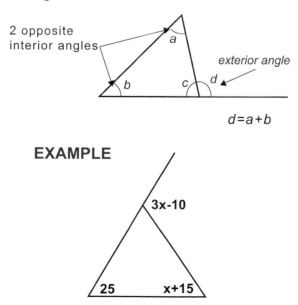

$d = a + b$

EXAMPLE

(iv) The perimeter of a triangle is equal to the sum of its sides.

(v) The area of a triangle is always half the product of the base and the height.

$$\text{Area} = \frac{1}{2} \text{Base} \times \text{Height}$$

You can pick any side of the triangle to function as the base, and the height will be the line perpendicular to that side that runs between it and the opposite vertex.

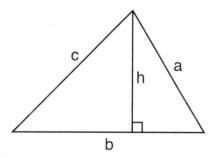

(vi) The sum of any two sides of a triangle is always greater than or equal to the third side. So if a, b, and c are the three sides of a triangle,

$$a + b \geq c.$$

If the sum of two sides is equal to the length of the third side, the triangle is a line segment. This property is known as the **triangle inequality**.

(vii) The difference of any two sides of a triangle is always smaller than the third side. So if a, b and c are three sides of a triangle, a − b < c.

What are the possible values for x?

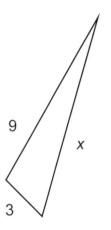

Therefore, x < (9 + 3) and x > (9 - 3), 6 < x < 12.

A. Right Triangles

A **right triangle** is a triangle that contains a right angle. The other two angles in a right triangle add up to 90°.

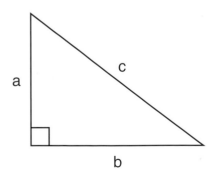

The two short legs of a right triangle (the legs that come together to form the right angle) and the hypotenuse (the side opposite the right angle) are related by the Pythagorean Theorem:

$$a^2 + b^2 = c^2$$

To find a missing side of the triangle, plug the values you have into the Pythagorean Theorem and solve algebraically.

The two legs of a right triangle are its base and height. So to find the area, compute as thus shown.

$$\text{Area} = \frac{1}{2}(a \times b)$$

Special Cases: There are a few cases of right triangles you should know. First, the ratios of side lengths 3:4:5 and 5:12:13 are often used. Identifying that a triangle corresponds to one of these cases can save you precious time since you will not have to solve the Pythagorean Theorem.

There are also two special ratios of interior angles for right triangles: 30°–60°–90° and 45°–45°–90°. The sides of a 30°–60°–90° triangle have the ratio $1:\sqrt{3}:2$ and the sides of a 45°–45°–90° triangle have the ratio $1:1:\sqrt{2}$.

> **NOTE**
>
> ### Pythagorean Theorem
>
> Knowing any two sides of a right triangle lets you find the third side by using the Pythagorean formula: $a^2 + b^2 = c^2$.
>
> 3-4-5 triangle: if a right triangle has two legs with a ratio of 3:4, or a leg to a hypotenuse ratio of either 3:5 or 4:5, then it is a 3-4-5 triangle.
>
> 5-12-13 triangle: if a right triangle has two legs with a ratio of 5:12, or a leg to a hypotenuse ratio of either 5:13 or 12:13, then it is a 5-12-13 triangle.
>
> 45°-45°-90° triangle: if a right triangle has two angles that are both 45°, then the ratio of the three legs is $1:1:\sqrt{(2)}$.
>
> 30°-60°-90° triangle: if a right triangle has two angles of 30° and 60°, then the ratio of the three legs is $1:\sqrt{(3)}:2$.

B. Isosceles Triangles

An **isosceles triangle** is a triangle that has two equal sides. The angles that sit opposite the equal sides are also equal.

For an isosceles triangle, use the odd side as the base and draw the height line to the odd vertex. This line will bisect the side, so it is simple to determine the height using the Pythagorean Theorem on one of the new right triangles formed.

C. Equilateral Triangles

An **equilateral triangle** is a triangle

with all three sides equal. All three interior angles are also equal, so they are all 60°.

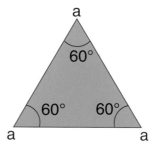

Drawing a height line from any vertex will divide the triangle into two 30°–60°–90° triangles, so you can easily solve for the area.

D. Scalene Triangles

A **scalene triangle** is any triangle that has no equal sides and no equal angles. To find the value for the height of this kind of triangle requires the use of trigonometric functions (see Chapter 6).

E. Similar Triangles

Two triangles are **similar** if they have the same values for interior angles. This means that ratios of corresponding sides will be equal. Similar triangles are triangles with the same shape that are scaled to different sizes.

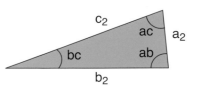

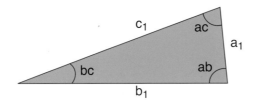

To solve for values in a triangle from information given about a similar triangle, you will need to use ratios. The ratios of corresponding sides are always equal, for example $\dfrac{a_1}{a_2} = \dfrac{b_1}{b_2}$. Also, the ratio of two sides in the same triangle is equal to the corresponding ratio in the similar triangle, for example $\dfrac{a_1}{b_1} = \dfrac{a_2}{b_2}$.

5.2.3 Circles

A **circle** is a figure in which every point is the same distance from the center. This distance from the center to the edge is known as the **radius** (r). The length of any straight line drawn from a point on the circle, through the center, and out to another point on the circle is known as the **diameter** (d). The diameter is twice the radius.

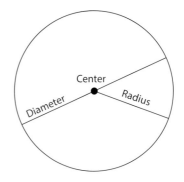

$$d = 2 \times r \quad \text{or} \quad r = \frac{1}{2}d$$

There are no angles in a circle.

Circumference: The circumference of a circle is the total distance around a circle. It is equal to pi times the diameter.

$$\text{Circumference} = \pi \times d = 2\pi \times r$$

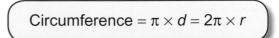

Area: The area of a circle is equal to pi times the square of the radius.

$$\text{Area} = \pi \times r^2 = \frac{1}{4}\pi \times d^2$$

Length: Length of an arc is defined as a piece of circumference formed by an angle of *n* degrees measured as the arc's central angle in a circle of radius *r*.

$$L = \frac{n°}{360°} \times 2\pi r$$

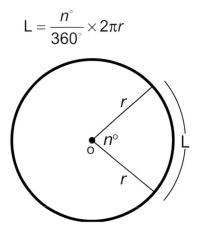

Area of a sector: The area of a sector is a portion of the circle formed by an angle of *n* degree measured as the sector's central angle in a circle of radius *r*.

$$\text{Area (sector)} = \frac{1}{2}r^2\theta \text{ (in radians)}$$

$$\text{Area (sector)} = \frac{n°}{360°} \times \pi r^2 \text{ (in degrees)}$$

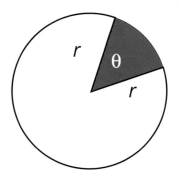

5.2.4 Trapezoids and Parallelograms

A. Trapezoids

A **trapezoid** is a four-sided figure with one pair of parallel sides and one pair of non-parallel sides.

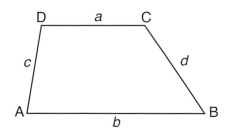

Usually the easiest way to solve trapezoid problems is to drop vertical lines down from the vertices on the smaller of the two parallel lines. This splits the figure into two right triangles on the ends and a rectangle in the middle. Then, to find information about the trapezoid, you can solve for the information (side length, area, angles, etc.) of these other shapes.

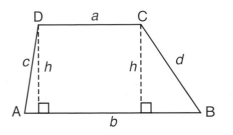

1. The area of a trapezoid is calculated as

$$\frac{a+b}{2}h$$

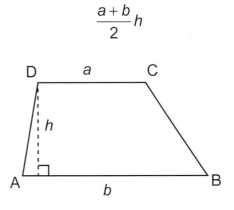

2. The upper and lower base angles are supplementary angles (i.e., they add up to 180°).

Angle A + Angle D = 180°
Angle B + Angle C = 180°

Sometimes it can be useful to draw a line from vertex to vertex and construct a triangle that way, but this usually only makes sense if the resulting triangle is special (i.e. isosceles).

Isosceles Trapezoids: Just like isosceles triangles, **isosceles trapezoids** are trapezoids with two equal sides. The sides that are equal are the parallel sides that form angles with the base of the trapezoid. Similarly, if the left and right sides are of the same lengths, these angles are the same as well.

In this isosceles trapezoid, ABCE means that Angle A = Angle D, Angle B = Angle C, and Diagonal AC = Diagonal BD.

The perimeter = $a + b + 2c$

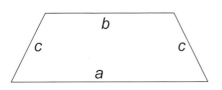

B. Parallelograms

A **parallelogram** is a quadrilateral that has two sets of parallel sides. A square, for example, is a special kind of parallelogram, as is a rhombus (which has four sides of equal length but, unlike a square, has two different pairs of angle values).

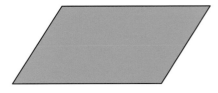

Area: The area of a parallelogram is simply the base times the height.

Area = (Base) × (Height)

The height of a parallelogram can be found by dropping a vertical from a vertex to the opposite side and evaluating the resulting right triangle.

The sum of all the angles in a parallelogram is 360°. Opposite angles are equivalent, and adjacent angles add up to 180°.

5.3 3D Solids

In three dimensions, it doesn't always make sense to talk about perimeters. Shapes with defined edges (such as boxes and pyramids) still have them, but rounded shapes (such as spheres) do not. Instead, we are generally concerned with the values of surface area and volume.

5.3.1 Boxes

Boxes are the three-dimensional extension of rectangles. Every angle in a box is 90°, and every box has six rectangular faces, twelve edges, and eight vertices. Opposite (and parallel) faces are always of the same length, height, and width, as are opposite (and parallel) edges.

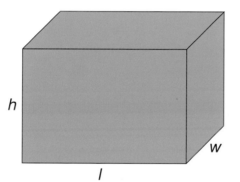

Perimeter: The perimeter of a box is the sum of its edges. There are, however, only three different lengths and four edges corresponding to each one. So to find the perimeter, we can simply take the sum of four times each the width, length, and height.

$$\text{Perimeter} = 4l + 4w + 4h = 4(l + w + h)$$

Surface Area: The surface area of a box is the sum of the area of each of its faces. Since there is one duplicate of each unique face, we only need to find three products, double them, and add them together.

$$\text{Surface Area} = 2lw + 2wh + 2lh$$
$$= 2(lw + wh + lh)$$

Volume: Calculating the volume of a box can be visualized as taking the surface of any of its rectangular faces and dragging it through space, like you were blowing a box-shaped bubble. So you start with the product of a width times a height, and then you multiply that by a length.

$$\text{Volume} = l \times w \times h$$

5.3.2 Spheres

The definition of a sphere is basically identical to that of a circle, except that it is applied in three dimensions rather than two: It is a collection of points in three dimensions that are all of the same distance from a particular center point. Again, we call this distance the radius, and twice the radius is the diameter. A sphere has no vertices or edges, so it has no circumference.

Surface Area:

$$\text{Surface Area} = 4\pi \times r^2$$

Volume:

$$\text{Volume} = (4/3)\pi \times r^3$$

5.3.3 Cylinders

Spheres may be the 3D equivalent of circles, but if you start with a circle and extend it into the third dimension, you obtain the tube shape known as a cylinder. Cylinders have two parallel circular faces, and their edges are connected by a smooth, edgeless surface.

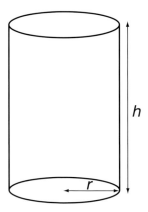

Surface Area: The surface area of a cylinder is composed of three parts: The two circular faces and the connecting portion. To find the total area of a cylinder, add the areas of these two parts. We already know how to calculate area for circles; and for the connecting surface, all we need to do is extend the circumference of one of the circles into three dimensions. So, multiply the circumference by the height of the cylinder.

$$\text{Surface Area} = 2(\pi \times r^2) + (2\pi \times r) \times h$$

Volume: The volume of a cylinder is equal to the area of one of its bases (circle) multiplied by the height.

$$\text{Volume} = (\pi \times r^2) \times h$$

5.3.4 Cones

A cone is like a cylinder, except that instead of having a circle on either end; it has a circle on one and a single point on the other. The height of the cone is the distance from the center of the circle to the single vertex, and the slant length is the distance from the edge of the circle to the vertex.

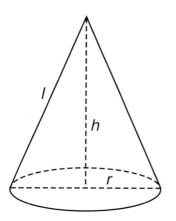

Surface Area: To find the surface area of a cone, we use the same strategy as we did with a cylinder. We find the surface area of the circle and add it to the surface area of the smooth lateral portion. The area of the circle can be found from the radius as usual, and the area of the lateral portion is ½ the circumference of the circle times the slant length.

$$\text{Surface Area} = (\pi \times r^2) + \frac{1}{2}c \times l$$
$$= (\pi \times r^2) + \frac{1}{2}(2\pi \times r) \times l$$

Volume: To find the volume of a cone, we need the radius of the circle and the cone's height.

$$\text{Volume} = (1/3)\pi \times r^2 \times h$$

There are all kinds of different solids

5.3.5 Other Solids

that can be constructed out of basic 2D figures and the solids we've already discussed. If you are able to deal with all of these individually though, you will be able to break down and tackle any wacky solid that might be thrown at you.

5.3.6 Vertices

You have now heard the word "vertex" used in different instances with similar meanings. Just for clarification, we may define the vertex as: (1) the point at which the sides of an angle intersect; (2) the points on a triangle or pyramid opposite to and farthest away from its base; and finally, (3) a point on a polyhedron (a solid bounded by faces/polygons) common to three or more sides.

GOLD STANDARD WARM-UP EXERCISES

CHAPTER 5: Geometry

1. The area of a circle is 144π. What is its circumference?
   A. 6π
   B. 24π
   C. 72π
   D. 12π
   E. 36π

2. How many cubes with edges of length 6 inches will fit inside a cubical box with an edge of length 1 yard?
   A. 216
   B. 36
   C. 18
   D. 108
   E. 72

3. The points (2,–3) and (2,5) are the endpoints of a diameter of a circle. What is the radius of the circle?
   A. 64
   B. 4π
   C. 16
   D. 8
   E. 4

4. A cylinder of radius 1 foot and height 1 foot is full of water. The water is poured into a cyclinder of radius 1 foot and height 6 inches until it is full. How many cubic feet of the water will be left over?
   A. 0.6π
   B. 0.4π
   C. 0.64π
   D. 0.5π
   E. 0.75π

5. A and B are similar 45°-45°-90° triangles. If B has an area of 12 square feet, and A has three times the area of B, what is the length of A's hypotenuse?
   A. $\sqrt{72}$ feet
   B. 36 feet
   C. 72 feet
   D. 12 feet
   E. 6 feet

6. Leslie drives from Highway 1 to the parallel Highway 2 using the road that crosses them, as in the given figure below. Leslie misses the turn onto Highway 1 at point Q and drives 2 km further, to point P. Driving in a straight line from point P to get back to Highway 1, how much further will Leslie travel?

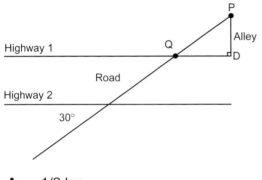

A. 1/2 km
B. $\sqrt{3}$ km
C. 1 km
D. 2 km
E. $2\sqrt{3}$ km

7. A circle is inscribed in a square with a diagonal of length 5. What is the area of the circle?

A. $\dfrac{25}{8}\pi$

B. $\dfrac{25}{2}\pi$

C. $\dfrac{25}{16}\pi$

D. $\dfrac{25}{4}\pi$

E. 50π

8. A circle is drawn inside a larger circle so that they have the same center. If the smaller circle has 25% the area of the larger circle, which of the following is the ratio of the radius of the small circle to that of the larger circle?

A. $\dfrac{1}{8}$

B. $\dfrac{3}{4}$

C. $\dfrac{1}{4}$

D. $\dfrac{1}{25}$

E. $\dfrac{1}{2}$

9. A circle passes through the point (0,0) and the point (10,0). Which of the following could NOT be a third point on the Circle?

A (1, –3)
B (2, 4)
C (7, 4)
D (5, 0)
E (2, –4)

10. A rectangular picture 4½ feet wide and 3½ feet long is enclosed by a border 3 inches wide. What is the total area, in square feet, of the picture and border?

A. 12
B. 15
C. 15¾
D. 17¹³⁄₁₆
E. 20

11. Mary wants to wallpaper a room. It has one bay window that measures 3 feet by 4 feet, and a door that measures 3 feet by 7 feet. The room is 12 feet by 12 feet, and is 10 feet tall. If only the walls are to be covered, and rolls of wallpaper are 100 square feet, what is the minimum number of rolls that she will need?

A. 4 rolls
B. 5 rolls
C. 6 rolls
D. 7 rolls
E. 8 rolls

12. In order to protect her new car, Stacey needs to build a new garage. The concrete floor needs to be 64.125 square feet and is 9.5 feet long. How wide does it need to be?

A. 7.25 feet
B. 8.25 feet
C. 6.75 feet
D. 6.25 feet
E. 7.50 feet

GS ANSWER KEY

CHAPTER 5

		Cross-Reference				Cross-Reference
1.	B	QR 5.2, 5.2.3		7.	A	QR 5.2, 5.2.1, 5.2.3
2.	A	QR 5.3, 5.3.1		8.	E	QR 5.2, 5.2.3
3.	E	QR 5.2, 5.2.3		9.	D	QR 5.1, 5.1.1, 5.2.3
4.	D	QR 5.3, 5.3.3		10.	E	QR 5.2, 5.2.1
5.	D	QR 5.2, 5.2.2		11.	B	QR 5.3, 5.3.1
6.	C	QR 5.1, 5.1.3		12.	C	QR 5.3, 5.3.1

* Explanations can be found at the back of the book.

Go online to DAT-prep.com for additional chapter review Q&A and forum.

TRIGONOMETRY
Chapter 6

Memorize	Understand	Importance
* Formulas for Sine, Cosine, and Tangent * Important Values of Sine and Cosine * Important Identities * Polar Coordinate Conversions	* Graphing Sine, Cosine, and Tangent * Secant, Cosecant, and Cotangent * The Unit Circle * Degrees vs. Radians * Inverse Trigonometric Functions * Graphing in Polar Coordinates * Distance and Midpoint Formulas	**3 to 5 out of the 40 QR** questions on the DAT are based on content from this chapter (in our estimation). * This will change in 2015.

DAT-Prep.com

Introduction

Trigonometry is the most conceptually advanced branch of mathematics with which you will need to be familiar for the Quantitative Reasoning test. But don't let that scare you. Basically, everything in this section boils down to right triangles, and after Chapter 6, you'd be a triangle pro!

Additional Resources

Free Online Forum

DAT-Prep.com
THE GOLD STANDARD

6.1 Basic Trigonometric Functions

The trigonometric functions describe the relationship between the angles and sides of right triangles. The angle in question is generally denoted by θ, the Greek letter theta, but you will never see the right angle used as θ.

We call the leg connecting to the vertex of θ the *adjacent side* ("b" in the diagram), and the leg that does not touch the *opposite side* ("a" in the diagram). The edge across from the right angle is called the *hypotenuse*.

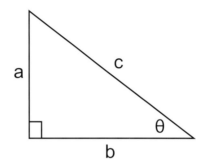

6.1.1 Sine

A lot of people like to use the mnemonic device "SOH-CAH-TOA" to remember how to evaluate the three basic trigonometric functions: Sine, cosine, and tangent. The first three letters, "SOH," refer to the first letter of each word in the following equation.

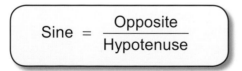

$$\text{Sine} = \frac{\text{Opposite}}{\text{Hypotenuse}}$$

Sine of an angle θ is written sin(θ). So to calculate this value, simply divide the length of the opposite side by the length of the hypotenuse.

EXAMPLE

What is sin(θ) in the following triangle?

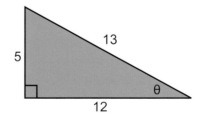

The opposite side has length 5, and the hypotenuse has length 13, so

$$\sin(\theta) = \frac{5}{13}$$

6.1.2 Cosine

The second set of three letters in SOH-CAH-TOA refers to the equation for the cosine of an angle.

$$\text{Cosine} = \frac{\text{Adjacent}}{\text{Hypotenuse}}$$

The abbreviation for the cosine of an angle is cos(θ).

EXAMPLE

In the 5–12–13 triangle in Section 6.1.1, what is cos(θ)?

Dividing the adjacent side by the hypotenuse, we obtain the following solution:

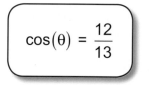

$$\cos(\theta) = \frac{12}{13}$$

6.1.3 Tangent

The final three letters in SOH-CAH-TOA refer to the equation for finding the tangent of an angle.

$$\text{Tangent} = \frac{\text{Opposite}}{\text{Adjacent}}$$

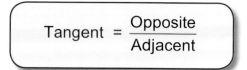

You can also find the tangent of an angle if you know the value for sine and cosine. Notice that the hypotenuse cancels out if you divide sine and cosine.

$$\text{Tangent} = \frac{\text{Sine}}{\text{Cosine}}$$

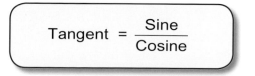

You can also manipulate this equation to express sine or cosine in terms of the tangent.

EXAMPLE

In the 5–12–13 triangle in Section 6.1.1, what is tan(θ)?

Dividing the opposite side by the adjacent side, we obtain:

$$\tan(\theta) = \frac{5}{12}$$

6.1.4 Secant, Cosecant, and Cotangent

These three functions are far less commonly used than sine, cosine, and tangent, but you should still be familiar with them. They are not very hard to remember because they are just the reciprocals of the main three functions.

$$\text{Secant} = \frac{1}{\text{Cosine}}$$

$$= \frac{\text{Hypotenuse}}{\text{Adjacent}}$$

$$\text{Cosecant} = \frac{1}{\text{Sine}}$$

$$= \frac{\text{Hypotenuse}}{\text{Opposite}}$$

$$\text{Cotangent} = \frac{1}{\text{Tangent}}$$

$$= \frac{\text{Adjacent}}{\text{Opposite}}$$

The abbreviations for these functions are sec, csc, and cot, respectively.

6.2 The Unit Circle

6.2.1 Trig Functions on a Circle

As you can see from the equations in Section 6.1, the trigonometric functions are ratios of side lengths. This means that every angle has a value for each of the functions that *does not* depend on the scale of the triangle.

In Section 6.1 we looked at examples with a 5–12–13 triangle. Our solutions were as follows:

$$\sin(\theta) = \frac{5}{13}$$

$$\cos(\theta) = \frac{12}{13}$$

$$\tan(\theta) = \frac{5}{12}$$

Let's compare these results with the trigonometric functions for the similar triangle 10, 24, 26, which clearly has longer sides but the same angle θ:

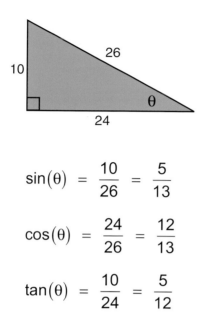

$$\sin(\theta) = \frac{10}{26} = \frac{5}{13}$$

$$\cos(\theta) = \frac{24}{26} = \frac{12}{13}$$

$$\tan(\theta) = \frac{10}{24} = \frac{5}{12}$$

As you can see, the trigonometric values for the angle remain the same.

Also, the absolute value of sine and cosine is never greater than 1 for any angle. This makes perfect sense because the hypotenuse of a triangle is always its longest side, and for sine and cosine, the hypotenuse is in the denominator.

If we plot the graph of sine and cosine for θ from 0° to 360° in Cartesian Coordinates with $x = \cos(\theta)$ and $y = \sin(\theta)$, we obtain a circle of radius 1. This is known as

the **unit circle**, as shown in the succeeding picture. The angle formed at the vertex of the x-axis is equal to θ.

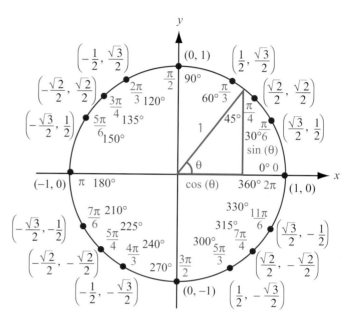

When simply dealing with right triangle figures, we never use negative numbers because negative length does not make sense. With the unit circle, though, legs of the triangle can be in negative space on the Cartesian plane. This can result in negative values for sine and cosine.

6.2.2 Degrees and Radians

Up until this point, we have measured angles using degrees. When dealing with trigonometric functions, however, it is

often more convenient to use the unit-less measurement of **radians**. There are 2π radians in 360°, so one trip around the unit circle is an increase in θ by 2π radians.

$$2\pi \text{ radians} = 360°$$

This translates to 1 radian = $\dfrac{360}{2\pi}$, but you will usually be working with radians in multiples of π, so it is not necessary to memorize this.

Here is a list of important angles (in degrees and radians) and their sine and cosine values to memorize from the unit circle:

Degrees	Radians	Sine	Cosine
0°	0	0	1
30°	$\dfrac{\pi}{6}$	$\dfrac{1}{2}$	$\dfrac{(\sqrt{3})}{2}$
45°	$\dfrac{\pi}{4}$	$\dfrac{1}{\sqrt{2}}$	$\dfrac{1}{\sqrt{2}}$
60°	$\dfrac{\pi}{3}$	$\dfrac{(\sqrt{3})}{2}$	$\dfrac{1}{2}$
90°	$\dfrac{\pi}{2}$	1	0

Note that $\dfrac{1}{\sqrt{2}}$ is the same as $\dfrac{\sqrt{2}}{2}$.

These major angles repeat for each quadrant of the unit circle, but the signs of the sine and cosine values change. Moving counterclockwise around the circle and beginning with the upper right, the quadrants are labeled I, II, III, and IV.

Quadrant	Sine	Cosine
I	+	+
II	+	−
III	−	−
IV	−	+

NOTE

How many degrees are there in $\dfrac{3(\pi)}{4}$ radians?

Because 2π radians = 360°, this makes 1(π) radian = 180°.

Solution:

1π radian = 180°

$$\frac{3\pi}{4} = \frac{3\pi}{4} \times \frac{180°}{\pi}$$
$$= 135°$$

How many radians are there in 270°?

Solution:

1π radian = 180°

$$270° \times \frac{\pi}{180°} = \frac{3\pi}{2}$$

6.2.3 Graphing Trig Functions

Looking at the unit circle, it is very apparent that the trigonometric functions are **periodic**. This means that they continue to repeat the same cycle infinitely. After you go once around the circle, a full 360°, you end up right back at the beginning and begin to cycle through again.

A. Sine

As you can see from the table in 6.2.2, the sine function increases for the first 90°. For the next 90° it decreases while staying positive, then it continues to decrease into the negatives, and finally for the last 90°, it increases from −1 back to 0. From this information, we can picture the general shape of the graph, and we know that the period of the function is a full 360° or 2π radians.

The graph itself looks like this:

$y = \sin(x)$

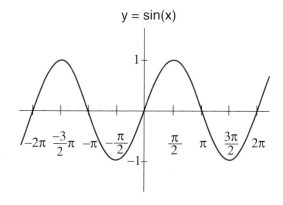

As you can see in the graph, the sine function reaches a maximum at $\frac{\pi}{2} + 2\pi \times n$, has an x-intercept at $\pi \times n$, and a minimum at $\frac{3\pi}{2} + 2\pi \times n$ where n is any integer.

B. Cosine

The cosine function is identical to the sine function, except that it is shifted along the x-axis by half a period. So rather than starting at 0 and increasing, it starts at one and decreases. The period is still 2π radians.

The graph looks like this:

$y = \cos(x)$

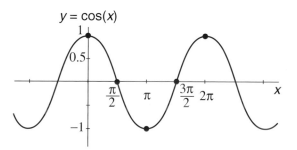

Just like with the sine function, you can see where the maxima, minima, and intercepts of the cosine function are from the graph. It reaches a maximum at $2\pi \times n$, an x-intercept at $\frac{\pi}{2} + \pi \times n$, and a minimum at $2\pi \times n + \pi \times n$ where n is any integer.

C. Tangent

The graph of the tangent function differs from sine and cosine graphs in a few important ways. First of all, the tangent function repeats itself every π radian instead of every 2π. So it is π-periodic rather than 2π-periodic. Also, it has vertical **asymptotes**, vertical lines that the function approaches but never crosses, at $(n)\left(\dfrac{\pi}{2}\right)$ for every odd integer n. The value of the tangent goes infinity as it approaches an asymptote from left to right; and negative infinity as it approaches from right to left.

Remember, the tangent function is the ratio of the sine function to the cosine function, so the asymptotes occur when the cosine of an angle is equal to zero, where $\cos(x) = 0$, because division by zero is undefined. 0/0 is never possible for the tangent function, so it is irrelevant.

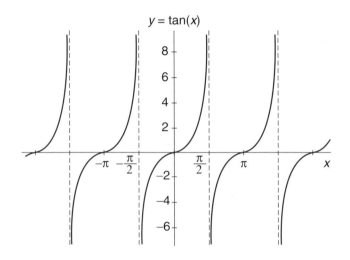

$y = \tan(x)$

6.3 Trigonometric Problems

6.3.1 Inverse Trig Functions

We have discussed the formulas for finding the value of trigonometric functions for different angles, but how can you find the value of an angle if all you know is the value of one of the functions? This is where the inverse trigonometric functions come into play.

The **inverse** of a trigonometric function takes an input value x and outputs an angle. The value of the inverse trigonometric function of x is equal to the angle. To represent an inverse function, we write -1 in superscript like we would an exponent. But remember, this is not actually an exponent.

Inverse sine is represented as $\sin^{-1}$ and it is defined as such:

$$\sin\left(\sin^{-1}(x)\right) = x$$

So, $\sin(\theta) = x$ and $\sin^{-1}(x) = \theta$.

Now that we have inverse functions in our toolbox, we can begin to solve algebraic problems that contain trigonometric functions.

Solve the following equation for x.

$$\pi - \tan 2x = \left(\frac{4}{3}\right)\pi$$

$$\Rightarrow -\tan 2x = \left(\frac{1}{3}\right)\pi$$

$$\Rightarrow \tan 2x = \frac{-\pi}{3}$$

$$\Rightarrow 2x = \tan^{-1}\left(\frac{-\pi}{3}\right)$$

We did not list values for tangent in the tables in Section 6.2.2, but we can use the sine and cosine values to find them. Remember that tan = sin/cos. We can use the values for $\frac{\pi}{3}$ in quadrant IV:

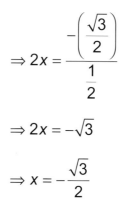

$$\Rightarrow 2x = \frac{-\left(\dfrac{\sqrt{3}}{2}\right)}{\dfrac{1}{2}}$$

$$\Rightarrow 2x = -\sqrt{3}$$

$$\Rightarrow x = -\frac{\sqrt{3}}{2}$$

6.3.2 Trigonometric Identities

There are a few other identities that can be extremely useful in the manipulation of equations involving trigonometric functions. If you encounter such an equation and it seems like it would be difficult to solve using only inverses, you should try to apply these identities. You may have to do some algebraic work, though, before you can apply them.

(i) $\quad \sin^2\theta + \cos^2\theta = 1$

This identity follows directly from the Pythagorean Theorem. Since the sine and cosine compose the legs of a right triangle and the hypotenuse has length 1, this identity always holds.

(ii) $\tan^2\theta + 1 = \sec^2\theta$

(iii) $\cot^2\theta + 1 = \csc^2\theta$

(iv) $\sin(2\theta) = 2\sin\theta\cos\theta$

(v) $\cos(2\theta) = 1 - 2\sin^2\theta$

(vi) $\tan(2\theta) = \dfrac{2\tan\theta}{1-\tan^2\theta}$

EXAMPLE

Simplify the following equation:

$$\sin^2(x) + \sin^2(x) \times \cos^2(x) = \sec^2(x)$$

Since the only functions on the left side at this point are sines and cosines, let's factor out a $\sin^2(x)$ and then try to use identity (i).

$$\sin^2(x)[\sin^2(x) + \cos^2(x)] = \sec^2(x)$$
$$\sin^2(x) \times 1 = \sec^2(x)$$

Now let's replace $\sec^2(x)$ using identity (ii).

$$\sin^2(x) = \tan^2(x) + 1$$

We can even simplify this further using the equation for tangent (= sin/cos) and then multiply each side by $\cos^2(x)$.

$$\sin^2(x) = \frac{\sin^2(x)}{\cos^2(x)} + 1$$

$$\sin^2(x)\cos^2(x) = \left(\frac{\sin^2(x)}{\cos^2(x)} + 1\right)\cos^2(x)$$

$$\sin^2(x)\cos^2(x) = \cos^2(x) + \sin^2(x)$$

By using identity (i) again, we have

$$\sin^2(x)\cos^2(x) = 1$$

6.3.3 The Pythagorean Theorem

The Pythagorean Theorem is fundamental to trigonometry.

If a problem requires you to set up an equation involving trigonometric functions, whether it is from an arbitrary right triangle or the unit circle, you will most likely need to use the Pythagorean Theorem. Remember, it is the primary relationship we have in relating the lengths of sides in a right triangle, so now we can relate side length to trigonometric functions.

6.4 Polar Coordinates

So far, we have only discussed graphs using Cartesian coordinates. As we have seen, the Cartesian system makes it easy to work with straight lines, but this does not hold true for all types of curves.

There is another important two-dimensional system that uses what are known as **polar coordinates**. Instead of plotting a point using the two legs of a right triangle (the x and y coordinates in the Cartesian system), polar coordinates use the hypotenuse of the triangle (r) and the angle from the x-axis (θ). Instead of two distance components, polar coordinates use one radial distance component (the distance from the origin) and an angle component. A point is written as the ordered pair (r, θ).

Conversions: Sometimes, it is necessary to convert points between polar and Cartesian coordinates. Here are the identities to use:

(i) $r^2 = x^2 + y^2$

(ii) $x = r \times \cos(\theta)$

(iii) $y = r \times \sin(\theta)$

EXAMPLE

Convert the Cartesian point (3,4) to polar coordinates.

Before we can find θ we need to find the value for r using (i).

$$r^2 = 3^2 + 4^2$$
$$\Rightarrow r^2 = 25$$
$$\Rightarrow r = 5$$

Now we can find θ using either (ii) or (iii).

$$3 = 5 \times \cos(\theta)$$
$$\Rightarrow 3/5 = \cos(\theta)$$
$$\Rightarrow \theta = \cos^{-1}(3/5)$$
$$\Rightarrow \theta \approx 53°$$

Combining this information, we see that the Cartesian point (3,4) is the point (5, 53°) in polar coordinates.

EXAMPLE

Convert $x^2 + y^2 = 4$ to polar coordinates and graph.

This conversion happens to be extremely simple. All we need to do is apply (i) directly.

$$\Rightarrow r^2 = 4$$
$$\Rightarrow r = 2$$

Notice that in this equation, r does not depend on θ. It contains simply all points that are 2 units away from the origin.

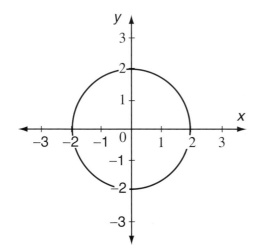

In polar coordinates, a circle of radius x centered at the origin results when $r = x$ for any constant x.

6.5 Additional Helpful Formulas

Sum or Difference of Two Angles

For angles α and β, the following sum and difference identities may be applied:

1. $\sin(\alpha + \beta) = \sin\alpha \cos\beta + \cos\alpha \sin\beta$

2. $\sin(\alpha - \beta) = \sin\alpha \cos\beta - \cos\alpha \sin\beta$

3. $\cos(\alpha + \beta) = \cos\alpha \cos\beta - \sin\alpha \sin\beta$

4. $\cos(\alpha - \beta) = \cos\alpha \cos\beta + \sin\alpha \sin\beta$

5. $\tan(\alpha + \beta) = \dfrac{\tan\alpha + \tan\beta}{1 - \tan\alpha\,\tan\beta}$

6. $\tan(\alpha - \beta) = \dfrac{\tan\alpha - \tan\beta}{1 + \tan\alpha\,\tan\beta}$

Cofunction Identities

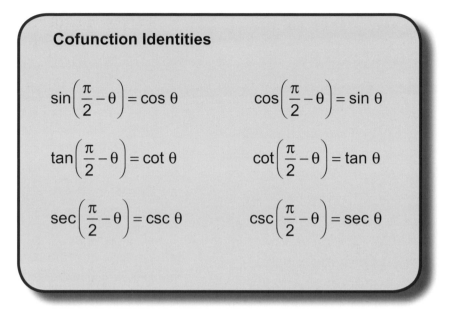

$$\sin\left(\frac{\pi}{2} - \theta\right) = \cos\theta \qquad \cos\left(\frac{\pi}{2} - \theta\right) = \sin\theta$$

$$\tan\left(\frac{\pi}{2} - \theta\right) = \cot\theta \qquad \cot\left(\frac{\pi}{2} - \theta\right) = \tan\theta$$

$$\sec\left(\frac{\pi}{2} - \theta\right) = \csc\theta \qquad \csc\left(\frac{\pi}{2} - \theta\right) = \sec\theta$$

Odd-Even Identities

For angle θ at which the functions are defined:

1. $\sin(-\theta) = -\sin(\theta)$

2. $\cos(-\theta) = \cos(\theta)$

3. $\tan(-\theta) = -\tan(\theta)$

4. $\cot(-\theta) = -\cot(\theta)$

5. $\sec(-\theta) = \sec(\theta)$

6. $\csc(-\theta) = -\csc(\theta)$

GOLD STANDARD WARM-UP EXERCISES

CHAPTER 6: Trigonometry

1. In a right triangle ABC with right angle at C, hypotenuse AB = 7 cm and side AC = 2 cm, approximately what is the measure of the angle at A?

   A. 17°

   B. 1°

   C. 0.5°

   D. 73°

   E. 16°

2. What percentage of the unit circle is represented by the angle 8π/5?

   A. 1.6%

   B. 80%

   C. 0.25%

   D. 160%

   E. 502%

3. Which of the following is the value of -cos(π/2)?

   A. 0

   B. −1

   C. 1

   D. $1/\sqrt{2}$

   E. $\sqrt{2}$

4. The tangent of one of the acute angles in a right triangle is 3/2. If the leg opposite this angle has a length of 12, what is the length of the hypotenuse?

   A. 8

   B. $6\sqrt{13}$

   C. $4\sqrt{13}$

   D. 18

   E. $3\sqrt{13}$

5. $\cos(x) - \sin(x) = 0$, $x = $?

   A. 45°

   B. 30°

   C. 180°

   D. 60°

   E. 270°

6. If the secant of an angle is 5/4, what is the tangent of the angle?

   A. 9/16

   B. 1/2

   C. 4/5

   D. 3/4

   E. $\sqrt{41}/25$

7. The value of cos(π/6) equals the value of:

    A. sin(π/2)

    B. sin (π/4)

    C. sin(π)

    D. sin (π/6)

    E. sin (π/3)

8. The sine of an angle is negative, and the tangent of the same angle is positive. In which quadrant does the angle lie?

    A. First

    B. Second

    C. Third

    D. Fourth

    E. Any

GS ANSWER KEY

CHAPTER 6

		Cross-Reference				*Cross-Reference*
1.	D	QR 6.3, 6.3.1	5.	A	QR 6.3, 6.3.2
2.	B	QR 6.2, 6.2.1	6.	D	QR 6.3, 6.3.2
3.	A	QR 6.5	7.	E	QR 6.2, 6.2.3
4.	C	QR 6.1, 6.1.3, 6.3, 6.3.3	8.	C	QR 6.2, 6.2.1

* Explanations can be found at the back of the book.

Go online to DAT-prep.com for additional chapter review Q&A and forum.

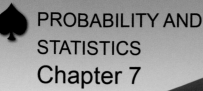

Memorize	Understand	Importance
* Formula for Average * Formula for Probability	* Determining Probabilities * Combining Probabilities of Multiple Events * Mode, Median, Variance, Standard Deviation and its Corresponding Graph * Correlation Coefficient * Permutations and Combinations	**3 to 5 out of the 40 QR** questions on the DAT are based on content from this chapter (in our estimation). * This will change in 2015.

DAT-Prep.com

Introduction

Probability and statistics are relatively minor subjects on the Quantitative Reasoning test, but they can be tricky. Please do note that effective 2015, more of these items will be given on the DAT.

This section will help you keep things straight such as when to multiply and when to add probabilities – simple questions that can often be the most confusing.

Additional Resources

Free Online Forum

7.1 Probability

7.1.1 What is Probability?

Probability is a measure of the likelihood that something will happen.

In mathematics, probability is represented as a ratio of two numbers. The second number - the denominator - corresponds to the total number of possible outcomes the situation can have. The first number - the numerator - corresponds to the number of ways the particular outcome in question can occur.

$$\text{Probability} = \frac{(\text{number of ways the outcome can occur})}{(\text{number of possible outcomes})}$$

Let's look at a simple example.

Let's consider the flipping of a coin. Of course, we know that there are only two possible outcomes of a coin flip, heads or tails. So the total number of outcomes is 2, which will be our denominator.

Say we want to find the probability that a flipped coin will be heads. There is only one way this outcome can come about, so the numerator will be 1. Therefore, the probability of flipping heads is 1 in 2:

$$\text{Probability of Heads} = \frac{1}{2}$$

It is important to note that the quantity in the numerator of a probability ratio is a subset of the quantity in the denominator. The number of ways an outcome can occur is always less than or equal to the total number of outcomes. This means that a probability will never be more than 1, since 1 would mean the outcome is the *only* possibility. Also, the sum of the probabilities of all possible outcomes will always be 1.

Let's look at a slightly more complicated example.

Say you have a typical six-sided die with the sides labeled 1 through 6. If you roll the die once, what is the probability that the number will not be divisible by 3?

Let's begin by finding the total number of outcomes. Be careful here. The only outcomes we wish to determine the probability of are rolls of numbers divisible by 3, but the total number of possible outcomes is not affected by this restriction. There are still 6 in total, one for each number it is possible to roll.

Now we want to know how many ways out of these 6 we can roll a number that is not divisible by 3. Well, the only two numbers that are divisible by 3 that are possibilities are 3 and 6. So 1, 2, 4, and 5 are not. This means that there are 4 ways for the outcome to occur.

$$\text{Probability} = \frac{4}{6}$$

Reducing fractions is usually fine when working with probability; just know that if you do, the numerator and denominator will not necessarily correspond to the number of possibilities anymore.

$$\text{Probability} = \frac{2}{3}$$

The simplest way to complicate a probability problem is to allow for multiple correct outcomes. To find the total probability, simply add the individual probabilities for each correct outcome. For the above example, the total probability is actually the sum of the probabilities of rolling 1, 2, 4, and 5.

7.1.2 Combining Probabilities

What if you are asked to find the probability that multiple events will occur?

The solution to such a problem will still be a ratio in which the numbers represent the same quantities as before. The new difficulty is figuring out how many different outcome possibilities there are. Luckily, there is an easy way to calculate this. All you have to do is find the probability of each individual event and then multiply them together.

Why does this work? Think about it this way: For each possible outcome of the first event, there is still every possible outcome for the second. So the total number of possibilities will be the number of outcomes in the first times the number of outcomes in the second.

EXAMPLE

Let's go back to the flipping coin! If you flip it twice, what is the probability that the first flip will turn up heads and the second tails?

When dealing with multiple events, always focus on one event at a time before combining. So start with the first flip. We know that the probability it will be heads is ½. Now for the second flip, the probability it will be tails is also ½.

Now to find the probability that both of the events will occur, we multiply the individual probabilities:

$$\text{Probability} = \frac{1}{2} \times \frac{1}{2}$$
$$= \frac{1}{4}$$

Probability questions will not always be as clear-cut as this. Let's look at another coin flip example.

EXAMPLE

If you flip a coin twice, what is the probability that it will come up heads exactly one time?

This question seems almost identical to the previous example, but be careful! The difference is that the phrasing of this question does not specify particular outcomes for the individual events.

Let's solve this in two ways:

(i) Let's combine both events into one. To find the total number of possible outcomes, multiply the totals of each event, so there are $2 \times 2 = 4$ possibilities. Now count the number of ways we can flip heads once. Well, we could have heads on the first flip and tails on the second, so that is 1, or we could have tails then heads, so that is 2. Therefore, the probability of flipping heads exactly once is 2 to 4.

$$\text{Probability} = \frac{2}{4}$$

(ii) Now let's treat the events separately. Ask yourself: What are the odds that an outcome of the first event will be compatible with flipping heads once? The answer is

$\frac{2}{2}$ since we can still achieve the overall desired outcome with the second flip no matter what the first flip is.

Now what are the odds that an outcome of the second event will be compatible with flipping heads once? Since you already have a first flip determined, there is only one outcome for the second flip that will give the desired result. If the first flip was heads we need a tails flip, and if the first flip was tails we need a heads flip. So the odds for the second flip are ½ .

$$\text{Probability} = \frac{2}{2} \times \frac{1}{2}$$
$$= \frac{2}{4}$$

There are all kinds of confusing ways probability problems can be written. You have to be extra careful to break them down and determine exactly what is being asked because the test writers love to try and trick you. Double and triple-check that you have the setup right for probability problems because it is so easy to accidentally overlook something.

NOTE

When you want to know the probability of event A or B, the probabilities must be added. If you want to know the probability of events A and B, the probabilities must be multiplied.

7.2 Statistics

7.2.1 Averages

When given a collection of numbers, the **average** is the sum of the numbers divided by the total number of numbers.

$$\text{Average} = \frac{(\text{sum of numbers})}{(\text{number of numbers})}$$

EXAMPLE

What is the average of the set {4, 7, 6, 7}?

Add up the numbers and, since there are 4 of them, divide by 4.

$$\text{Average} = \frac{(4+7+6+7)}{4}$$
$$= \frac{24}{4}$$
$$= 6$$

The average may or may not actually appear in the set of numbers, but it is a common way to think of the typical value for the set.

7.2.2 Mode, Median, Mean

Here are a few other statistics terms you should know:

The **mode** of a set of values is the number that appears the most times. Mode can be bimodal or multimodal. Simply stated, bimodal means that two numbers are repeated the most while multimodal indicates two or more numbers are repeated the most.

The **median** of a set of values is the number that appears exactly in the center of the distribution. This means there are an equal number of values greater than and less than the median.

Arithmetic mean is just another name for the average of a set of numbers. The terms are interchangeable.

EXAMPLE

Find the mode, median, and mean of the following set: {3, 5, 11, 3, 8}.

Let's begin with the mode. All we need

to do is see which value or values repeat the most times. In this case, the only one that repeats is 3.

$$Mode = 3$$

To find the median we always need to first arrange the set in numerical order.

$$\{3, 3, 5, 8, 11\}$$

Now the median is whichever number lies in the exact center.

$$Median = 5$$

Since the mean is the same as the average, we add the values and divide by 5.

$$Mean = \frac{(3+3+5+8+11)}{5}$$
$$= \frac{30}{5}$$
$$= 6$$

NOTE

If a set has an even number of values, there will be no value exactly in the center. In this case, the median is the average of the two values that straddle the center.

Example

Given: 3, 4, 5, 6, 6, 8, 9, 10, 10, 12

The median is the average of the two middle data: $\frac{(6+8)}{2} = 7$

7.3 More Tools for Probability and Statistics

7.3.1 The Correlation Coefficient

The correlation coefficient r indicates whether two sets of data are associated or *correlated*. The value of r ranges from -1.0 to 1.0. The larger the absolute value of r, the stronger the association. Given two sets of data X and Y, a positive value for r indicates

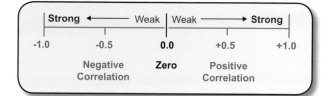

that as *X* increases, *Y* increases. A negative value for *r* indicates that as *X* increases, *Y* decreases.

Imagine that the weight (*X*) and height (*Y*) of everyone in the entire country was determined. There would be a strong positive correlation between a person's weight and their height. In general, as weight increases, height increases (*in a population*). However, the correlation would not be perfect (i.e. r < 1.0). After all, there would be some people who are very tall but very thin, and others who would be very short but overweight. We might find that *r* = 0.7. This would suggest there is a strong positive association between weight and height, but it is not a perfect association.

If two sets of data are correlated, does that mean that one *causes* the other? Not necessarily; simply because weight and height are correlated does not mean that if you gained weight you will necessarily gain height! Thus association does not imply causality.

Note that a correlation greater than 0.8 is generally described as strong, whereas a correlation that is less than 0.5 is generally described as weak. However, the interpretation and use of these values can vary based upon the "type" of data being examined. For example, a study based on chemical or biological data may require a stronger correlation than a study using social science data.

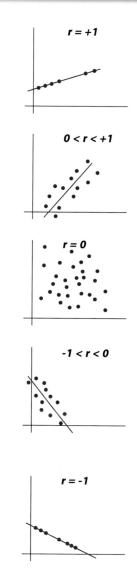

Varying values of the correlation coefficient (r) based on data plotted for two variables (= scatter diagrams). In red is the line of "best fit" (= *regression line;* Appendix A.1.3).

7.3.2 The Standard Deviation

When given a set of data, it is often useful to know the average value, *the mean*, and the *range* of values. As previously discussed, the mean is simply the sum of the data values divided by the number of data values. The range is the numerical difference between the largest value and the smallest value.

Another useful measurement is the *standard deviation*. The standard deviation indicates the dispersion of values around the mean. Given a bell-shaped distribution of data (i.e., the height and weight of a population, the GPA of undergraduate students, etc.), each standard deviation (SD) includes a given percentage of data. For example, the mean +/− 1 SD includes

approximately 68% of the data values, the mean +/− 2 SD includes 95% of the data values, and the mean +/− 3 SD includes 99.7% of the data values.

For example, imagine that you read that the mean GPA required for admission to Belcurve University's Dental School is 3.5 with a standard deviation of 0.2 (SD = 0.2). Thus approximately 68% of the students admitted have a GPA of 3.5 +/− 0.2, which means between 3.3 and 3.7. We can also conclude that approximately 95% of the students admitted have a GPA of 3.5 +/− 2(0.2), which means between 3.1 and 3.9. Therefore the standard deviation becomes a useful measure of the dispersion of values around the mean 3.5.

Green Area = 68% or 1 Standard Deviation
Green + Blue = 95% or 2 Standard Deviations
Green + Blue + Red = 99% or 3 Standard Deviations

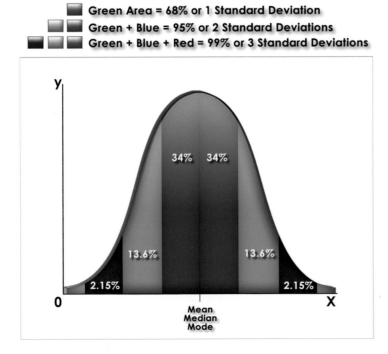

Figure 7.1: The Normal Curve (also referred to as: the Normal Distribution Curve).

7.3.3 Variance

Variance is another measure of how far a set of numbers is spread out or, in other words, how far numbers are from the mean. Thus variance is calculated as the average of the squared differences from the mean.

There are three steps to calculate the variance:

1. Determine the mean (the simple average of all the numbers)
2. For each number: subtract the mean and square the result (the squared difference)
3. Determine the average of those squared differences

The variance is also defined as the square of the standard deviation. Thus unlike standard deviation, the variance has units that are the square of the units of the variable itself. For example, a variable measured in meters will have a variance measured in meters squared. Note: for those of you aiming for a perfect QR score, the equations for standard deviation and variance can be found at the end of this chapter.

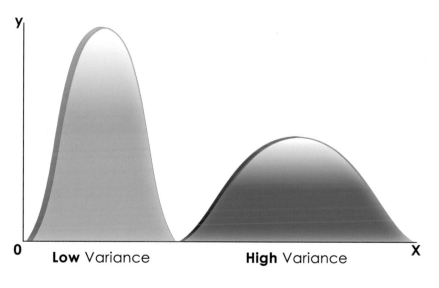

Figure 7.2: Variance.

7.3.4 Equations for Standard Deviation and Variance

Standard deviation and variance problems are common for DAT QR; however, because of time constraints, it is not likely that you would need to calculate the standard deviation or variance using the formulas in this section. However, if you are aiming for a perfect score then it is prudent to have all the tools at your disposal.

First, let's revisit the mean or average of a data set.

In statistics, a sample is a subset of a population. Typically, the population is very large, making an analysis of all the values in the population impractical or impossible. The sample is a subset of manageable size. Samples are collected and statistics are calculated so one can make inferences or extrapolations from the sample to the population.

For any data set, the mean can be calculated:

Sample Mean	Population Mean
$\bar{X} = \dfrac{\sum x}{n}$	$\mu = \dfrac{\sum x}{N}$

$\sum$ = the sum of

$\sum x$ = the sum of all data values

n = the number of data items in the sample

N = the number of data items in the population

The standard deviation (SD) - a measure of the dispersion of a set of data from its mean - is calculated using the following formula:

Sample SD	Population SD
$s = \sqrt{\dfrac{\sum \left(x - \bar{X}\right)^2}{n-1}}$	$\sigma = \sqrt{\dfrac{\sum \left(x - \mu\right)^2}{N}}$

x = each value in the sample or population

n - 1 = "degrees of freedom" and is used to compensate for the fact that the more accurate population mean (μ) is usually unknown.

HYPOTHETICAL EXAMPLE

The number of times students completed the DAT before obtaining a QR score of 25 or higher: 3, 2, 4, 1, 4, 4. Find the standard deviation and variance of the data set.

Step 1: Calculate the mean and deviation of this small data set. Note that because $n = 6$, this is very likely a subset of all students who scored 25 or higher in QR, we regard this as a sample size and we use the equations accordingly.

x	$\bar{X}$	$(x - \bar{X})$	$(x - \bar{X})^2$
3	3	0	0
2	3	-1	1
4	3	1	1
1	3	-2	4
4	3	1	1
4	3	1	1

Step 2: Using the deviation, calculate the standard deviation by squaring both sides of the relevant equation:

$$s^2 = \frac{(0 + 1 + 1 + 4 + 1 + 1)}{(6 - 1)} = \frac{8}{5}$$

$$= 1.6$$

Since $s^2 = 1.6$, the standard deviation of the sample $s = 1.265$. And the variance of the sample $(= s^2) = 1.6$.

The Coefficient of Variation

A standard deviation of 1.265 with a mean of 3, as we calculated, is much different than a standard deviation of 1.265 with a mean of 20. By calculating how the standard deviation relates to the mean (= coefficient of variation = CV), we can have a standard way of determining the relevance of the standard deviation and what it suggests about the sample. The closer the CV is to 0, the greater the uniformity of the data. The closer the CV is to 1, the greater the variability of the data.

$$CV = \frac{s}{\bar{X}}$$

Using our example of a standard deviation of 1.265 and a mean of 3, you will see that the coefficient of variation is rather large, indicating that the data has a great deal of variability with respect to the mean and there is no general consensus among the sample.

$$CV = \frac{s}{\bar{X}} = \frac{(1.265)}{(3)} = 0.42$$

Using the example of a standard deviation of 1.265 and a mean of 20, we see that the coefficient of variation is rather small, indicating that the data has a greater deal of uniformity with respect to the mean and there is a general consensus among the sample.

$$CV = \frac{s}{\bar{X}} = \frac{(1.265)}{(20)} = 0.06$$

7.3.5 Simple Probability Revisited

Let's apply a formula to simple probability. If a phenomenon or experiment has n equally likely outcomes, s of which are called successes, then the probability P of success is given by $P = \dfrac{s}{n}$.

EXAMPLE

- if "heads" in a coin toss is considered a success, then

  $P(\text{success}) = \dfrac{1}{2}$;

- if a card is drawn from a deck and diamonds are considered successes, then

  $P(\text{success}) = \dfrac{13}{52}$. It follows that $P(\text{success}) = 1 - P(\text{failure})$.

7.3.6 Permutations

Suppose n is a positive integer. The symbol $n!$, read *n-factorial*, is defined as follows:

$$n! = (n)(n-1)(n-2) \dots (3)(2)(1)$$

By definition $0! = 1$.

A permutation of a set is an *ordered* arrangement of the elements in that set. The number of permutations of n objects is $n!$. For example, using 5 different amino acids, the number of possible permutations creating different outcomes (*oligopeptides*) is: $5! = (5)(4)(3)(2)(1) = 120$.

Suppose you have 7 books and place 3 on a shelf. The first slot can be filled by any of 7 choices, the second slot can be filled by one less or 6 choices, and again there is one less choice for the third slot leaving 5 books from which to choose. The total number of ways to fill the 3 slots on the shelf is thus $(7)(6)(5) = 210$.

The general rule is that the number of permutations of n things taken r at a time is n_r, where $n_r = n!/(n-r)!$. In the preceding example, $n = 7$ and $r = 3$ thus,

$$
\begin{aligned}
n_r &= 7!/(7-3)! \\
&= (7)(6)(5)(4)(3)(2)(1)/(4)(3)(2)(1) \\
&= (7)(6)(5)(4!)/(4!) \\
&= (7)(6)(5) = 210
\end{aligned}
$$

NOTE

Permutations may be simplified if it is found in both the numerator and the denominator.

In the given example, $4!$ could be canceled out, leaving you with $(7)(6)(5) = 210$. This will save you time on the DAT and you will not have to waste too much effort expanding a permutation.

For the DAT, it is very important to pay

attention to the wording of the problem and identify what is known about the problem. In this example, we know that there are 7 books and as each is placed on the shelf, there is 1 less book to choose from. Since the outcome of the first depends on the outcome of the second, these events are considered dependent. This is called sampling without replacement.

In the case where the object is being put back into your sample after each event, the amount of possible outcomes does not change from one event to another. If the outcome of the first event does not affect the outcome of the second, the two events are independent of each other. This is called sampling with replacement.

7.3.7 Combinations

Permutations are important when the *order* of selection matters (e.g., *simply by changing the order of the amino acids, the activity of the oligopeptide or the* outcome *changes*). Combinations are important when the order of selection does not matter (e.g., *as long as there is a red book, a green book, and a blue book on the shelf, the order does not matter*).

Since the order does not matter, there are fewer combinations than permutations. In fact, the combination C_r is given by:

$$C_r = \frac{n_r}{r!} = \frac{n!}{\left[r!(n-r)! \right]}$$

For example, once again consider a total of 7 books where there are only 3 slots on the shelf. This time you are told that the order the books appear on the shelf is not relevant. The number of different combinations is therefore

$$C_r = \frac{n_r}{r!} = \frac{n!}{\left[r!(n-r)! \right]} = \frac{7!}{\left[3!(7-3)! \right]}$$
$$= \frac{210}{3!} = \frac{210}{6} = 35$$

7.3.8 Probability Tree

The probability tree may be used as another means to solve probability of independent and dependent events. It is a very useful visual that will show all possible events. Each branch represents a possible outcome and its probability. Depending on what the question is asking for, the probabilities of each event may be added or multiplied to determine the combined probability of events.

Suppose that you were observing the probability of choosing 2 balls from a basket that contained 8 red and 4 white balls. What is the probability of picking 2 red balls without replacement?

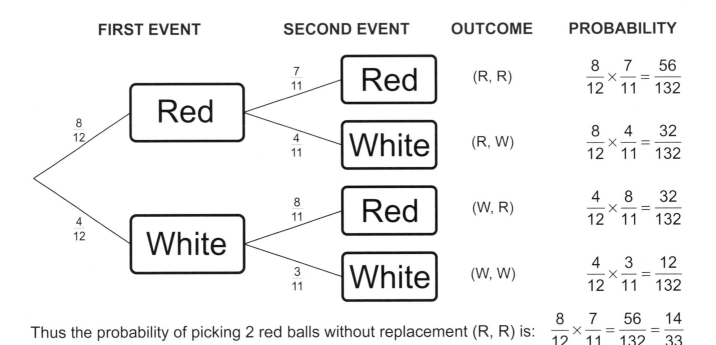

FIRST EVENT	SECOND EVENT	OUTCOME	PROBABILITY
Red ($\frac{8}{12}$)	Red ($\frac{7}{11}$)	(R, R)	$\frac{8}{12} \times \frac{7}{11} = \frac{56}{132}$
	White ($\frac{4}{11}$)	(R, W)	$\frac{8}{12} \times \frac{4}{11} = \frac{32}{132}$
White ($\frac{4}{12}$)	Red ($\frac{8}{11}$)	(W, R)	$\frac{4}{12} \times \frac{8}{11} = \frac{32}{132}$
	White ($\frac{3}{11}$)	(W, W)	$\frac{4}{12} \times \frac{3}{11} = \frac{12}{132}$

Thus the probability of picking 2 red balls without replacement (R, R) is: $\frac{8}{12} \times \frac{7}{11} = \frac{56}{132} = \frac{14}{33}$

If the question had asked the probability of having at least 1 white ball without replacement, the answer would be $\frac{8}{12} \times \frac{4}{11} + \frac{4}{12} \times \frac{8}{11} + \frac{4}{12} \times \frac{3}{11} = \frac{76}{132} = \frac{19}{33}$. Notice that this answer represents all outcomes NOT given by (R, R) and so it is numerically 1 - P(R, R).

GOLD STANDARD WARM-UP EXERCISES

CHAPTER 7: Probability and Statistics

1. A jar contains 4 red marbles and 6 blue marbles. What is the probability that a marble chosen at random will be red?

   A. 4/6
   B. 4/10
   C. 2/6
   D. 6/10
   E. 2/4

2. In how many different ways can six different objects be arranged in a line?

   A. 120
   B. 30
   C. 720
   D. 36
   E. 6

3. A box contains 6 yellow balls and 4 green balls. Two balls are chosen at random without replacement. What is the probability that the first ball is yellow and the second ball is green?

   A. 5/12
   B. 1/10
   C. 6/25
   D. 1
   E. 4/15

4. An English teacher wants to prepare a class reading list that includes 1 philosophy book, 1 work of historical fiction, and 1 biography. She has 3 philosophy books, 2 works of historical fiction, and 4 biographies to choose from. How many different combinations of books can she put together for her list?

   A. 32
   B. 288
   C. 28
   D. 9
   E. 24

5. An unemployment office's survey shows that the distribution of the local residents' annual income is a bell curve. 2,516 residents are within one standard deviation of the local average annual income. How many residents were in the survey's sample?

   A. 3,700
   B. 2,648
   C. 2,524
   D. 2,523
   E. 7,862

6. The average time it takes 3 students to complete a test is 35 minutes. If 1 student takes 41 minutes to complete the test and another takes 37 minutes, how many minutes does the third student take to complete the test?

   A. 4
   B. 38
   C. 27
   D. 39
   E. 43

7. A small library receives a shipment of gray books, blue books, black books, and brown books. If the librarian decides to shelve all the books of one color on Monday, all of the books of another color on Tuesday, and the rest of the books on Wednesday, in how many different ways can the book shelving be completed?

   A. 3
   B. 4
   C. 8
   D. 12
   E. 24

8. A list of four integers has the following properties: the range is equal to 14, the median is equal to 7, and the mean is equal to 8. One of the numbers is 9. What are the other three numbers?

   A. 1, 7, 15
   B. 2, 5, 16
   C. −11, 3, 7
   D. 0, 0, 23
   E. −12, 2, 7

9. When you roll a die, what is the probability to first get a 3 and then a 1 or a 2?

   A. 1/6
   B. 1/8
   C. 1/32
   D. 1/16
   E. 1/18

GS ANSWER KEY

CHAPTER 7

Cross-Reference

1. B QR 7.1.1
2. C QR 7.3.4
3. E QR 7.1, 7.1.2
4. E QR 7.3, 7.3.5
5. A QR 7.3.2

Cross-Reference

6. C QR 7.2, 7.2.1
7. D QR 7.3.5
8. B QR 7.2
9. E QR 7.1, 7.1.2

★ Explanations can be found at the back of the book.

Go online to DAT-prep.com for additional chapter review Q&A and forum.

APPENDIX
CHAPTER 7: Probability and Statistics

Advanced DAT-30 Passage: ANOVA, Scheffe Test and Chi-Square

> **NOTE**
>
> This section is not for all students. This content is "low yield" meaning that it takes a lot of energy to review it properly but the questions pop up on the DAT rarely. If you have the time and the will to aim for a perfect score, this additional statistics review is followed by questions so that the material can be learned in an interactive way. As per usual, explanations are at the back of the book. You should decide if you wish to read these sections based on the requirements of the dental program(s) you wish to attend. If you are preparing for the 2015 DAT or beyond, we suggest that you review this section and go online to dat-prep.com for further suggested reading.

Student's *t*-test and ANOVA

The *t*-test (= Student's t-test) and analysis of variance (= ANOVA) are statistical procedures that assume normal distributions (= *parametric*) and make use of the mean and variance to determine the significance of the differences of the means of two or more groups of values.

The *t*-test uses the mean, the variance and a "Table of Critical Values" for the "*t*" distribution. The *t*-test is used to determine the significance of the difference between the means of two groups based on a standard that no more than 5% of the difference is due to chance or sampling error, and that the same difference would occur 95% of the time should the test be repeated. Rarely, a more rigorous standard of 1% (= .01 level) is used and, as a result, the same difference would occur 99% of the time should the test be repeated.

EXAMPLE

The experiment or treatment group ($\bar{X}$ = 73.30, SD = 3.91) scored significantly higher than the control group ($\bar{X}$ = 67.30, SD = 4.32), $t(75) = 4.90$, $p < .05$. Note that the number in parenthesis (75) after the *t* value is the number of cases adjusted for the values that are free to vary = "degrees of freedom" = $n - 1$. The *p* value (= probability value or alpha level) expresses statistical significance.

In the preceding example, *p* is most important and indicates at what level a statistically significant difference exists (i.e .05 level; this will be discussed further).

There are one sample and two sample *t*-tests:

1. a one sample *t*-test is a hypothesis test for answering questions about the mean where the data are a random sample of independent observations from an underlying normal distribution where the variance is unknown;

2. a two sample *t*-test is a hypothesis test for answering questions about the mean where the data are collected from two random samples of independent observations, each from an underlying normal distribution where the variances of the 2 populations are assumed to be equal.

Analysis of variance (ANOVA) is a parametric statistical measure used for determining whether differences exist among two or more groups. ANOVA uses the mean, the variance and a "Table of Critical Values for the *F* Distribution". Statistical significance is usually based on the .05 level.

ANOVA can be used for several different types of analyses:

- One-way ANOVA - assumes there are two variables with one variable a dependent, interval or ratio variable (numerical data that show quantity and direction), and one variable, an independent, nominal variable or factor such as an ethnicity code or sex code.

- *N*-way ANOVA - assumes there are more than two variables with one variable a dependent, interval or ratio variable and two or more, independent, nominal variables or factors such as ethnicity code or sex code.

- Multiple Regression - assumes there are more than two variables with one variable a dependent, interval or ratio variable and two or more, independent, interval or ratio variables such as test scores, income, GPA, etc.

- Analysis of Covariance - assumes there are more than two variables with one variable a dependent, interval or variable and two or more variables are a combination of independent, nominal, interval or ratio variables.

Scheffe Test

The Scheffe test is used with ANOVA to determine which variable among several independent variables is statistically the most different.

Effect Size

For both *t*-test and one-way ANOVA procedures, a secondary statistical procedure called effect size is sometimes used to determine the level of significance. This could be used in an experimental study comparing the means of two groups, a control group and an experimental group. Effect size is calculated by taking the difference in the means of the two groups and dividing it by the standard deviation of the control group. In education experiments, an effect size of +.20 (20% of the standard deviation) would be considered a minimum for significance; an effect size above +.50 is considered very strong.

Chi-Square

t-test and analysis of variance are parametric statistical procedures that assume that the distributions are normal or nearly normal and is used when variables are continuous such as test scores and GPAs. Chi-square is a nonparametric statistical procedure used to determine the significance of the difference between groups when data are nominal and placed in categories such as gender or ethnicity. This procedure compares what is observed against what was expected.

Categories of Chi-Square (χ^2):

1. Chi-Squared Goodness of Fit Test is a test for comparing a theoretical distribution, such as a Normal distribution, with the observed data from a sample.

2. Chi-Squared Test of Association allows the comparison of two attributes in a sample of data to determine if there is any relationship between them. If the value of the test statistic for the chi-squared test of association is too large, then there is a poor agreement between the observed and expected frequencies and the null hypothesis of independence or no association is rejected.

3. Chi-Squared Test of Homogeneity is used to determine if a single categorical variable has the same distribution in 2 (or more) distinct populations from 2 (or more) samples.

Null Hypothesis, Alternative Hypothesis

Consider the following two types of statistical hypotheses:

- **Null hypothesis** (= H_0) is usually the hypothesis that sample observations result purely from chance. {Remember: "If *p* is low, H_0 has to go!"}

- **Alternative hypothesis** (= H_1 or H_a) is the hypothesis that sample observations are influenced by some non-random cause.

For example, suppose we wanted to determine whether a coin was fair and balanced. A null hypothesis might be that half the flips would result in heads and half, in tails. The alternative hypothesis might be that the number of heads and tails would be very different. Symbolically, these hypotheses would be expressed as

H_0: probability = 0.5
H_a: probability < 0.5 or > 0.5

Suppose we flipped the coin 100 times, resulting in 85 heads and 15 tails. Given this result, we would be inclined to reject the null hypothesis. That is, we would conclude that the coin was probably not fair and balanced.

Z Scores and p values

The z score (= standard score = z value) is a test of statistical significance that helps you decide whether or not to reject the null hypothesis. The p-value is the probability that you have falsely rejected the null hypothesis. Z scores are measures of standard deviation. For example, a Z score of +3.0 is interpreted as "+3.0 standard deviations away from the mean". P values are probabilities. Both statistics are associated with the standard normal distribution.

Very high or a very low (negative) z scores (i.e. very small p values) are found in the tails of the normal distribution. The p value associated with a 95% confidence level is 0.05 and the associated z values are approximately -2 and +2 (see the normal curve in section 7.3.2).

One and Two-sided Tests

A one-sided test (= one-tailed test of significance) is a statistical hypothesis test in which the values for which we can reject the null hypothesis H_0 are located entirely in one tail of the probability distribution. In other words, the critical region for a one-sided test is the set of values less than the critical value of the test, or the set of values greater than the critical value of the test.

A two-sided test (= two-tailed test of significance) is a statistical hypothesis test in which the values for which we can reject the null hypothesis, H_0 are located in both tails of the probability distribution. In other words, the critical region for a two-sided test is the set of values less than a first critical value of the test and the set of values greater than a second critical value of the test.

Errors

Two types of errors can result from a decision rule:

- **Type I error.** A Type I error occurs when the researcher rejects a null hypothesis when it is true. The probability of committing a Type I error is called the significance level or alpha (= α). The confidence level is $1 - \alpha$.

- **Type II error.** A Type II error occurs when the researcher accepts a null hypothesis that is false. The probability of committing a Type II error is called beta (= β). The probability of not committing a Type II error is called the "power of the test" = $1 - \beta$.

10. What is the meaning of $p < .05$?
    A. The probability of obtaining the data if the null hypothesis were true is less than 5%.
    B. There is a 5% chance of making a type I error.
    C. There is a less than a 1 in 20 probability of the result occurring by chance alone if the null hypothesis were true.
    D. All of the above.

11. The ANOVA test is based on which assumption(s)?

    I.   The samples are randomly selected

    II.   The populations are statistically significant

    III. The populations are normally distributed

    A. III only

    B. II and III only

    C. I, II, and III only

    D. I, and III only

12. The chi-square goodness of fit test can be used to test for:

    A. credibility.

    B. probability.

    C. differentiability.

    D. normality.

13. The null hypothesis is:

    A. the assumption that a significant result is very unlikely.

    B. the analysis of the pattern between the variables being tested.

    C. the assumption there is no relationship or difference between the variables being tested.

    D. the assumption that there is a relationship or difference between the variables being tested.

14. Which of the following is consistent with the null hypothesis and the alternative hypothesis?

    A. It is possible for neither hypothesis to be true

    B. Exactly one hypothesis must be true

    C. Both hypotheses must be true

    D. It is possible for both hypotheses to be true

15. In a two-tailed test of significance:

    A. results in either of two directions can lead to the rejection of the null hypothesis.

    B. no results lead to the rejection of the null hypothesis.

    C. results in only one direction can lead to the rejection of the null hypothesis.

    D. a standard deviation leads to the rejection of the null hypothesis.

16. If the Gold Standard was trying to prove that their materials are more effective at getting high DAT scores compared to older methods of preparation, they would conduct a:

    A. one-tailed test.

    B. two-tailed test.

    C. Chi-Squared Test of Homogeneity.

    D. Chi-Squared Test of Association.

17. The alternative hypothesis can be:
    A. one-sided.
    B. two- sided.
    C. one or two- sided.
    D. neither one nor two- sided.

18. A type II error occurs when:
    A. the test is biased.
    B. the sample mean differs from the population mean.
    C. the null hypothesis is incorrectly accepted when it is false.
    D. the null hypothesis is incorrectly rejected when it is true.

19. The value set for α is known as:
    A. the significance level.
    B. the rejection level.
    C. the confidence level.
    D. the acceptance level.

20. When someone asks "how significant" the sample evidence is, they are referring to the:
    A. causality.
    B. value of β.
    C. sample value.
    D. p-value.

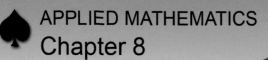
Memorize	Understand	Importance
* Law of Reflection * Property of Elliptical Mirrors * Equations for Velocity and Interest	* Ellipses * Rates of Change * Velocity Problems, Interest Problems, Work Problems, Age Problems * Strategies for Word Problems	**8 to 12 out of the 40 QR** questions on the DAT are based on content from this chapter (in our estimation). * This will change in 2015.

DAT-Prep.com

Introduction ▮▮▮▮

Ten of the forty Quantitative Reasoning questions on the DAT are applied mathematics or word problems. There is a huge range of types of word problems that you might encounter on the test. This chapter covers those that require extra explanation, as well as convenient strategies for dealing with any type that gets thrown your way.

Additional Resources

Free Online Forum

8.1 Optics

Optics is the branch of physics that deals with light. Problems of this variety show up on the Quantitative Reasoning test because reflection of light is all about angles.

8.1.1 Reflection

Reflection occurs when light hits a surface and bounces off. An uneven surface reflects light diffusely, scattering it, but an even surface like a mirror reflects light in a very precise way. This is why you can see your image in a mirror but not in, say, a wall.

Law of Reflection: This law says that the angle of incidence is always equal to the angle of reflection.

If you draw a line perpendicular to the mirror at the point where the light hits (= the "normal" line), the **angle of incidence** (θ_i) is the angle formed by that line and the incoming light ray. Similarly, the **angle of reflection** (θ_r) is the angle formed by the perpendicular and the reflected light ray.

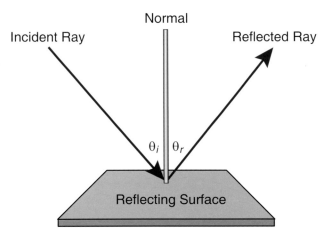

Using the law of reflection, you can easily turn any plane mirror problem into a geometry and/or trigonometry problem involving lines and angles.

8.1.2 Elliptical Mirrors

The law of reflection still applies to curved mirror surfaces. The only problem is knowing how to draw the perpendicular line at the point of incidence. Dealing with unusually curved mirrors is usually too complicated for the Quantitative Reasoning test, but you may still encounter questions about an elliptical mirror.

An **ellipse** is an oval-shaped figure. It has two points in its interior that are equally spaced on either side of the center (called the **foci**) such that, for any point on the perimeter of the ellipse, the sum of the distances to the foci is always the same. The line passing through both foci from one end of the perimeter to the other is known as the **major axis**. The line perpendicular to the major axis passing through the midpoint is the **minor axis**. A circle is a special ellipse for which both foci are the same point.

Property: If a light ray passes through a focus of an elliptical mirror, it will always reflect off the inside of the mirror and pass through the other focus.

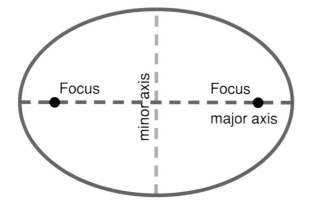

> ### NOTE
>
> The length of the major axis is the same as the distance a light ray will travel between one focus and the other if it is reflected once on the way.

8.2 Word Problems

8.2.1 Rates of Change

A rate of change is an amount by which one variable changes in relationship to another variable. Usually, a rate of change specifies how some value changes as time progresses. All rates of change can be written as fractions, so rate of change problems almost always boil down to algebra problems involving fraction manipulation.

EXAMPLE

A glass can hold 10 oz of liquid. Water is being poured in at a rate of 3 oz every 2 seconds. How long will it take for the glass to reach $^2/_3$ full?

The rate in this problem translates to the fraction 3 oz/2 sec. We want to find the time "t" it will take for $^2/_3$ of 10 oz to be poured in, so we set up an algebraic equation:

$$\frac{3\text{ oz}}{2\text{ sec}} \times t = \frac{2}{3} \times 10\text{ oz}$$

$$\Rightarrow t = \frac{2\text{ sec}}{3\text{ oz}} \times \frac{20\text{ oz}}{3}$$

$$\Rightarrow t = \frac{40}{9}\text{ sec}$$

8.2.2 Distance, Time and Velocity

A specific type of rate of change with which you should be familiar is **velocity**. Velocity is the distance an object travels in a specific direction per unit of time. Do not get this confused with **speed,** which is a value that is independent of the direction of travel.

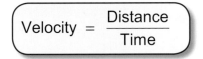

$$\text{Velocity} = \frac{\text{Distance}}{\text{Time}}$$

You can use this equation to solve for any one of the three values if you know the other two.

EXAMPLE

A jogger runs the first 100 meters of a 5 km race in 24 seconds. If the jogger maintains the same pace until the end of the race, how long will it take him to run the entire race?

We are given a distance and a time, so we can easily find the velocity of the jogger.

$$V = \frac{100\text{ m}}{24\text{ sec}}$$

The distance in question is in kilometers, so we need to convert this velocity.

$$V = \frac{.1\text{ km}}{24\text{ sec}}$$

Now we need to apply our velocity formula once more. We have a velocity and a distance, but we ultimately want to find the time.

$$\frac{.1\ km}{24\ sec} = \frac{5\ km}{t}$$
$$\Rightarrow 5\ km \times 24\ sec = .1\ km \times t$$
$$\Rightarrow \frac{(5 \times 24\ sec)}{.1} = t$$
$$\Rightarrow t = 1200\ sec = 20\ min$$

Velocity problems can also involve a geometric component if a specific direction (or directions) of travel is included, so be on the lookout! {Vectors are discussed in the QR Appendix (A.6)}

8.2.3 Simple and Compound Interests

Questions dealing with simple and compound interests are very straightforward on the DAT. These questions are essentially plug-and-chug problems. Make sure you differentiate between simple and compound interests.

Simple interest is calculated based on just the initial amount of money invested. Thus the formula for simple interest can be expressed as:

I = PRT

where I is the interest earned from the investment, P is the principal or the amount of money invested, R is the rate of interest (usually in the form of percentage) charged on the principal, and T is the time.

EXAMPLE

Johnny borrowed $15,000 from the bank at 5% simple interest per year. How much does Johnny owe the bank in one year?

I = PRT

= ($15,000)(0.05)(1)

= $750 owed

Compound interest is computed based on the amount of money invested and all interests accumulated during the past periods. Interests may be compounded monthly, semiannually, or annually. The simplest way to approach these questions is to treat each period as a simple interest problem.

EXAMPLE

Joe borrowed $12,000 from the bank at 10% interest compounded annually. How much does he owe the bank in 3 years?

After the first year:

$I = PRT$

$= (\$12{,}000)(0.1)(1)$

$= \$1{,}200$ in interest for the first year.

After the second year:

$I = PRT$

$= (\$12{,}000 + \$1{,}200)(0.1)(1)$

$= \$1{,}320$ in interest for the second year.

After the third year:

$I = PRT$

$= (\$12{,}000 + \$1{,}200 + \$1{,}320)(0.1)(1)$

$= \$1{,}452$ in interest for the third year.

Total interest:

$\$1{,}200 + \$1{,}320 + \$1{,}452 = \$3{,}972$ total interest owed after three years.

> **NOTE**
>
> Be comfortable with rearranging the Interest equation. The DAT can ask you to solve for any one of the interest rate, time, or principal.

8.2.4 Work Problems

Work problems are almost guaranteed to show up on the DAT. Fortunately, they are rather simple and can be solved with the following equation:

$$\frac{1}{(t1)} + \frac{1}{(t2)} = \frac{1}{(T)}$$

where $t1$ = time it takes for A to finish the task, $t2$ = time it takes for B to finish the task, and T = total time.

EXAMPLE

Jack takes 5 hours to paint a house while Joan takes 10 hours to do the same task. How long would it take to paint one house if Jack and Joan worked together?

$$\left(\frac{1}{5 \text{ hours}}\right) + \left(\frac{1}{10 \text{ hours}}\right) = \left(\frac{1}{\text{total time}}\right)$$

$$\left(\frac{2}{10 \text{ hours}}\right) + \left(\frac{1}{10 \text{ hours}}\right) = \left(\frac{1}{\text{total time}}\right)$$

$$\left(\frac{3}{10 \text{ hours}}\right) = \left(\frac{1}{\text{total time}}\right)$$

Cross multiply:

3(total time) = 10 hours

total time = 10/3 or 3 ⅓ hours if Jack and Joan work together.

8.2.5 Age Problems

Age problems are simply algebraic expressions disguised as word problems. There are two methods in approaching these problems.

Problem: Kim is 20 years older than Joe. In 5 years, Kim will be 5 years older than twice Joe's age. How old is Kim today?

Method 1:

Let K = Kim's age and J = Joe's age

We can set up the first statement as:

K = J + 20

The second statement can be set up as:

$$(K + 5) - 5 = 2(J + 5)$$

Let's rearrange the first equation to K - 20 = J since we are solving for Kim's age. Then substitute the first equation into the second equation. We get,

$$(K + 5) - 5 = 2(K - 20 + 5)$$
$$K = 2(K - 15)$$
$$K = 2K - 30$$
$$K = 30$$

Kim is 30 years old while Joe is 10 years old.

Method 2:

Plug and chug the answers provided. Sometimes the quickest way to solving these types of problems are through trial and error.

8.3 Word Problem Strategies

8.3.1 What You Need and What You Know

Identify the Problem Type: The first thing you should do when you encounter a word problem is ask, "What type of problem is it?" If you can identify it as a rate, geometry, probability, or some other kind of problem, you will have an immediate idea of what might need to be done.

What You Need: Next, go through the problem and pick out exactly what information the problem is asking you to find. Are you looking for the distance traveled, the probability of heads, the measure of an angle? Whatever it may be, write it down on the laminated note board provided during the test.

What You Know: After you have identified what you are looking for, you should go back and look at what information you are given. The problem will always provide enough information to solve the problem (sometimes even more than enough), but it can often be a little confusing to keep all of it in your mind at once. It may not even be presented in an easy to understand form; for example, ratios and rates are much clearer if you rewrite them as concise fractions. It can be extremely helpful to quickly list out what you know on the note board.

8.3.2 Draw a Picture

If a word problem has any kind of geometric component, it can be difficult to keep it straight in your mind. Drawing a simple picture of the situation will solve this problem, but beyond that, a picture can even help you to see connections you would not have otherwise noticed.

Some problems do not lend themselves to pictorial representations. In such cases, you should not spend time worrying about drawing one. If it seems difficult to draw or if you can't even figure out what to draw, then a picture probably would not be helpful.

8.3.3 Set Up the Math

This is the part where you have to bring your math knowledge and skills to the table. You have your lists of what you need and know, you have your picture, and now you have to find a way to solve the problem.

It is up to you to make the connections, but before you start tossing numbers around you should take a moment to set up the math. This means you should write out the equations and relationships you will need before you start evaluating. This way, you can easily keep track of the work you are doing in case you make a mistake, and all you need to do in the end to find the solution is plug in values and crank out some basic algebra and arithmetic.

GOLD STANDARD WARM-UP EXERCISES

CHAPTER 8: Applied Mathematics

1. If it takes thirty minutes to walk 1.5 miles, how many miles will be covered in 3 hours?

    A. 12
    B. 4.5
    C. 9
    D. 7.5
    E. 2.25

2. A ray of light passes through one focus of an elliptical mirror with a major axis of length 8. At the point of reflection, it is 6 units away from the other focus. At this point, how far is the ray of light from the first focus?

    A. 2
    B. 4
    C. 6
    D. 8
    E. 10

3. A ray of light passes through the foci of an elliptical mirror at $(\sqrt{5}, 0)$. It is reflected at the endpoint of the minor axis, the point (0, 2). What is the length of the major axis?

    A. $2\sqrt{5}$
    B. 3
    C. 4
    D. 6
    E. $\sqrt{29}$

4. A small pipe allows water to flow at 5 gallons per minute. A larger pipe allows water to flow at 15 gallons per minute. If both pipes are used, how many minutes will it take to fill a 180 gallon tank with water?

    A. 18
    B. 9
    C. 24
    D. 12
    E. 30

5. A beam of light originates at the outer edge of a circular mirror of radius 5 and passes through the center. How far does it travel before being reflected?

    A. 10
    B. 1
    C. 5
    D. 2.5
    E. 15

6. A truck travels 150 miles in 3 hours during the morning, and 180 miles in 3 hours during the afternoon. What is its average speed for the day?

    A. 37 mph
    B. 36 mph
    C. 65 mph
    D. 110 mph
    E. 55 mph

7. The beam from a lighthouse sweeps out $\frac{\pi}{4}$ radians every 5 seconds. 500 meters away from the shore, a ship is directly approaching at a rate of 100 meters per minute. If this speed is maintained, how many complete revolutions will the beam make before the ship reaches the shore?

   A. 5
   B. 60
   C. 7.5
   D. 75
   E. 300

8. The bottom of a square basement window with a diagonal length of 1 meter is level with the ground, as shown in the following figure. A ray of light originates at its lower left-hand corner and travels diagonally up to the upper right-hand corner, where it is reflected downwards. How many meters from the corner of the window (point D) is the ray when it reaches the ground again, at point E?

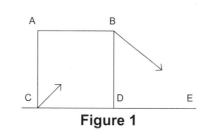

Figure 1

   A. $2/\sqrt{2}$
   B. $1/2$
   C. 1
   D. $1/\sqrt{2}$
   E. 2

9. The average age of a wife, her husband and daughter three years ago was 27 years and that of her husband and daughter five years ago was 20 years. What is the wife's present age?

   A. 36
   B. 40
   C. 37
   D. 42
   E. 38

10. Hiking up a mountain took 5 hours, but down only 1½ hours. If the distance each way was 3.3 miles, what is the difference between the two hiking rates in km/s?

   A. 5.63×10^{-4} km/s
   B. 6.84×10^{-4} km/s
   C. 9.03×10^{-4} km/s
   D. 6.16×10^{-4} km/s
   E. 6.43×10^{-4} km/s

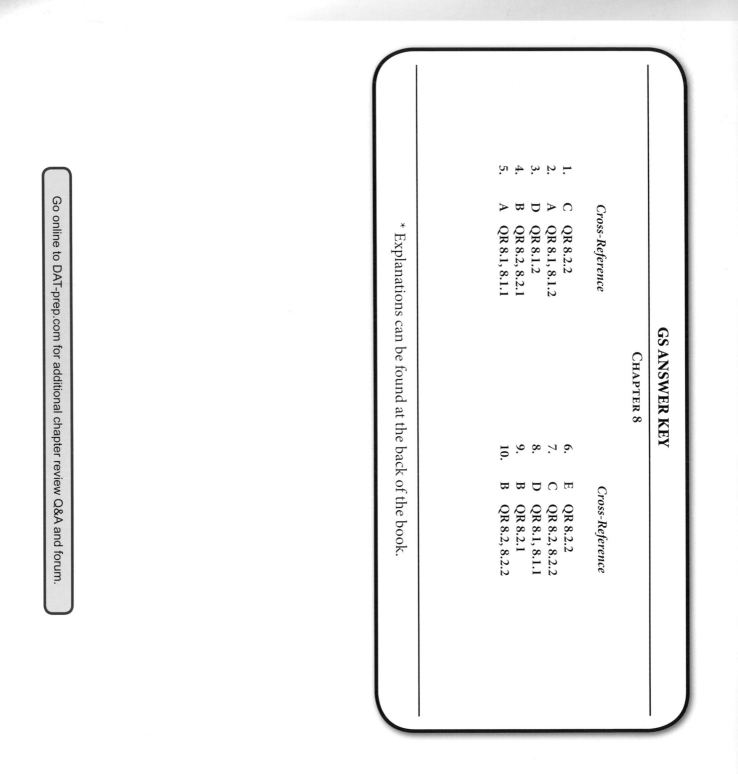

GS ANSWER KEY

CHAPTER 8

Cross-Reference

1. C   QR 8.2.2
2. A   QR 8.1, 8.1.2
3. D   QR 8.1.2
4. B   QR 8.2, 8.2.1
5. A   QR 8.1, 8.1.1

Cross-Reference

6. E   QR 8.2.2
7. C   QR 8.2, 8.2.2
8. D   QR 8.1, 8.1.1
9. B   QR 8.2.1
10. B   QR 8.2, 8.2.2

* Explanations can be found at the back of the book.

Go online to DAT-prep.com for additional chapter review Q&A and forum.

Appendix A

DAT MATH REVIEW

In the preceding science review and QR sections, several mathematical concepts were presented (i.e. trigonometry, rules of logarithms, the quadratic equation, statistics, etc.). The purpose of this section is to review the DAT mathematical concepts *not* presented elsewhere, though there may be some overlap for emphasis.

A.1 Basic Graphs

A.1.1 The Graph of a Linear Equation

Equations of the type $y = ax + b$ are known as *linear equations* since the graph of y (= *the ordinate*) versus x (= *the abscissa*) is a straight line. The value of y where the line intersects the y axis is called the *intercept b*. The constant a is the *slope* of the line. Given any two points (x_1, y_1) and (x_2, y_2) on the line, we have:

$$y_1 = ax_1 + b$$

and

$$y_2 = ax_2 + b.$$

Subtracting the upper equation from the lower one and dividing through by $x_2 - x_1$ gives the value of the slope,

$$a = (y_2 - y_1)/(x_2 - x_1).$$

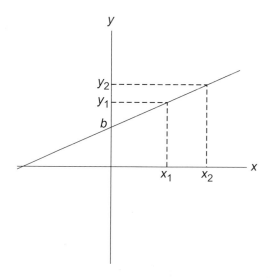

A.1.2 Reciprocal Curve

For any real number x, there exists a unique real number called the multiplicative inverse or *reciprocal* of x denoted $1/x$ or x^{-1} such that $x\,(1/x) = 1$. The graph of the reciprocal $1/x$ for any x is:

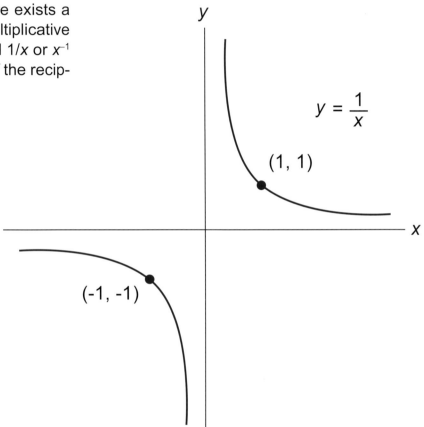

$$y = \frac{1}{x}$$

(1, 1)

(-1, -1)

A.1.3 Miscellaneous Graphs

There are classical curves which are represented or approximated in the science text as follows: Sigmoidal curve (CHM 6.9.1, BIO 7.5.1), sinusoidal curve (QR 6.2.3), and hyperbolic curves (CHM 9.7 Fig III.A.9.3, BIO 1.1.2).

If you were to plot a set of experimental data, often one can draw a line (A.1.1) or curve (A.1.2/3, A.2.2) which can "best fit" the data. The preceding defines a *regression* line or curve. The main purpose of the regression graph is to predict what would likely occur outside of the experimental data.

A.2 Exponents and Logarithms

A.2.1 Rules of Exponents

$$a^0 = 1 \qquad\qquad a^1 = a$$

$$a^n\, a^m = a^{n+m} \qquad a^n/a^m = a^{n-m}$$

$$(a^n)^m = a^{nm} \qquad a^{\frac{1}{n}} = \sqrt[n]{a}$$

A.2.2 Exponential and Logarithmic Curves

The exponential and logarithmic functions are *inverse functions*. That is, their graphs can be reflected about the $y = x$ line.

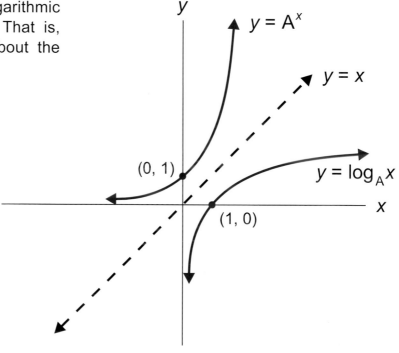

Figure A.1: Exponential and Logarithmic Graphs. $A > 0$, $A \neq 1$.

A.2.3 Log Rules and Logarithmic Scales

The rules of logarithms were discussed in context of Acids and Bases in General Chemistry (CHM 6.5.1). These rules also apply to the "natural logarithm" which is the logarithm to the base e, where "e" is an irrational constant approximately equal to 2.7182818. The natural logarithm is usually written as ln x or loge x . The natural logarithm is used in the Nernst equation (BIO 5 Appendix). In general, the power of logarithms is to reduce wide-ranging numbers to quantities with a far smaller range.

For example, the graphs commonly seen in this text, including the preceding one, are drawn to a unit or *arithmetic scale*. In other words, each unit on the x and y axes represents exactly *one* unit. This scale can be adjusted to accommodate rapidly changing curves. For example, in a unit scale the numbers 1 ($= 10^0$), 10 ($= 10^1$), 100 ($= 10^2$), and 1000 ($= 10^3$), are all far apart with varying intervals. Using a logarithmic scale, the sparse values suddenly become separated by one unit: Log $10^0 = 0$, log $10^1 = 1$, log $10^2 = 2$, log $10^3 = 3$, and so on.

In practice, logarithmic scales are often used to convert a rapidly changing curve (e.g. an exponential curve) to a straight line. It is called a *semi-log* scale when either the abscissa *or* the ordinate is logarithmic. It is called a *log-log* scale when both the abscissa *and* the ordinate are logarithmic.

A.3 Simplifying Algebraic Expressions

Algebraic expressions can be factored or simplified using standard formulae:

$$a(b + c) = ab + ac$$
$$(a + b)(a - b) = a^2 - b^2$$
$$(a + b)(a + b) = (a + b)^2 = a^2 + 2ab + b^2$$
$$(a - b)(a - b) = (a - b)^2 = a^2 - 2ab + b^2$$
$$(a + b)(c + d) = ac + ad + bc + bd$$

QUANTITATIVE REASONING

A.4 Significant Digits, Experimental Error

If we divide 2 by 3 on a calculator, the answer on the display would be 0.6666666667. The leftmost digit is the *most significant digit* and the rightmost digit is the *least significant digit*. The number of digits which are really significant depends on the accuracy with which the values 2 and 3 are known.

For example, suppose we wish to find the sum of two numbers *a* and *b* with experimental errors (or *uncertainties*) Δa and Δb, respectively. The uncertainty of the sum *c* can be determined as follows:

$$c \pm \Delta c = (a \pm \Delta a) + (b \pm \Delta b)$$

$$= a + b \pm (\Delta a + \Delta b)$$

thus

$$\Delta c = \Delta a + \Delta b.$$

The sign of the uncertainties are not correlated, so the same rule applies to subtraction. Therefore, *the uncertainty of either the sum or difference is the sum of the uncertainties*.

Now we will apply the preceding to significant digits. A measurement or calculation of 3.7 has an implicit uncertainty. Any number between 3.65000... and 3.74999... rounds off to 3.7, thus 3.7 really means 3.7 $\pm$ 0.05. Similarly, 68.21 really means 68.21

$\pm$ 0.005. Adding the two values and their uncertainties we get: (3.7 $\pm$ 0.05) + (68.21 $\pm$ 0.005) = 71.91 $\pm$ 0.055. The error is large enough to affect the first digit to the right of the decimal point; therefore, the last digit to the right is not significant. The answer is thus 71.9.

The rule for significant digits states that *the sum or difference of two numbers carries the same number of significant digits to the right of the decimal as the number with the least significant digits to the right of the decimal*. For example, 105.64 − 3.092 = 102.55.

Multiplication and division is somewhat different. Through algebraic manipulation, the uncertainty or experimental error can be determined:

$$c \pm \Delta c = (a \pm \Delta a)(b \pm \Delta b)$$

After some manipulation we get

$$\Delta c/c = \Delta a/a + \Delta b/b.$$

The preceding result also holds true for division. Thus for $(10 \pm 0.5)/(20 \pm 1)$, the fractional error in the quotient is:

$$\Delta c/c = \Delta a/a + \Delta b/b = 0.5/10 + 1/20$$
$$= 0.1 \ (10\% \ \text{error})$$

Thus the quotient including its absolute error is $c \pm \Delta c = 0.5(1 \pm 0.1) = 0.5 \pm 0.05$.

The <u>rule for significant digits</u> can be derived from the preceding and it states that *the product or quotient of two numbers has the same number of significant digits as the number with the least number of significant digits.*

A.5 Properties of Negative and Positive Integers

Positive + Positive = Positive

$$5 + 4 = 9$$

Negative + Negative = Negative

$$(-6) + (-2) = -8$$

Positive + Negative = Sign of the highest number and then subtract

$$(-5) + 4 = -1$$
$$(-8) + 10 = 2$$

Negative − Positive = Negative

$$(-7) - 10 = -17$$

Positive − Negative = Positive + Positive = Positive

$$6 - (-4) = 6 + 4 = 10$$

Negative − Negative = Negative + Positive = Sign of the highest number and then subtract

$$(-8) - (-7) = (-8) + 7 = -1$$

Negative × Negative = Positive

$$(-2) \times (-5) = 10$$

Positive/Positive = Positive

$$8/2 = 4$$

Negative × Positive = Negative

$$(-9) \times 3 = -27$$

Positive/Negative = Negative

$$64/(-8) = -8$$

A.6 Scalars and Vectors

> **NOTE**
>
> Translational motion is the movement of an object (or particle) through space without turning (rotation). Displacement, velocity and acceleration are key vectors - specified by magnitude and direction - often used to describe translational motion. Being able to manipulate and resolve vectors is helpful for some DAT problems. For example, vectors are useful to determine if a molecule has a dipole based on bond polarity (i.e. CHM, ORG). They also help resolve a boat's velocity while it is moving across a river with a downstream current (QR). Because of its rarity on the DAT, we consider acceleration to be an Advanced DAT-30 Topic.

Scalars, such as speed, have magnitude only and are specified by a number with a unit (55 miles/hour). Scalars obey the rules of ordinary algebra. Vectors, like velocity, have both magnitude and direction (100 km/hour, west). Vectors are represented by arrows where:

(i) the length of the arrow indicates the magnitude of the vector, and;

(ii) the arrowhead indicates the direction of the vector. Vectors obey the special rules of vector algebra. Thus vectors can be moved in space but their orientation must be kept the same.

Addition of Vectors: Two vectors a and b can be added geometrically by drawing them to a common scale and placing them head to tail. The vector connecting the tail of a to the head of b is the sum or resultant vector r.

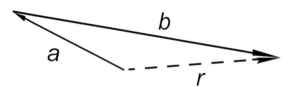

Figure III.B.1.1: The vector sum $a + b = r$.

Subtraction of Vectors: To subtract the vector b from a, reverse the direction of b then add to a.

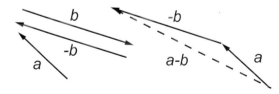

Figure III.B.1.2: The vector difference $a - b = a + (-b)$.

Resolution of Vectors: Perpendicular projections of a vector can be made on a coordinate axis. Thus the vector a can be resolved into its x–component (a_x) and its y–component (a_y).

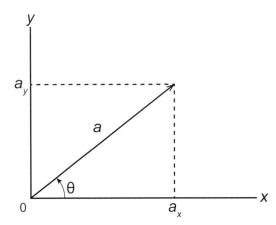

Figure III.B.1.3: The resolution of a vector into its scalar components in a coordinate system.

Analytically, the resolution of vector a is as follows:

$$a_x = a \cos \theta \text{ and } a_y = a \sin \theta$$

Conversely, given the components, we can reconstruct vector *a*:

$$a = \sqrt{a_x^2 + a_y^2} \text{ and } \tan \theta = a_y / a_x$$

A.7 Common Values of Trigonometric Functions

There are special angles which produce standard values of the trigonometric functions. These values should be memorized. Several of the values are derived from the following triangles:

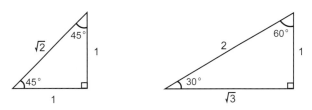

Table III.B.1.1: Common values of trigonometric functions. The angle θ may be given in radians (R) where $2\pi^R = 360° = 1$ revolution. Recall $\sqrt{3} \approx 1.7$, $\sqrt{2} \approx 1.4$.

Note that 1° = 60 arcminutes, 1 arcminute = 60 arcseconds

θ	sin θ	cos θ	tan θ
0°	0	1	0
30°	1/2	$\sqrt{3}/2$	$1\sqrt{3}$
45°	$1\sqrt{2}$	$1\sqrt{2}$	1
60°	$\sqrt{3}/2$	1/2	$\sqrt{3}$
90°	1	0	∞
180°	0	-1	0

Each trigonometric function (i.e. sine) contains an inverse function (i.e. $\sin^{-1}$), where if $\sin \theta = x$, $\theta = \sin^{-1}x$. Thus $\cos 60° = 1/2$, and $60° = \cos^{-1}(1/2)$. Some texts denote the inverse function with "arc" as a prefix. Thus arcsec $(2) = \sec^{-1}(2)$.

A.8 Distance and Displacement

Distance is the amount of separation between two points in space. It has a magnitude but no direction. It is a scalar quantity and is always positive.

Displacement of an object between two points is the difference between the final position and the initial position of the object in a given referential system. Thus, a displacement has an origin, a direction and a magnitude. It is a vector.

The sign of the coordinates of the vector displacement depends on the system under study and the chosen referential system. The sign will be positive (+) if the system is moving towards the positive axis of the referential system and negative (−) if not.

The units of distance and displacement are expressed in length units such as feet (ft), meters (m), miles and kilometers (km).

A.9 Speed and Velocity

Speed is the rate of change of distance with respect to time. It is a scalar quantity, it has a magnitude but no direction, like distance, and it is always positive.

Velocity is the rate of change of displacement with respect to time. It is a vector, and like the displacement, it has a direction and a magnitude. Its value depends on the position of the object. The sign of the coordinates of the vector velocity is the same as that of the displacement.

The **instantaneous velocity** of a system at a given time is the slope of the graph of the displacement of that system vs. time at that time. The magnitude of the

velocity decreases if the vector velocity and the vector acceleration have opposite directions.

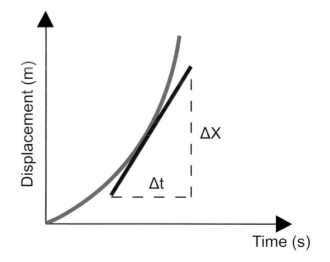

Figure III.B.1.4: Displacement vs. time.

The units of speed and velocity are expressed in length divided by time such as feet/sec., meters/sec. (m/s) and miles/hour.

Dimensional Analysis: remember from High School math that a slope is "rise over run" meaning it is the <u>change in the y-axis divided by the change in the x-axis</u> (see Appendix A.1.1). This means when we pay attention to the units, we get, for example, m/s which is velocity.

A.10 Acceleration: Advanced DAT-30 Content from A.10 to A.12

Acceleration (*a*) is the rate of change of the velocity (*v*) with respect to time (*t*):

$$a = v/t$$

Like the velocity, it is a vector and it has a direction and a magnitude.

The sign of the vector acceleration depends on the net force applied to the system and the chosen referential system. The units of acceleration are expressed as velocity divided by time such as meters/sec². The term for negative acceleration is **deceleration**.

A.10.1 Average and Instantaneous Acceleration

The average acceleration *av* between two instants *t* and *t'* = *t* + Δ*t*, measures the result of the increase in the speed divided by the time difference,

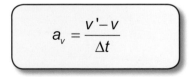

$$a_v = \frac{v' - v}{\Delta t}$$

The instantaneous acceleration can be determined either by calculating the slope (*see* Appendix A.1.1) of a velocity vs. time graph at any time, or by taking the limit when Δt approaches zero of the preceding expression.

$$av = \lim_{\Delta t \to 0} \frac{v' - v}{\Delta t}$$

Math involving "limits" does not exist on the DAT. So let's discuss what this definition is describing in informal terms. The limit is the value of the change in velocity over the change in time as the time approaches 0. It's like saying that the change in velocity is happening in an instant. This allows us to talk about the acceleration in that incredibly fast moment: the instantaneous acceleration which can be determined graphically.

Consider the following events illustrated in the graph (Fig. III.B.1.4): your car starts at rest (0 velocity and time = 0); you steadily accelerate out of the parking lot (the change in velocity increases over time = acceleration); you are driving down the street at constant velocity (change in velocity = 0 and thus acceleration is 0 divided by the change in time which means: a = 0); you see a cat dart across the street safely which made you slow

down temporarily (change in velocity is negative thus negative acceleration which, by definition, is deceleration); you now enter the on-ramp for the highway so your velocity is now increasing at a faster and faster rate (increasing acceleration). You can examine the instantaneous acceleration at any one point (or instant) during the period that your acceleration is increasing.

To determine the displacement (*not* distance), take the area under the graph or curve. To calculate area: a rectangle is base (*b*) times height (*h*); a triangle is ½*b* × *h*; and for a curve, they can use graph paper and expect you would count the boxes under the curve to estimate the area.

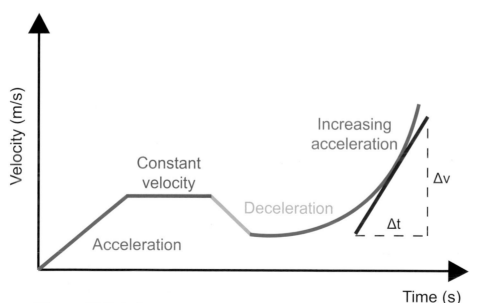

Figure III.B.1.4: Velocity vs. time. Note that at constant velocity, the slope and thus the acceleration are both equal to zero.

A.11 Uniformly Accelerated Motion

The magnitude and direction of the acceleration of a system are solely determined by the exterior forces acting upon the system. If the magnitude of these forces is constant, the magnitude of the acceleration will be constant and the resulting motion is a **uniformly accelerated motion**. The initial displacement, the velocity and the acceleration at any given time contribute to the overall displacement of the system:

$x = x_0$ – displacement due to the initial displacement x_0.

$x = v_0 t$ – displacement due to the initial velocity v_0 at time t.

$x = \frac{1}{2}at^2$ – displacement due the acceleration at time t.

The total displacement of the uniformly-accelerated motion is given by the following formula:

$$x = x_0 + v_0 t + \frac{1}{2}at^2$$

The translational motion is the motion of the center of gravity of a system through space, illustrated by the above equation.

A.12 Equations of Kinematics

Kinematics is the study of objects in motion with respect to space and time. There are three related equations. The first is above, the others are:

$$v = v_0 + at \quad \text{and} \quad v^2 = v_0^2 + 2ax$$

where v is the final velocity.

CHAPTER REVIEW
SOLUTIONS - QR

Question 1   B

See: QR 2.2.3, 2.4.3

According to the rules of order of operations, we work with the square root first: $0.125 + \sqrt{\dfrac{1}{9}} = 0.125 + \dfrac{1}{3}$. Since the answers are in decimal form, this problem is easiest to solve if all values are in decimal form. From the list of fraction-to-decimal conversions, $\dfrac{1}{3} \approx 0.33$, and so, $0.125 + \dfrac{1}{3} \approx 0.125 + 0.33 = 0.455$.

All of the answers have only two decimal places, so we must round this answer off to the hundredths decimal place. The digit in the thousandths decimal place is a 5, and so the digit in the hundredths decimal place increases by 1 to become 6. 0.455 therefore rounds off to 0.46.

Quick Solution:

$$0.125 + \sqrt{\dfrac{1}{9}} = 0.125 + \dfrac{1}{3} \approx 0.125 + 0.333$$

$$= 0.458 \approx 0.46.$$

Question 2   E

See: QR 2.6.2

This is a proportion problem, so there will be two equivalent ratios. We construct the first ratio as $\dfrac{0.8}{0.9}$ and the second as $\dfrac{80}{x}$. If we set them equal, we get $\dfrac{0.8}{0.9} = \dfrac{80}{90}$, and cross-multiplication gives us $0.8x = (0.9)(80)$, or $0.8x = 72$. Therefore, $x = \dfrac{72}{0.8} = 90$.

> **Quick Solution:** 80 differs from 0.8 by a factor of 100. This means that the answer must be related to 0.9 by the same factor: $x = 100(0.9) = 90$

Question 3   A

See: QR 2.4.3

The interest earned by investing \$5,897 in Bank B is 21% of \$5,897, or $(0.21)(\$5,897) = \$1238.37$. The interest earned by investing \$6,430 in Bank A is 19% of \$6,430, or $(0.19)(\$6,430) = \$1221.70$. Subtracting the smaller from the larger, we get $\$1238.37 - \$1221.70 = \$16.67$.

Question 4   C

See: QR 2.4.2

We must work backwards to find the lengths of boards B and C.

Board B is 4/5 as long as Board A, which is $\dfrac{4}{5}(100m) = 80m$.

Board C is 3/4 as long as this, which is $\dfrac{3}{4}(80m) = 60m$. To find the sum of these lengths, we add the three values: 100m + 80m + 60m = 240m.

Question 5   B

See: QR 2.6.2

This is a proportion problem in which the following are given: The proportion of the yellow marbles in the jar of yellow and green marbles is 7 out of 9. This makes the ratio of the number of yellow marbles to green marbles 7:2. The total number of marbles is 999. Therefore, the number of yellow marbles = (7/9) × 999 = 777 marbles.

Question 6   E

See: QR 2.6.1

This is a ratio problem involving different units. The given ratio is 0.25 months per week. We need to re-write this as a fraction: 0.25 months per week $= \dfrac{25}{100}$ months$/$week $= \dfrac{1}{4}$ months$/$week. This ratio tells us that there are four weeks in one month. We can express the number of months corresponding to one day using an intermediate relationship. There are 7 days in one week, which we can express with the ratio $\dfrac{1}{7}$ weeks$/$day. To express the number of months per day, we must multiply the first ratio by the second: $(\dfrac{1}{4}$ months$/$week$)(\dfrac{1}{7}$ weeks$/$day$) = \dfrac{1}{28}$ months$/$day. Notice that the weeks units cancel so that the only units left are months and days. If we had used a ratio expressing the number of days per week (the reciprocal of weeks per day), $\dfrac{7}{1}$ days$/$week, this cancellation would not occur and the final answer would not have the correct units of months per day.

> **Quick Solution:** To convert a ratio that expresses a relationship between months and weeks to one that expresses a relationship between months and days, multiply it by a ratio that expresses a relationship between weeks and days:
>
> $(\dfrac{1}{4}$ months$/$week$)(\dfrac{1}{7}$ weeks$/$day$) = \dfrac{1}{28}$ months$/$day.

Question 7   B

See: QR 2.2.3, 2.4.3, 2.5.2

The first step in this problem is to find the value of 6.4% of 1,000. We convert the percentage to a decimal (0.064) and multiply by 1,000: 0.064(1,000) = 64. Next, we find which of the answer choices is equal to this value. Choice A is obviously incorrect because 64 taken to any power besides 1 does not equal 64. The order of operations tells us that we must perform the calculation inside the parentheses first in choice C, which is a decimal (0.64). Squaring this value does not give us 64. It is easy to see that choice D will also be a decimal. Choice E begins with a small number (6.4) and divides it by a much larger number, so we know that the answer will be even smaller, and therefore not equal to 64. The correct choice is B. To check this, note that $256^{3/4} = (256^{1/4})^3 = (4)^3$ (because $4 \times 4 \times 4 \times 4 = 256$) and $(4)^3 = 64$.

Question 8   D

See: QR 2.2.3, 2.4.3
First, simplify the expressions according to the rules of the order of operations:

$$2 + \left[71 - 8\left(\frac{6}{2}\right)^2\right] = 2 + (70 - 8(3)^2)$$
$$= 2 + (71 - 8(9))$$
$$= 2 + (71 - 72)$$
$$= 2 + (-1) = 1$$

and $\sqrt{2500} = 50$. So, we need to find the percentage of 50 that is constituted by 1. Using the formula

$$\text{Percent} = \text{Part/Whole} \times 100$$

$$\frac{1}{50} \times 100 = 0.02 \times 100 = 2,$$

we see that the answer is 2%.

Question 9   A

See: QR 2.4.3
The tenths decimal place is the largest occupied in each number. Comparing the digits in this decimal place, it is clear that the .6 in .636 is the largest.

Question 10   D

See: QR 2.2.1
Following the rule of adding like and unlike signs:

$$= 9 + -5 + 6$$
$$= 4 + 6$$
$$= 10$$

Question 11   B

See: QR 2.5.2
Dividing the coefficients 1.5 and 3.0 gives an answer of 0.5. Then the correct exponent value is determined by subtracting the exponents involved, which are 7 and 4. The final answer in scientific notation is 0.5×10^3.

CHAPTER REVIEW SOLUTIONS   CHAPTER 3

Question 1   D

See: QR 3.2.2
Construct a ratio comparing millimeters to meters using the definition of the prefix "milli." Remember that we want to convert from meters to millimeters, so the denominator of the

fraction we use for this ratio must contain the units of meters:

$\frac{1000\,\text{mm}}{1\text{m}}$. Now multiply this ratio and the given value:

$$75\,\text{m}\left(\frac{1000\,\text{mm}}{1\text{m}}\right) = 75,000\,\text{mm}.$$

Question 2   C

See: QR 3.1.2
Start with any of the choices and compare it to the rest:

$$0.1\text{km} = 100\text{m} > 10\,\text{m}$$

$$0.5\,\text{km} > 0.1\,\text{km} > 10\,\text{m}$$

$$10\,\text{cm} < 10\,\text{m}$$

$$1000\text{mm} = 1\text{m} > 10\,\text{cm}$$

Question 3   A

See: QR 3.2
The total length of the triathlon is $12\,\text{km} + 10\,\text{km} + 15\,\text{km} = 37\,\text{km}$. Express the ratio of kilometers to meters as a fraction, with kilometers in the denominator to cancel the units of 37 km: $\frac{1000\,\text{m}}{1\,\text{km}}$.

Now multiply: $37\,\text{km}\left(\frac{1000\,\text{m}}{1\,\text{km}}\right) = 37,000\,\text{m}.$

Question 4   C

See: QR 3.1
Construct an equation that expresses an unknown number of staples, times the weight of each, equals the weight of one paper-clip:

$$0.05x = 1$$

$$x = \frac{1}{0.05} = 20$$

Question 5   E

See: QR 3.2.2

Convert the mixed number to an improper fraction:

$$17\frac{5}{6} = \frac{107}{6}$$

Convert using the fact that 60 minutes equals 1 hour:

$$\left(\frac{107}{6}\,\text{hours}\right)\left(\frac{60\,\text{minute}}{1\,\text{hour}}\right) = 1070\,\text{minutes}$$

Question 6   B

See: QR 3.2.2

Add like units:

$$67\,\text{lbs.} + 93\,\text{lbs.} + 18\,\text{lbs.} = 178\,\text{lbs.}$$

$$1\,\text{oz.} + 2\text{oz.} + 5\text{oz.} = 8\text{oz.}$$

Convert to pounds the part of the total weight that is in ounces and add to the rest of the weight:

$$(8\,\text{oz.})\left(\frac{1\,\text{lbs.}}{16\,\text{0z.}}\right) = 0.5\,\text{lbs.}$$

$$178\,\text{lbs.} + 0.5\,\text{lbs.} = 178.5\,\text{lbs.}$$

Question 7   D

See: QR 3.1.1, 3.2

Given that the charges are:

> $20.50 per hour to file paper,
> $55 per hour for time in court,
> $30 per hour for consultations,

a 90-minute consultation = $30 + $15 = $45.

8 /6   hours = 80 minutes time filing paper work = $20.50 + $6.83 = $27.33

Since 20 minutes = $6.83

1 hour in court = $55

Total charges = $45 + $27.33 + $55 = $127.33

Question 8   A

See: QR 3.2.2

Multiply by all ratios necessary to convert centimeters to feet (via inches) and seconds to minutes, and divide by 4 to calculate the speed for only 25% of a minute:

$$(20\,\text{cm/sec.})\left(\frac{1}{2.54}\,\text{in./cm}\right)$$

$$\left(\frac{1}{12}\,\text{ft./in.}\right)(60\,\text{sec./min.})\left(\frac{1}{4}\right) \approx 10\,\text{ft./min.}$$

Question 1   C

See: QR 4.2.2A

Combine like terms:

$$\frac{x}{2} - 1 - \frac{x}{2} < x - \frac{x}{2}$$

$$-1 < \frac{x}{2}$$

$$-1(2) < \left(\frac{x}{2}\right)(2)$$

$$-2 < x$$

Question 2   E

See: QR 4.1.4

Substitute 2 for x in the function:

$$f(2) = \frac{12}{4(2)^3 - 6(2) + 5}$$

$$= \frac{12}{4(8) - 12 + 5}$$

$$= \frac{12}{32 - 12 + 5} = \frac{12}{25}$$

Question 3 D

See: QR 4.3.2, 4.3.3

Create a ratio with the first two values and simplify:

$$\frac{13xy^2z}{39y} = \frac{xyz}{3}$$

The unknown ratio must also be equal to this value. Let k represent the variable and cross-multiply:

$$\frac{9xyz^6}{k} = \frac{xyz}{3}$$

$$3(9xyz^6) = (xyz)k$$

$$\frac{27xyz^6}{xyz} = k$$

$$27z^5 = k$$

Question 4 A

See: QR 4.4.2A, 4.4.2B

Substitute the first equation into the second, replacing y:

$$6x - 5y = -3$$
$$6x - 5(2x - 1) = -3$$
$$6x - 10x + 5 = -3$$
$$-4x + 5 = -3$$
$$-4x = -8$$
$$x = 2$$

Substitute this value back into either equation to find y:

$$y = 2x - 1$$
$$y = 2(2) - 1$$
$$y = 3$$

Question 5 E

See: QR 4.4.2B

We will need to write equations that correspond to the sentences. Let d represent the number of dimes, and n represent the number of nickels. Since there are two less dimes than nickels,

$$d = n - 2.$$

The amount of money a group of coins is worth is equal to the value of the coins times the number of coins. The total value of Loubha's nickels is $\$0.05n$ and the total value of her dimes is $\$0.10d$. These add up to all of the money she has:

$$\$0.05n + \$0.10d = \$0.85.$$

Substitute the first equation into the second for n:

$$\$0.05n + \$0.10(n - 2) = \$0.85$$
$$\$0.05n + \$0.10n - \$0.20 = \$0.85$$
$$\$0.15n = \$0.85 + \$0.20$$
$$\$0.15n = \$1.05$$

$$n = \$1.05 / \$0.15$$
$$n = 7$$

There are 7 nickels. We can plug this into either of the two original equations, but the first is easiest to use:

$$d = n - 2$$
$$d = 7 - 2$$
$$d = 5$$

NOTE: In this particular problem, the fastest way is to just try the different answers until one fits the requirements. We have shown the work in case it was a different question type then you would still know the approach.

Question 6 B

See: QR 4.3.1

Simplify the expression:

$$(2.5 \times 10^3)(3 \times 10^x) = 0.075$$
$$(2.5 \times 3)(10^3 \times 10^x) = 0.075$$
$$(7.5)(10^{3+x}) = 0.075$$

Divide both sides of the equation 7.5, or simply note that 0.075 is one–hundredth $(\frac{1}{100}) = 10^{-2}$ of 7.5:

$$10^{3+x} = 10^{-2}$$
$$3 + x = -2$$
$$x = -5$$

Question 7 B

See: QR 4.6.2

y is a quadratic equation, so we can use the quadratic formula to solve for x, but, first, the equation must be in standard form:

$$3x^2 - 5x - 7 - y = 0$$

The term $-y$ does not have any powers of x, so it becomes part of the constant term: $a = 3, b = -5, c = -7 - y$. Applying the quadratic formula,

$$\frac{-(-5) \pm \sqrt{(-5)^2 - 4(3)(-7-y)}}{2(3)}$$

$$= \frac{5 \pm \sqrt{25 + 84 + 12y}}{6}$$

$$= \frac{5 \pm \sqrt{109 + 12y}}{6}$$

Question 8   D

See: QR 4.5.4

If we think of the plank as a straight line in a coordinate system, we can use the points at which its ends are located to find its slope. The origin can be anywhere we choose, and the base of the house's left wall is a good choice. This point of the house must be located at $(0, 0)$, and so the base of the plank, 7 feet to the left, is located at $(-7, 0)$. The point at which the plank touches the left wall is 5 feet above the origin, at $(0, 5)$. The slope of the plank

is therefore

$$m = \frac{0 - 5}{-7 - 0} = \frac{-5}{-7} = \frac{5}{7}$$

Question 9   D

See: QR 4.3.1, 4.4.2A, 4.4.2B

It is given that $2n = 3k$, which implies that $\frac{2}{3}n = k$. $n + k = 5$ can therefore be rewritten:

$$n + \frac{2}{3}n = 5$$
$$\frac{5}{3}n = 5$$
$$n = 3$$

CHAPTER REVIEW SOLUTIONS   CHAPTER 5

Question 1   B

See: QR 5.2, 5.2.3

Using the given information to write an equation, we have:

$$\pi r^2 = 144\pi$$

We need the value of the radius to find the circumference, so we solve for r:

$$r^2 = \frac{144\pi}{\pi}$$
$$r = \sqrt{144}$$
$$r = 12$$

The formula for the circumference of a circle gives us:

$$2\pi r = 2\pi(12) = 24\pi$$

Question 2   A

See: QR 5.3, 5.3.1

We need to divide the volume of the box by the volume of one of the smaller cubes. One edge of the large box is 1 yard, or 36 inches, so its volume is $(36 \text{ in})^3 = 46656$ in. The volume of the cube is $(6 \text{ in})^3 = 216$ in^3

$$\frac{46656 \, \text{in}^3}{216 \, \text{in}^3} = 216$$

Question 3   E

See: QR 5.2, 5.2.3

The length of the radius is half of the length of the diameter, which is $d = \sqrt{(2 - 2)^2 + (-3 - 5)^2} = \sqrt{0 + 64} = 8$

units long. The radius is therefore equal to 4.

Question 4   D

See: QR 5.3, 5.3.3

The difference in volume of the cylinders will give us the difference in the amount of water they can hold. The larger cylinder has volume $\pi(1)^2(1)^2 = \pi$ ft^3 and the smaller cylinder has volume $\pi(1)^2(0.5) = 0.5\pi$ ft^3. The difference is π ft^3 $- 0.5\pi$ ft^3 $= 0.5\pi$ ft^3.

Question 5   D

See: QR 5.2, 5.2.2

Triangle A has an area of $\frac{bh}{2} = 3(12 \text{ ft}^2) = 36\text{ft}^2$, which means that its base times its height is equal to 72 square feet. The base and height of all $45°$–$45°$–$90°$ triangles are the same, so

$(b \times h)/2 = (b \times b)/2 = 36$. Solving for b gives us b $= \sqrt{72}$. Using the Pythagorean Theorem, we can solve for the hypotenuse. h2 $= (\sqrt{72})2 + (\sqrt{72})2 = 144$, therefore h $= \sqrt{144} = 12$.

Question 6   C

See: QR 5.1, 5.1.3

The angle PQD has a measure equal to that of the given angle, 30 degrees, because the highways are parallel and the road forms a transversal across them. The hypotenuse of the right triangle PQD is 2 km long, and the alley, which forms the leg of the triangle that is opposite angle PQD, has a length of

$$(2 \text{ km}) \sin(30°) = 1 \text{ km}$$

Question 7   A

See: QR 5.2, 5.2.1, 5.2.3
The relationship between the length of a side s and the length of the diagonal d of a square is

$$d = s\sqrt{2}$$

The length of a side of the given square is therefore

$$s = \frac{d}{\sqrt{2}} = \frac{5}{\sqrt{2}}$$

This is always the length of the diagonal of the inscribed circle, which has a radius of length $\frac{5}{\sqrt{2}} \div 2 = \frac{5}{2\sqrt{2}}$. The area of the circle is therefore

$$\pi\left(\frac{5}{2\sqrt{2}}\right)^2 = \frac{25\pi}{8}$$

Question 8   E

See: QR 5.2, 5.2.3
Represent the areas of the large and small circle by πr_L^2 and πr_S^2, respectively. 25% is equivalent to $\frac{1}{4}$, so

$$\pi r_S^2 = \frac{1}{4}(\pi r_L^2)$$

$$r_S^2 = \frac{1}{4}r_L^2$$

$$\sqrt{r_S^2} = \sqrt{\frac{1}{4}r_L^2}$$

$$r_S = \frac{1}{2}r_L$$

and the ratio of the radii is $\frac{r_S}{r_L} = \frac{\frac{1}{2}r_L}{r_L} = \frac{1}{2}$.

Question 9   D

See: QR 5.1, 5.1.1, 5.2.3
(0, 0), (10, 0), and any given point except (5, 0) can be connected by an arc, which can form part of a circle. (0, 0), (10, 0), and (5, 0) can only be connected by a line, which can never form part of a circle.

Question 10   E

See: QR 5.2, 5.2.1
The 3-inch border at each end of both dimensions adds 6 in., or 0.5 ft. to both the length and the width of the picture. The total area of both picture and border is therefore: (5)(4) = 20 sq. ft.

Question 11   B

See: QR 5.3, 5.3.1
The four walls have a total area of 4(10)(12) = 480 sq. ft. The total area of the door and bay window are (3)(7) + (3)(4) = 21 + 12 = 33 sq. ft. The total surface area that needs to be covered with wallpaper is therefore 480 − 33 = 447 sq. ft. The number of wallpaper rolls needed is $\frac{447}{100} = 4.47$, which rounds up to 5.

Question 12   C

See: QR 5.3, 5.3.1
The surface area of the floor is given by its length times its width, so its width is given by the surface area divided by the length:

$$\frac{64.125}{9.5} = 6.75 \text{ feet}$$

Question 1   D

See: QR 6.3, 6.3.1

The lengths of the hypotenuse and the side adjacent to angle A are given, so we can use the inverse cosine of the ratio of these sides to fnd the angle:

$$\cos^{-1}\left(\frac{2}{7}\right) \approx 73°$$

Question 2   B

See: QR 6.2, 6.2.1

A circle covers a total of 2π radians, and

$$\frac{\frac{8\pi}{5}}{2\pi} = \frac{4}{5}$$

which is equivalent to 80%.

Question 3   A

See: QR 6.5

$$-\cos\left(\frac{\pi}{2}\right) = \cos\left(\frac{\pi}{2}\right) = 0$$

Question 4   C

See: QR 6.1, 6.1.3, 6.3, 6.3.3

In a right triangle, the tangent of an angle represents the ratio of sides $\frac{opposite}{adjacent}$, so the given values form the proportion $\frac{3}{2} = \frac{12}{x}$, where x is the side adjacent the angle in Question. Cross-multiplication gives us 3x = 24, or x = 8, and we can fnd the length of the hypotenuse using the Pythagorean Theorem:

$$12^2 + 8^2 = c^2$$
$$144 + 64 = c^2$$
$$\sqrt{208} = c$$
$$\sqrt{4 \times 4 \times 13} = c$$
$$4\sqrt{13} = c$$

Question 5   A

See: QR 6.3, 6.3.2

Simplifying the expression, we get: Cos (x) = sin(x). The only angle for which the sine and cosine are equal is 45°. This can be inferred from the fact that the legs of a 45°–45°–90° triangle are of equal lengths.

Question 6   D

See: QR 6.3, 6.3.2

Using the identity $\tan^2(x) + 1 = \sec^2(x)$,

$$\tan^2(x) + 1 = \left(\frac{5}{4}\right)^2$$

$$\tan^2(x) = \frac{25}{16} - \frac{16}{16}$$

$$\tan(x) = \sqrt{\frac{9}{16}}$$

$$\tan(x) = \frac{3}{4}$$

Question 7   E

See: QR 6.2, 6.2.3

The cosine of an angle is equal to the sine of its complement. $\frac{\pi}{6}$, or $\left(\frac{\pi}{6}\right)\left(\frac{180°}{\pi}\right) = 30°$, is the complement of $\frac{\pi}{3} = 60°$.

Question 8   C

See: QR 6.2, 6.2.1

On the unit circle, the sine of an angle is equivalent to the y-coordinate of the terminal side of the angle, so the angle must lie in one of the quadrants in which y is negative: The third or fourth. The tangent of an angle is represented by the quotient of the y-coordinate and x-coordinate of the angle's terminal side, so it is positive in quadrants in which x and y have the same sign: The third and first. Therefore, the angle must be located where the two possible regions overlap: The third quadrant.

Question 1   B

See: QR 7.1.1

There are four red marbles, and a total of 4 red + 6 blue = 10 marbles, so the probability is $\dfrac{4}{10}$.

Question 2   C

See: QR 7.3.4

Each ordering of the objects is different, so it is necessary to calculate of the number of permutations in which all 6 objects are used. 6! = 720

Question 3   E

See: QR 7.1, 7.1.2

With a total of 10 balls and 6 yellow balls, the probability that the first ball is yellow is $\dfrac{6}{10} = \dfrac{3}{5}$. After the first ball is chosen, there are 9 left, of which 4 are green. The probability of choosing a green ball at this point is therefore $\dfrac{4}{9}$. The total probability is

$$\left(\dfrac{3}{5}\right)\left(\dfrac{4}{9}\right) = \dfrac{4}{15}$$

Question 4   E

See: QR 7.3, 7.3.5

Multiply all possible choices: $3 \times 2 \times 4 = 24$

Question 5   A

See: QR 7.3.2

The 2516 residents represent 68% of the total number of residents x:

$$2516 = 0.68x$$

$$3700 = x$$

Question 6   C

See: QR 7.2, 7.2.1

If the third student takes x minutes to complete the test:

$$\dfrac{41 + 37 + x}{3} = 35$$

$$78 + x = 105$$

$$x = 27$$

Question 7   D

See: QR 7.3.5

There are 4 different book colors, so there are 4 different choices for books to shelve on Monday. There are only 3 choices on Tuesday. On Wednesday, the rest of the books will be shelved, so there is only 1 choice. This gives a total of $4 \times 3 \times 1 = 12$ different ways to shelve the books.

Question 8   B

See: QR 7.2

Label the numbers a, b, c, d from smallest to largest. The range is the difference between the largest and smallest:

$$d - a = 14$$

The median is the average of the two middle numbers:

$$\dfrac{b + c}{2} = 7$$

and so

$$b + c = 14$$

The mean is the average of all of the numbers:

$$\dfrac{a + b + c + d}{4} = 8$$

Simplifying this equation and substituting 14 for $b + c$:

$$a + b + c + d = 32$$

$$a + 14 + d = 32$$

$$a + d = 18$$

Adding this equation and the equation that represents the range:

$$(a + d) + (d - a) = 18 + 14$$

$$2d = 32$$

$$d = 16$$

Therefore:

$$16 - a = 14$$

$$a = 2$$

Now, we have 3 of the numbers and can use the simplified equation for the mean to find the fourth, which we can call x:

$$2 + 9 + 16 + x = 32$$

$$x = 5$$

Question 9   E

See: QR 7.1, 7.1.2

A die has a total of 6 possible sides. There is only one side that displays a 3, so the probability of rolling a 3 is $\frac{1}{6}$. Similarly, the probability of rolling any other number is also $\frac{1}{6}$. The probability of rolling a 1 or a 2 is the sum of their individual probabilities: $\frac{1}{6} + \frac{1}{6} = \frac{1}{3}$. Because this probability is independent of the probability of first rolling a 3, we multiply the results to get the total probability: $\left(\frac{1}{6}\right)\left(\frac{1}{3}\right) = \frac{1}{18}$.

Question 10   D

See: QR Chap 7 Appendix

The p value (= **p**robability value or alpha level) expresses statistical significance. The probability of committing a Type I error is called the significance level or alpha (= α). All answer choices are accurately describing p<.05.

Question 11   A

See: QR Chap 7 Appendix

The t-test (= Student's t-test) and analysis of variance (= ANOVA) are statistical procedures that assume normal distributions (= *parametric*) and make use of the mean and variance to determine the significance of the differences of the means of two or more groups of values. Whether there is evidence that the samples or data were random or that differences in the populations are significant would be the result of a statistical analysis but not an assumption.

Question 12   D

See: QR Chap 7 Appendix

Chi-Squared Goodness of Fit Test is a test for comparing a theoretical distribution, such as a Normal distribution, with the observed data from a sample.

Question 13   C

See: QR Chap 7 Appendix

Null hypothesis (= H_0) is usually the hypothesis that sample observations result purely from chance. In other words, the null hypothesis says that there is no significant difference between specified populations, any observed difference being due to sampling or experimental error. This is most consistent with answer choice C which states that it is "the assumption that there is no relationship or difference between the variables being tested".

Question 14   B

See: QR Chap 7 Appendix

Either the null hypothesis is true or the alternative hypothesis is true but never both.

Question 15   A

See: QR Chap 7 Appendix

A two-sided test (= two-tailed test of significance) is a statistical hypothesis test in which the values for which we can reject the null hypothesis, H_0 are located in both tails of the probability distribution.

Question 16   A

See: QR Chap 7 Appendix

Test scores follow a normal curve or normal distributions (= *parametric*). Chi-square is a nonparametric statistical procedure. The question is looking at one parameter: are Gold Standard students scoring higher than other students: one-tailed test.

Question 17   C

See: QR Chap 7 Appendix

Again, let's return to flipping a coin.

H_0: probability = 0.5

H_a: probability < 0.5 or > 0.5

Thus the alternative hypothesis could be that heads occur more often, or that heads occur less often as would be predicted by the null hypothesis would suggest that the event is not random.

Question 18   C

See: QR Chap 7 Appendix

A Type II error occurs when the researcher accepts a null hypothesis that is false. Traditionally, a Type I error is considered to be more serious.

Question 19   A

See: QR Chap 7 Appendix

A Type I error occurs when the researcher rejects a null hypothesis when it is true. The probability of committing a Type I error is called the significance level or alpha (= α). The confidence level is $1 - \alpha$.

Question 20   D

See: QR Chap 7 Appendix

The p value (= **p**robability value or alpha level) expresses statistical significance. The probability of committing a Type II error is called beta (= β).

Question 1   C

See: QR 8.2.2

The walking speed is $\dfrac{1.5\,\text{mi}}{0.5\,\text{hr.}}$ = 3 mi./hr., and in 3 hours, (3

hr.) (3 mi./hr.) = 9 mi. will be covered.

Question 2   A

See: QR 8.1, 8.1.2

Since the ray passes through one focus, it must pass through the other after being reflected. The length of any such path is always equal to the length of the major axis, so if the distance between the point of reflection and the second focus is 6, the distance between the point of reflection and the first focus must be 8 − 6 = 2.

Question 3   D

See: QR 8.1.2

The distance from the given focus to the point of reflection is

$$\sqrt{(\sqrt{5} - 0)^2 + (0 - 2)^2}$$
$$= \sqrt{(\sqrt{5})^2 + (2)^2}$$
$$= \sqrt{5 + 4}$$
$$= \sqrt{9} = 3$$

The second focus must be located at $(-\sqrt{5}, 0)$. By symmetry, this focus is also 3 units from the point of reflection. The sum of these lengths is the total distance traveled by the ray of light, and is equal to the length of the major axis.

Question 4   B

See: QR 8.2, 8.2.1

Combined, the two pipes fill the tank at a rate of 5 + 15 = 20 gal./min.. The time t needed to fill the tank is:

$$t = \frac{180\,\text{gal.}}{20\,\text{gal.} / \text{min.}} = 9\,\text{min.}$$

Question 5   A

See: QR 8.1, 8.1.1

The beam of light will be reflected on the opposite side of the mirror, and because it passes through the center, its path is a diagonal of the circle, which has length $2r = 2(5) = 10$.

Question 6   E

See: QR 8.2.2

The truck's speed during the morning is

$$\frac{150\,\text{mi}}{3\,\text{hrs}} = 50\,\text{mph}$$

and its speed during the afternoon is

$$\frac{180\,\text{mi}}{3\,\text{hrs}} = 60\,\text{mph}$$

The average speed is

$$\frac{50\,\text{mph} + 60\,\text{mph}}{2} = 55\,\text{mph}$$

Question 7   C

See: QR 8.2, 8.2.2

The ship will reach the shore in

$$\frac{500\,\text{km}}{100\,\text{km} / \text{min}} = 5\,\text{min}$$

This is a total of

$$(5\,\text{min.}) (60\,\text{sec./min.}) = 300\,\text{sec},$$

which makes up

$$\frac{300\,\text{sec}}{5\,\text{sec}} = 60$$

intervals of 5 seconds each. In this time, the lighthouse beam sweeps out

$$60\left(\frac{\pi}{4}\right) = 15\pi\,\text{radians},$$

which is equivalent to

$$\frac{15\pi}{2\pi} = 7.5\,\text{revolutions.}$$

Question 8   D

See: QR 8.1, 8.1.1

As the diagonal of a square intercepts the corners of the square at a 45° angle, a ray travelling diagonally across a square must intercept the corner at the same angle. The Law of Reflection tells us that the ray is reflected at 45° as well, so BDC and BED are congruent 45°–45°–90° triangles. The distance DE, which represents the ray's distance from point D, must be equal to CD. The length of the diagonal of a square is the length of the side times the square root 2, so CD and DE must have length $\dfrac{1}{\sqrt{2}}$.

Question 9   B

See: QR 8.2.1

Let w, h, d represent the current ages of the wife, husband, and daughter, respectively. Three years ago, they were $w - 3$, $h - 3$, $d - 3$ years old. The average of these is:

$$\frac{(w - 3) + (h - 3) + (d - 3)}{3} = 27$$

Five years ago, the husband and daughter were $h - 5, d - 5$ years old, and the average of these ages is:

$$\frac{(h - 5) + (d - 5)}{2} = 20$$

Simplify these fractions to get:

$$w + h + d = 90,$$
$$h + d = 50$$

Now, subtract the second equation from the first:

$$w + h + d - (h + d) = 90 - (50)$$
$$w = 40$$

Question 10   B

See: QR 8.2, 8.2.2

Use the formula $\text{rate} = \dfrac{\text{distance}}{\text{time}}$, where the distance is 3.3 miles. The downhill rate minus the uphill rate is:

$$r_2 - r_1 = \frac{3.3}{1.5} - \frac{3.3}{5}$$

$$= \frac{10(3.3)}{15} - \frac{3(3.3)}{15}$$

$$= \frac{7(3.3)}{15}$$

$$= 1.54 \text{ miles per hour}$$

Given that 1 mile = 1.6 km:

$$\frac{1.54\text{mi}}{1\text{hr}} \times \frac{1.6\text{km}}{1\text{mi}} \times \frac{1\text{ hr}}{3600\text{ s}}$$

$$= \frac{2.464 \text{ km}}{3600\text{ s}}$$

$$= 6.84 \times 10^{-4} \text{ km/s}$$

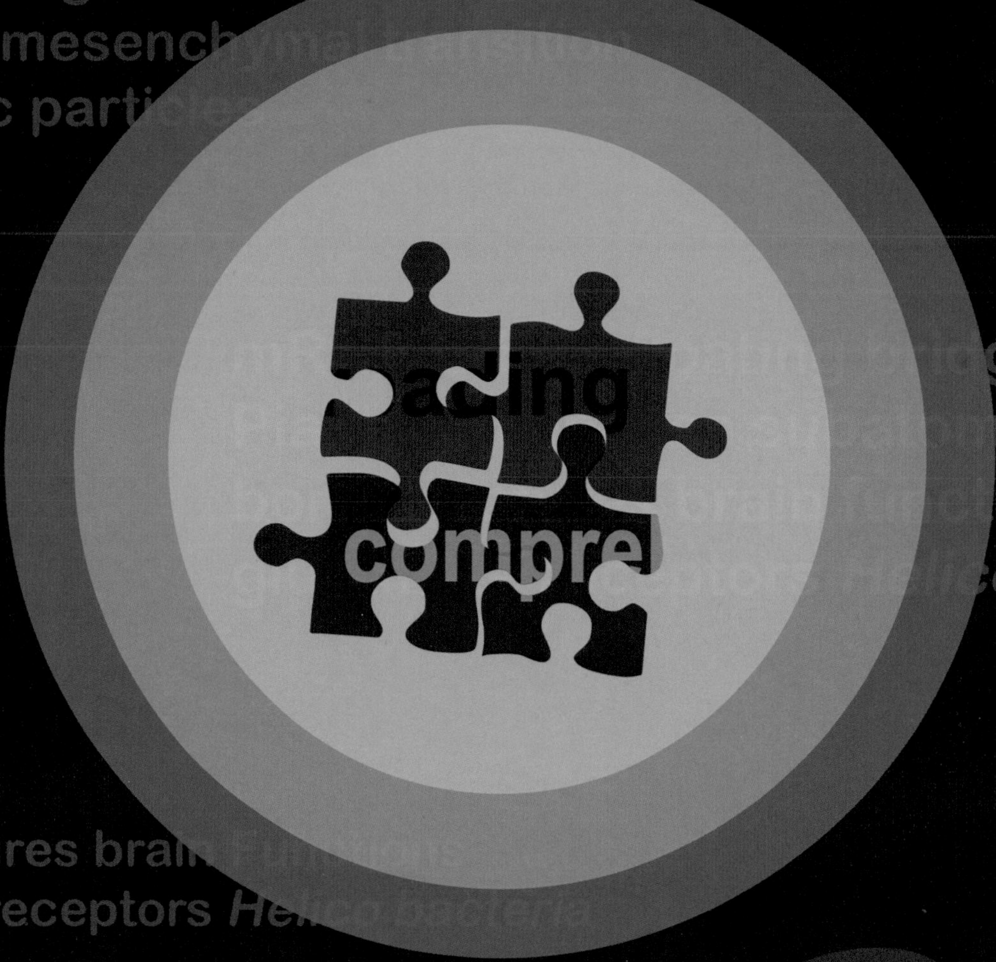

DAT-Prep.com

READING COMPREHENSION

Understand

* Key concepts in academic reading,
   question types, study reading strategies

DAT-Prep.com

Introduction ▮▮▮▮

The DAT Reading Comprehension entails two main tasks: (1) locating key information in academic texts and (2) identifying concepts in order to make reasonable inferences about the subject under discussion. These require certain skills that some candidates may already have while others may still need to develop.

In any case, your first step in confronting this section is to familiarize yourself with the features and structure of the test. This will help you determine the approach that you need to adopt in your RC preparation.

Let's start reading!

Additional Resources

Free Online Forum

1.1 Overview

The third section of the DAT is the **Reading Comprehension Test**. This section primarily assesses your ability to locate key details and infer fundamental concepts in scholarly texts. Recall and analysis of written information are skills that are requisite to the problem-solving demands in the basic sciences. Thus the stimulus passages given in the Reading Comprehension section replicate the kind of scientific reading required in dental college.

Prior knowledge of science topics and concepts is NOT REQUIRED to competently answer the test questions, and the best preparation really is, well...reading. However, it is regular study reading from a variety of academic references throughout your high-school and undergraduate studies that makes for a strong foundation in this section. Nevertheless, you should not neglect to prepare for this test as it accounts for one of the five standard scores that make up the Academic Average score in the DAT.

In a report published by the ADA in May 2011, 39 of the 58 surveyed U.S. dental schools indicated that they consider the Reading Comprehension as the third most important DAT score of an applicant, following the Academic Average and Total Science scores, in their admissions criteria.[1] Half of the 10 Canadian dental schools likewise include this score in the DAT, next to Perceptual Ability and Academic Average, as a significant factor in their selection process.

By acquainting yourself with the nature and scope of this section, you will be able to anticipate vulnerable areas. As long as you are quick to address your weaknesses, increasing your chances of doing well in this section is very much possible.

---

[1] ADA Survey Center, *2009-10 Survey of Dental Education Tuition, Admission, and Attrition Volume 2* (Chicago, Illinois: American Dental Association, 2011), http://www.ada.org/sections/professionalResources/pdfs/survey_ed_vol2.pdf.

1.2 Format and Content of the Test

The Reading Comprehension Test is composed of 50 multiple-choice questions and has a time limit of 60 minutes. It consists of three reading passages of approximately 1,500 words in length.

This section comes right after the optional 15-minute break subsequent to the Perceptual Ability Test. A passage is then presented on the computer screen in full-page view. {Please note that the Canadian

DAT remains a paper test and is 50 minutes long. The Reading Comprehension Test is only included in the English DAT in Canada.}

The subsequent screens will show one question at a time, with the reading passage in a parallel window right under it. Every time the page moves to the next question, the reading passage reloads and goes back to its beginning sentence or paragraph.

On average, there are 16 to 17 questions per passage, although this can occasionally range from 15 to 20. Each question requires an answer choice from four to five options.

The Reading Passage

A passage is placed in a smaller window with a vertical scroll bar that allows the test-taker to move the text up and down. Paragraphs are also numbered. The "NEXT" button at the bottom-center of the window leads to the questions in the succeeding pages.

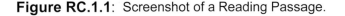

Page 15 of 19   Dental Admission Test   Time Remaining 8:00

(1). Another one of the devious little mysteries of science are the strange stones of Death Valley in California. These stones sit on sun-baked, flat, cracked earth, and they have trails they have left as they have moved, for some baffling reason, across the wasteland. The home of these mysterious stones is known, logically, as the "Racetrack Playa", a dry lakebed occasionally dampened by flash storms. The Racetrack measures 4.5 kilometers by 2.1 kilometers (2.8 by 1.3 miles), and is only about 5 centimeters (2 inches) higher at one end than the other.

(2). The trails left by the stones vary from a few meters to almost a kilometer in length. Some of the trails are straight, some zigzagged, some go in circles. In some cases the trails vary in width, meaning the stones must have rotated as they moved. 162 of the Racetrack's moving stones have been documented, and many of them have names, always female. They range from fist-sized to the size of an ice chest.

Click on the 'Next' button to continue.

PREVIOUS   NEXT   END

Figure RC.1.1: Screenshot of a Reading Passage.

Figure RC.1.2: Screen Window View of the Questions. Take note that for each question, the entire reading passage is still provided in a smaller screen with the scroll bar.

Unlike the Biology, Chemistry and Quantitative Reasoning sections, the ADA has not published any recommended text to review for the Reading Comprehension Test. However, the DAT User's Manual describes the subject matter as "developed from aspects of dental, basic, or clinical science not covered in an undergraduate college curriculum."[2]

In addition, students who have taken the past exams reported coming across the following topics:

---

[2] Dental Admission Testing Program, *Report 3 2011: User's Manual 2009* (Chicago, Illinois: American Dental Association Department of Testing Services, 2011), http://www.ada.org/sections/educationAndCareers/pdfs/dat_users_manual.pdf.

Science Topics

- Aging
- Antibiotics
- Bone fractures
- Brain functions, glutamate receptors
- Contraception
- Einstein-related topic
- Enzymes, telomerases
- Fungi
- Gene therapy, genetic cancer, epithelial-mesenchymal transition

- Helico bacteria (H.Pylori)
- Herbal medicine
- Hurricanes
- Physics involving calculations
- Subatomic particles
- Tooth development
- Transcription/Translation, recent studies on mRNA, voltage-gated ion channels, messenger

Non-science topics

- Ethics
- Floating Bridges

- Piano
- The Stock Market

Please note that you do neither have to know nor study these topics in order to do well on the exam. Rather, these merely serve as examples to give you a glimpse of the subject matters typically found on the test.

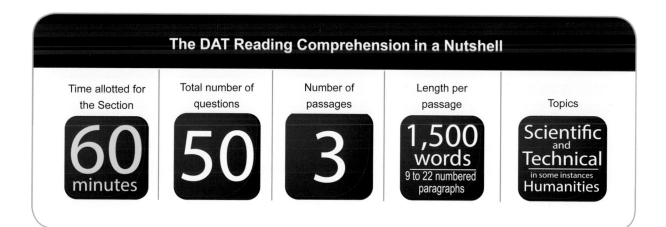

The DAT Reading Comprehension in a Nutshell

Time allotted for the Section	Total number of questions	Number of passages	Length per passage	Topics
60 minutes	**50**	**3**	**1,500** words 9 to 22 numbered paragraphs	Scientific and Technical in some instances Humanities

Understand

* Reading comprehension techniques:
  predicting, skimming, paraphrasing,
  visualizing, contextual clues

DAT-Prep.com

Introduction ▮▮▮▮

Questions in the DAT Reading Comprehension test mostly require careful attention to specific terms, methods and or core ideas in a passage. On some occasions, you may need to slow down and evaluate certain details with an analytical perspective.

Reading techniques such as predicting, skimming, and paraphrasing should form the backbone of your preparation. The earlier you utilize these skills, The earlier you utilize these skills, the earlier you will be able to identify which strategies are the most effective for you.

Additional Resources

Free Online Forum

2.1 Factors Affecting Preparation and Performance in the Test

In the preceding chapter, we have discussed the format and content of the DAT Reading Comprehension test.

Knowing what to expect in this section is quite important because the difficulty of a test is oftentimes subjective to the test-taker. For instance, some passages may appear lengthy because paragraphs in the RC section are numbered, making short but several paragraphs look longer. Being confronted with a seemingly lengthy passage may set an anxious examinee to panic, consequentially affecting focus and confidence in overcoming the whole test.

However, if you very well know beforehand that a reading passage will only have 1500 words at the maximum, and assuming that you have adequately practiced your reading speed for this section, you can calmly proceed with the exam.

Likewise, the difficulty of a specific passage depends on a candidate's background. Someone who is not used to reading dense articles whether in the sciences or humanities often find the RC section a real challenge. Moreover, humanities in the DAT RC context specifically refer to philosophical texts that deal with moral values or socio-political principles. Readings based on culture or the arts are also common. A student with a strong science background may find these readings difficult because of limited exposure to such topics.

Applicants who have English as their second language doubly struggle in the RC section because the language used in these passages is largely technical.

Building your skills effectively for this section indeed depends on a number of factors. However, familiarity with science topics, exposure to technical and scholarly reading, timing and the ability to focus are all key components to success. While no specific presumed knowledge is required to answer any of the questions, you still need to remain focused on cultivating these core skills, which will be tested in the actual exam.

2.2 Developing Comprehension Skills

2.2.1 One Year or More before the DAT

Strengthening your reading comprehension skills is beneficial to your overall preparation for the DAT: you are more likely to overcome better the cognitive rigor of the different test sections. By exposing yourself to various topics, your stored knowledge will also expand. This will be particularly important when you start interviewing for dental school and present yourself as a well-rounded individual.

Therefore, read! Be known as a "voracious reader"! Read materials that interest you, as well as those that DO NOT necessarily excite you. After all, dental school involves a lot of reading and absorbing enormous amounts of information.

Contrary to approaching creative and opinion pieces, some extent of background knowledge makes reading scientific articles a less agonizing experience. You tend to understand technical concepts better and quicker if you have been introduced to the topic before. At least once every week, for 1 – 3 hours, you should read among the following (either from a university library or online):

- **Scientific Articles**

Suggested Resources:

✓ **Dental Journals**
The Journal of the American Dental Association (http://jada.ada.org/)
The Journal of Contemporary Dental Practice (http://www.thejcdp.com/)
Journal of Dental Research (http://jdr.sagepub.com/)
The Directory of Open Access Journals (http://www.doaj.org/) This free-access site lists the links to online dental journals.

✓ **Dental Research and News Sources**
Pubmed has several articles that have free Full Text content: http://www.ncbi.nlm.nih.gov/pubmed/
ADA Science News (http://ada.org/272.aspx)
ADA Publications and Resources (http://ada.org/293.aspx)

✓ **Science Magazines**
The Scientific American (http://www.scientificamerican.com/sciammag/)
Discover Magazine (http://discovermagazine.com/)

Active reading tends to improve comprehension and speed. With scientific articles, the following techniques usually prove to be helpful:

1. **Predicting**

   This is equivalent to preliminary skimming. Upon seeing the title of what you are about to read, you can usually guess the article's content, especially if you are familiar with the subject matter from prior knowledge. Likewise, awareness of textual types (e.g., expository*, argumentative) could help predict to which the succeeding discussions may lead.

2. **Skimming**

   This is a technique for spotting clues within the text itself. You run your eyes quickly through the content for an overview of what to expect in the material, occasionally slowing down on seemingly salient parts. As you skim over the words and the paragraphs, you should continually ask yourself…

   - Is this article about a description of some characteristic?
   - Is the article about an origin, a discovery or a scientific process or method?

   - Does the author organize his or her ideas through definitions and examples, classification, or cause and effect?

   By using this technique, you can figure out certain parts that are not essential and detect parts where you need to dedicate some attention for a better understanding of the details. Lastly, skimming will confirm your earlier prediction, which was initially based on the article's title.

3. **Paraphrasing**

   In order to test your general understanding of reading material, restate the main idea of each relevant paragraph. By the end of the article, you will have a clearer outline of the author's central point. Taking the whole by its smaller parts is less overwhelming than having to swallow everything in a single glance.

4. **Visualizing**

   Quite frequently, the procedures and the apparatus described in scientific papers are very specific. For descriptions of the parts of an instrument, doing a sketch proves to be of great benefit. Similarly, you can create a skeletal outline of the steps in an experiment, a research investigation, or a process.

---

*Expository texts can range from textbooks to scientific journals, encyclopedia, and biographies. These articles are meant to inform, describe, explain or define concepts, theories and methods.

- **Humanities Articles**

For exposure to a variety of the humanities topics and themes, include Arts and Culture articles in your weekly plate of exploratory reading:

✓ **Humanities and Culture Magazines or Journals**
The New Yorker - Culture section
(http://www.newyorker.com/arts/)
Digital Humanities
(http://www.digitalhumanities.org/dhq/)
The Culture Magazine
(http://www.culturemachine.net/)

Paraphrasing is a reading technique that is highly applicable to selections from the humanities and any texts that demand inference. However, you should go beyond just getting the main idea. The following are also vital questions that you need to actively ask yourself when reading non-scientific articles:

- What are the primary supporting facts and/or evidences that support the author's thesis?
- For which type of audience would the article appeal?
- What is the author's tone?
- What is the author's attitude or opinion toward the subject?
- What is the author's purpose for writing the article?

2.3 One Year or Less before the DAT

Read section 2.2.1 one more time! Even at this point in your preparation, being a voracious reader - with all that it entails - should be your goal. Besides reading, you need to practice.

The best strategy is to take the ADA's *DAT Sample Test Items*, which can be downloaded for free from the ADA website. Although this is not a full-length test, you should still do this section within the prescribed time limit (approximately 1.2 minutes per question). Your main objective is to gauge your current skills against the

requirements of the real test. You should be able to determine this by reviewing your mistakes.

If you performed well and understood the source of your errors then you will only require ADA and the Gold Standard (GS) DATs in order to complete your preparation. If, on the other hand, you struggled in the test or struggled to understand your mistakes then you may need additional work on strategies, practice or a formal course for or without credit. An optional RC program can be found at DAT-prep.com.

Basic Preparation Tools	Practice Exams (Full-length)
• ADA *DAT Sample Items* • GS book and online	• DAT Practice Test (ADA) • GS QR/RC + PAT/GS-1 books and online • Top Score Pro

2.3 Advice for ESL Students

The same preparation applies for candidates with English as a second language (ESL). Depending on your English skills, you may or may not benefit from an English reading or writing summer course. Of course, you would have the option of deciding whether or not you would want to take such a course for credit.

However, vocabulary may be a chief obstacle, so getting used to academic and rhetorical language is imperative. The dictionary will have to be a constant help buddy in the beginning; but as you progress in your speed and vocabulary, you need to wean yourself from the dictionary and start counting on context clues.

2.4 Contextual Reading

Contextual reading compels you to make a logical guess about the meaning of an unknown word based on the other words and phrases found within the immediate sentences in the paragraph. Writers themselves use this technique to make lucid points. Several cues easily offer probable definitions to uncommon terms:

1) Examples
   Cue words: includes, consists of, such as

   Equine animals, such as horses and zebras, have long been used not only to aid in man's work but also to assist in therapy.

Using the example clue (use of "such as"), the word *equine* means:
A. mammal.
B. reptile.
C. horse group.
D. dog.

2) Synonyms
Cue words: is similar to, just as, also means

*Calling my cousin an "eccentric weirdo" is **tautologous**! It is similar to telling a ghost that he is dead twice.*

The cue word "is similar to" indicates that tautologous means:
A. repetitive.
B. alien.
C. scary.
D. ridiculous.

3) Antonyms and Contrasts
Cue words: unlike, contrary to/in contrast, on the other hand, as opposed to

*Contrary to the playwright's **euphemisms** about the King's corrupt leadership, the merchant was quite direct in criticizing the latter's injustices.*

Based on the contrasting descriptions used in the sentence, the word *euphemism* refers to:

A. corruption.
B. indirect speech.
C. criticism.
D. politics.

Answers:
1. C
2. A
3. B

4) Sense of the sentence
Oftentimes, you only need to observe how the words or phrases relate within the sentence in order to fairly conclude what the difficult word means. Take careful note of the descriptions in the paragraph. Use your logic in determining the most probable meaning of a newly-encountered term.

*March 21, 1894 marks a rare series of **syzygies** in the history of astronomical events. A few hours before Mercury transits the sun as seen from Venus, a partial lunar eclipse is witnessed from Earth. From Saturn, both Mercury and Venus could be seen simultaneously transiting the* *sun. Such planetary spectacles can also be observed by the naked human eye during full moons and new moons as the sun, our planet Earth, and the moon periodically aligns.*

Based on the context of the discussion in the paragraph, the closest meaning of syzygies could be:

A. planetary collisions.
B. lunar eclipses.
C. planetary alignments.
D. historical changes.

5) Root Words, Prefixes, and Suffixes

Certain root words and word parts carry specific meanings. Being acquainted with these, combined with the other clues discussed earlier, helps you figure out the most probable meaning of an unfamiliar word.

Answer: C

Descriptions in the paragraph mention "lunar eclipse," "Mercury transits the sun," and "the sun, our planet earth, and the moon periodically aligns." These should serve as primary clues in determining a general definition of syzygies.

(D) Historical changes is obviously the least likely option. (A) Planetary collisions may sound related; however, nothing in the paragraph indicates a collision of the planets. This should now narrow down your choice between (B) lunar eclipses and (C) planetary alignments. Now common knowledge tells us that a lunar eclipse occurs when three celestial bodies such as the sun, the moon and the Earth align. On the other hand, a full moon or a new moon does not necessarily result to a lunar eclipse. This makes C the more logical answer!

Common Root Words of Scientific Terms

The following is a list of root words, prefixes, and suffixes, which you would generally find in scientific literature. A prefix is a group of letters added to the beginning of a word; a suffix is added to the end of a word.

Prefixes

A
aden- gland
adip- fat
aero- air
agri- field; soil
alb- white
alg-/algia- pain
alto- high
ambi- both
ameb- change; alternation
amni- fetal membrane
amphi-; ampho- both
amyl- starch
ana- up; back; again
andro- man; masculine
anemo- wind
angi- blood vessel; duct
ante- before; ahead of time
anter- front
antho- flower
anthropo- man; human
aqu- water
archaeo- primitive; ancient
arteri- artery
arthr- joint; articulation
aster-; astr- ; astro- star
ather- fatty deposit
atmo- vapor

audi- hear
aur- ear
auto- self

B
bacter-/bactr- bacterium; stick; club
baro- weight
bath- depth; height
bene- well; good
bi- (Latin) two; twice
bi-/bio- (Greek) life; living
brachi- arm
brachy- short
brady- slow
branchi- fin
bronch- windpipe

C
calor- heat
capill- hair
capit- head
carcin- cancer
cardi-/cardio- heart
carn- meat; flesh
carp- fruit
carpal- wrist
cata- breakdown; downward
caud- tail

Prefixes

cente- pierce
centi- hundredth
centr- center
cephal- head
cerat- horn
cerebr- brain
cervic- neck
chel- claw
chem- dealing with chemicals
chir- hand
chlor- green
chondr- cartilage
chrom-/chromo- color
chron- time
circa-; circum- around; about
cirru- hairlike curls
co- with; together
cocc- seed; berry
coel- hollow
coll- glue
coni- cone
contra- against
corp- body
cort-/cortic- outer layer
cosmo- world; order; form
cotyl- cup
counter- against
crani- skull
cresc-/cret- begin to grow
crypt- hidden; covered
cumul- heaped
cuti- skin
cyt- cell; hollow container

D

dactyl- finger
deca- ten
deci- tenth
deliquesc- become fluid
demi- half
dendr- tree
dent- tooth
derm- skin
di-/dipl- (Latin) two; double
di-/dia- (Greek) through; across; apart
dia- (Latin) day
digit- finger; toe
din- terrible
dis- apart; out
dorm- sleep
dors- back
du-/duo- two
dynam- power
dys- bad; abnormal; difficult

E

ec- out of; away from
echin- spiny; prickly
eco- house
ecto- outside of
en-/endo-/ent- in; into; within
encephal- brain
enter- intestine; gut
entom- insects
epi- upon; above; over
erythro- red
eso- inward; within; inner

Prefixes

F
ferro- iron
fibr- fiber; thread
fiss- split
flor- flower
flu-; fluct-; flux flow
foli- leaf
fract- break

G
gastr- stomach
geo- land; earth
gloss- tongue
gluc-/glyc- sweet; sugar
glut- buttock
gnath- jaw
gymno- naked; bare
gyn- female
gyr- ring; circle; spiral

H
halo- salt
hapl- simple
hecto- hundred
hem- blood
hemi- half
hepar/hepat- liver
herb- grass; plants
hetero- different; other
hex- six
hibern- winter
hidr- sweat
hipp- horse
hist- tissue

holo- entire; whole
homo- (Latin) man; human
homo- (Greek) same; alike
hort- garden
hydr- water
hygr- moist; wet
hyper- above; beyond; over
hyph- weaving; web
hypno- sleep
hypo- below; under; less
hyster- womb; uterus

I
ichthy- fish
infra- below; beneath
inter- between
intra- within; inside
iso- equal; same

K
kel- tumor; swelling
kerat- horn
kilo- thousand
kine- move

L
lachry- tear
lact- milk
lat- side
leio- smooth
leuc-/leuk- white; bright; light
lign- wood
lin- line

Prefixes

lingu- tongue
lip- fat
lith-; -lite stone; petrifying
loc- place
lumin- light

M
macr- large
malac- soft
malle- hammer
mamm- breast
marg- border; edge
mast- breast
med- middle
meg- million; great
mela-/melan- black; dark
mes- middle; half; intermediate
met-/meta- between; along; after
micro- small; millionth
milli- thousandth
mis- wrong; incorrect
mito- thread
mole- mass
mono- one; single
mort- death
morph- shape; form
multi- many
mut- change
my- muscle
myc- fungus
mycel- threadlike
myria- many
moll- soft

N
nas- nose
necr- corpse; dead
nemat- thread
neo- new; recent
nephro- kidney
neur- nerve
noct-/nox- night
non- not
not- back
nuc- center

O
ob- against
ocul- eye
oct- eight
odont- tooth
olf- smell
oligo- few; little
omni- all
onc- mass; tumor
opthalm- eye
opt- eye
orb- circle; round; ring
ornith- bird
orth- straight; correct; right
oscu- mouth
oste- bone
oto- ear
ov-/ovi- egg
oxy- sharp; acid; oxygen

P
pachy - thick

Prefixes

paleo- old; ancient
palm- broad; flat
pan- all
par-/para- beside; near; equal
path- disease; suffering
pent- five
per- through
peri- around
permea- pass; go
phag- eat
pheno- show
phon- sound
photo- light
phren- mind; diaphragm
phyc- seaweed; algae
phyl- related group
physi- nature; natural qualities
phyt- plant
pino- drink
pinni- feather
plan- roaming; wandering
plasm- formed into
platy- flat
pleur- lung; rib; side
pneumo- lungs; air
poly- many; several
por- opening
port- carry
post- after; behind
pom- fruit
pre- before; ahead of time
prim- first
pro- forward; favoring; before
proto- first; primary

pseudo- false; deceptive
psych- mind
pter- having wings or fins
pulmo- lung
puls- drive; push
pyr- heat; fire

Q
quadr- four
quin- five

R
radi- ray
ren- kidney
ret- net; made like a net
rhe- flow
rhin- nose
rhiz- root
rhodo- rose
roto- wheel
rubr- red

S
sacchar- sugar
sapr- rotten
sarc- flesh
saur- lizard
schis-/schiz- split; divide
sci- know
scler- hard
semi- half; partly
sept- partition; seven
sex- six
sol- sun

Prefixes

solv- loosen; free
som-/somat- body
somn- sleep
son- sound
spec-/spic- look at
spir- breathe
stat- standing; staying
stell- stars
sten- narrow
stern- chest; breast
stom- mouth
strat- layer
stereo- solid; 3-dimensional
strict- drawn tight
styl- pillar
sub- under; below
super-/sur- over; above; on top
sym-/syn- together

T
tachy- quick; swift
tarso- ankle
tax- arrange; put in order
tele- far off; distant
telo- end
terr- earth; land
tetr- four
thall- young shoot
toxico- poison
top- place
trache- windpipe
trans- across
tri- three
trich- hair

turb- whirl

U
ultra- beyond
uni- one
ur- urine

V
vas- vessel
vect- carry
ven-/vent- come
ventr- belly; underside
vig- strong
vit-/viv- life
volv- roll; wander

X
xanth- yellow
xero- dry
xyl- wood

Z
zo- animal
zyg- joined together
zym- yeast

Suffixes

A
-ap/-aph -touch
-ary/-arium -place for something
-ase -forms names of enzymes

B
-blast -sprout; germ; bud

C
-cell -chamber; small room
-chrome -color
-chym -juice
-cid/-cis -cut; kill; fall
-cul/-cule -small; diminutive
-cyst -sac; pouch; bladder
-cyte -cell; hollow container

D
-duct -lead
E
-elle -small
-emia -blood
-en -made of
-eous -nature of; like
-err -wander; go astray

F
-fer -bear; carry; produce
-fid -divided into
-flect/-flex -bend

G
-gam -marriage
-gene -origin; birth

-gest -carry; produce; bear
-glen -eyeball
-glob -ball; round
-gon -angle; corner

H
-hal/-hale -breathe; breath
-helminth -worm

I
-iac -person afflicted with disease
-iasis -disease; abnormal condition
-ism -a state or condition
-ist -person who deals with...
-itis -inflammation; disease
-ium -refers to a part of the body

K
-kary -cell nucleus

L
-less -without
-log -word; speech
-logist -one who studies...
-logy -study of...
-lys/-lyt/-lyst -decompose; split; dissolve

M
-mer -part
-meter/-metry measurement
-mot -move

Suffixes

N
-ner -moist; liquid
-node -knot
-nom/-nomy -ordered knowledge; law

O
-oid -form; appearance
-oma -abnormal condition; tumor
-orium/-ory -place for something
-osis -abnormal condition

P
-pathy -disease; suffering
-ped -foot
-ped -child
-phil -loving; fond of
-phone -sound
-phore; pher -bear; carry
-phyll -leaf
-phyte -plant
-plast -form
-pod -foot

R
-rrhage -burst forth
-rrhea -flow

S
-scop -look; device for seeing
-septic -infection; putrefaction
-sis -condition; state
-sperm -seed
-spher -ball; round
-spire -breathe
-spor -seed

-stasis -placed
-stome -mouth

T
-the/-thes -put
-thel -cover a surface
-therm -heat
-tom -cut; slice
-trop -turn; change
-troph -nourishment; one who feeds

U
-ul/-ule -diminutive; small
-ura -tail
-verge -turn; slant
-vor -devour; eat

Z
-zoa -animal

Understand

* DAT-specific exam strategies and approaches
* Types of questions

DAT-Prep.com

Introduction ▮▮▮▮

Speed reading is a critical skill in the Reading Comprehension test. The DAT RC specifically calls for mental endurance and efficiency. For one, this section comes after the Perceptual Ability Test – which can already be mentally exhausting! For another, questions on the DAT RC require you to QUICKLY spot key details, delineate facts from opinion, and as the term "comprehension" implies, understand the central point of the written piece.

In this chapter, we will show you clear and specific strategies and build your skills with dozens of exercises. This will be followed by three separate mini-RC tests and then a full-length practice RC test. Let's begin . . .

Additional Resources

Free Online Forum

3.1 How to Approach the Reading Comprehension Section

Three passages to read – each with approximately 1500 words – and a total of 50 questions to answer in 60 minutes! How do you complete this test on time and ace it?

Indeed, time management poses a major challenge to many test-takers. The DAT RC, however, is not merely about speed reading. This section will also require mental endurance after a demanding one-hour Perceptual Ability Test. Likewise, efficiency in locating relevant information and understanding key ideas are integral factors that will help you overcome the demands of this section.

Nevertheless, students have aced the section using different strategies. There is no "one size fits all" strategy to obtain a great score. The key is to be able to start early with your preparation so you can identify which strategy specifically works for you. A systematic approach with clear strategies – some sort of a game plan – is vital in achieving an excellent RC score.

Ideally, you should make a concerted effort to try the various strategies that we present to you during separate timed practice tests. Then you can compare the various scores which you have obtained. This will help you narrow down the specific strategies that apply to your own experience. From that point onward, you should remain consistent.

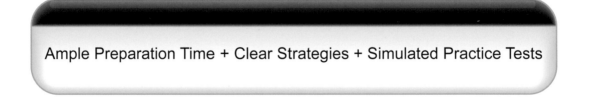

Ample Preparation Time + Clear Strategies + Simulated Practice Tests

3.1.1 Methods in Reading Passages during the Exam

Generally, you would need to read carefully but swiftly. You will have about 20 minutes per passage. Every 30 minutes, you should check the timer on the computer to be sure that you have completed approximately 25 questions. Of course you can judge time in any way you want (20, 25, 30-minute intervals, etc.). But decide on a system during practice and commit to that system on test day.

Be sure to reach a speed where you have at least 10 minutes to spare. If you have time at the end, you can return to properly evaluate the questions you skipped or marked. Of course, if you find that you are getting behind the set pace, then you consistently guess the answers to time-consuming questions in order to catch up.

In the meantime, you should try to apply each of the strategies that we will discuss in this section in order to determine which gives you your optimal performance. Different DAT students have boosted their RC scores with completely different techniques. With constant practice, you will be able to determine which of the following is best for you.

1. Questions First, Passage Once

Some candidates like to get a glimpse of the questions prior to reading the text. Others read the questions but not the answer choices yet. Then they read the passage and answer questions as they read the information. The point of doing this is to survey the kind of reading technique that will work best in attacking the passage and which other strategy to employ.

You may find it more efficient to work in this manner. Try one of the practice exams using this strategy and if you find it easier to answer the questions correctly, you should use the same method on the actual DAT.

2. Passage First, Questions Next

Some examinees prefer to carefully read through the passage once while noting the key details. Remember that the DAT is a computerized exam, and you will be provided with laminated note boards at your test center upon request. You can take brief notes of the major ideas and concepts in each paragraph along with their keywords. You can use boxes and or circles to categorize the important details and then, make meaningful connections between the main concepts and their supporting information by using arrows. This is also called "mapping."

This strategy allows you to mark significant information in specific paragraphs so that they are easier to locate when answering relevant questions later. At the same time, you can see where the discussion is going as you construct each part of the "map." Ideally, you should be able to make a reasonable conclusion of the author's central thesis once you complete the "map."

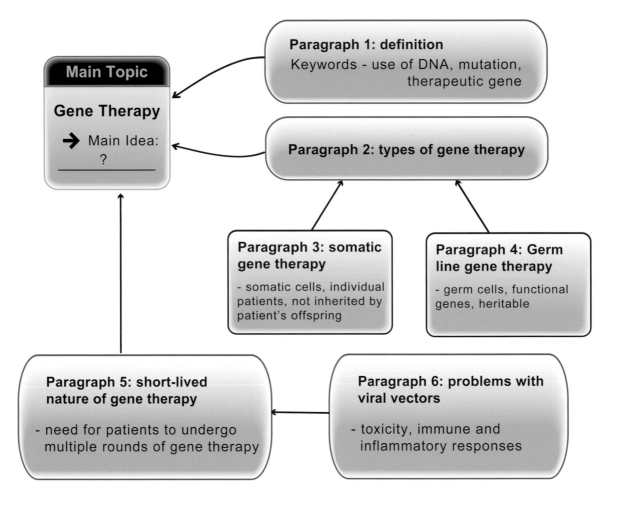

Figure RC 3.1: Mapping a Passage. Start with the main box using the passage's title as the main topic. You can then use circles and boxes to help you categorize the main concepts and their supporting details respectively. By the time that you complete "mapping" Paragraph 6, you can safely infer that the passage's main idea is roughly about the disadvantages of gene therapy.

3. Questions and Passage at the Same Time

This approach may not always work with questions that greatly require identifying the central idea of a passage. However, for questions that merely ask you to locate data such as dates, names, terminologies or definitions, this exam reading method is time-saving.

You read each question as you proceed with the test, and then skim through the different paragraphs to find the correct answer.

4. Read the Opening and Closing Paragraphs

In many cases, you would need to combine one or two of the preceding approaches in dealing with the passages. Going over the first and last paragraphs of a passage gives you a "bracket" to work within.

Once you get an initial feel of the passage, you can decide on the appropriate strategy that will speed up your performance during the exam.

We have also established that reading diverse material in the period leading up to the exam will be useful since the stimulus material will be from a variety of sources. Create a mindset that, in the exam, you are prepared for "edutainment": After completing a passage, look forward to what you can learn and discover in the next one. Having properly prepared and then begin the exam with the right attitude will give you an edge.

In any case, the most logical means to find out which strategy or which combination of strategies would augment your test-taking skills is to do simulated practice. The more you practice, the more you are inclined to be comfortable with a particular strategy or modify a technique to suit your own strengths or weaknesses.

3.1.2 Basic Question and Answer Techniques

Understanding the "science" of answering multiple choice questions is another vital skill in dealing with not only the Reading Comprehension section, but also with the DAT exam as a whole. The following are general techniques used in answering such questions.

1. Process of Elimination (PoE): eliminate any answers that are obviously

wrong. In many cases, there may be two very similar answer choices that appear to be correct. You would need to pay close attention to the subtle differences in order to determine the actual answer. Dismissing the obvious ones first from your choices would certainly save you a lot of precious time. If you have second thoughts about your remaining choices, the exam's program allows you to mark an answer so you can go back to it later - if you have enough time left - and decide on your final choice.

2. **Never lose sight of the question:** by the time students read answer choices C and D, some have forgotten the question and are simply looking for "true" sounding statements. Therefore, they tend to choose an option, which presents a statement that may be true but does not answer the question, and is therefore incorrect. For example,

Answer Choice D: Most people are of average height. → This is a true statement.

However, the question was: What is the weight of most people?

Therefore, the true statement becomes the incorrect answer!

Continually check the question and check or cross out right or wrong answers.

3. **Paying attention to details:** a common decoy in most timed multiple-choice exams, and especially in the DAT RC, is to offer options that are in close proximity – either within the same sentence or paragraph – where the correct answer is found. At other times, either the phrasing of the statements in the answer choices or the language used in the passage itself is complicated. Hence you need to stay focused on the facts and thoroughly understand both the information and the question presented.

EXAMPLE

Question: What is the most effective treatment for OLP?

A. Corrective dentistry
B. Regular dental consultations
C. Systemic corticosteroids
D. Non-randomized clinical trials

Text: Although systemic corticosteroids are probably the most effective treatment modality for patients with diffuse erosive OLP (oral lichen planus) or multi-site disease, the literature on their use is limited to non-randomized clinical trials. Thus oral hygiene and corrective dentistry play a major role in the management of OLP and consultation with a dentist or oral medicine specialist is helpful.

Answer: Getting the facts straight in this test item can be tricky. The question is simply asking for the most effective treatment, regardless of its actual use or availability of helpful alternatives. Thus the correct answer is C.

4. Verbatim Statements: Literal and direct quotes from the stimulus material characterize several of the correct answer choices in the real DAT. This is because topics in the reading passages mostly deal with scientific and literal matters.

The next question-and-answer techniques, which we will discuss, are rarely required in the DAT RC. However, these are common "tricks" in multiple choice questions, which are worth getting yourself familiar with – just in case they do come up in the exam.

5. Beware of the extreme: words such as always, never, perfect, totally, and completely are often (but not always) clues that the answer choice is incorrect.

6. Mean Statements: mean or politically incorrect statements are unlikely to be included in a correct answer choice. For example, if you see any of the following statements in an answer choice, you can pretty much guarantee that it is not the correct answer:

Parents should abuse their children.
Poor people are lazy.
Religion is socially destructive.
Torture is usually necessary.

3.2 DAT-specific RC Exam Strategies

While the preceding methods and techniques are effective in tackling the RC section, there are strategies that specifically address the types of questions presented in the DAT.

1. **Scan and Locate (SaL)**

You will most probably make the most use of this strategy. When you scan, you simply locate specific details that ask the basic "who, what, when, where, and how." Basically, you will be looking for proper nouns and numerical figures. It is similar to browsing the telephone directory to look up an address or contact number.

If you have been practicing the reading techniques recommended in Chapter 2, this strategy might become almost second nature to you. This is probably the easiest skill to develop, yet a very important one. Efficiently locating a specific detail trains you to differentiate material information from immaterial ones; those that add something new from those that simply restate an idea.

Scanning will work even without a preview of the questions. You simply proceed with each question – one at a time – and rapidly find the data being asked by scrolling down and up the passage, then move on to the next. Note the scanned details – either mentally or by writing them down – and remember that these are key to the passage's overall discussion. For example, the answer to a question "Which of the following experiments resulted in the widespread cure of such disease?" must be pertinent to the passage. You can then use this as one of your bases to understand the main idea better or to determine the author's purpose.

2. Skim for Ideas (SI)

The main difference between scanning and skimming is that you search for words or numerical values in the former while sentences and ideas in the latter. Skimming is mostly useful when the information that you are looking for is not explicitly stated in the passage. Therefore, you randomly seek for supporting data, more keywords, examples or explanations. Whenever you find one, slow down and read for the precise information you need.

3. Outline and Annotate (OA)

Outlining is more or less the same as the reading technique "paraphrasing" discussed in Chapter 2. You can use this strategy as a conjunction either after you have shortly gone over the questions or as you go along assessing the passage first. The advantage, on the other hand, of doing an initial glimpse of the different questions is that you get to have a heads-up as to whether the passage will simply require scanning information or demand an in-depth understanding of concepts. In most instances, this strategy tends to work best with inference questions.

Essentially, you jot down key terms and ideas of each numbered paragraph. Please note, however, that the Canadian

DAT does not allow the use of any paper other than the answer sheet provided. For the American DAT, as mentioned earlier, you can ask for a note board, which is provided in the test center. Doing so helps you to read actively and then later, to find keywords or points without having to search aimlessly. Your notes can also include any one or more of the following that you deem relevant:

- brief remarks of each paragraph's main idea
- definition of key terms
- hypothetical examples or inter- pretations of important concepts
- your observations of the author's tone, writing style, attitude toward the subject, or devices used to illustrate a point
- your own questions or doubts

about ambiguous points in the paragraph

Some candidates also find it helpful to do the following: just before you read from each passage, think of someone young that you know - for example, a younger brother, sister, cousin, etc. Imagine that once you finish reading the stimulus material, you will have to explain it to them in words that they understand. The idea is to encourage active reading, attention and focus.

An alternative scenario, if it does not stress you out too much, would be to imagine that you will need to give a speech in class regarding the passage right after you read it once. Keep that imagery during your evaluation of the material, so you have a heightened sense of awareness of what you are reading.

Gold Standard DAT RC
Key Methods and Strategies

- Scan and Locate (SaL)
- Skim for Ideas (SI)
- Outline and Annotate (OA)
- Process of Elimination (PoE)
- Attention to Details
- Never lose sight of the question

3.3 Types of Questions

Questions in the DAT Reading Comprehension section can be loosely classified into two main categories: detail-oriented and concept-oriented.

1. Detail-oriented

Questions of this type chiefly test your accurate identification of facts or key concepts found in the passage.

A. Recall Questions

You will need to search the passage for terms, synonyms, proper names, dates, statistical numbers, locations, characteristics, descriptions, definitions, etc.

B. Exception or Negative Questions

These are fundamentally the same as the Recall Questions; but this time, the false statement serves as the correct answer.

2. Concept-oriented

These require you to understand, conclude, or judge what could be reasonably inferred from the author's views or from the evidence demonstrated in the passage.

A. Math-related Questions

This question type occasionally comes out in the RC section and calls for simple math logic, interpretation, or a quick calculation of numerical data mentioned in the passage.

B. True or False Statements

These come in two forms:

- Two Statements

Normally, a test question presents two statements, which are derived from the passage. You need to evaluate them as either both true or false, or either one of them is true or false.

- Statement and Reason

You will be presented with a cause and effect statement that requires you to judge whether the reason supports the statement or not, or both are unrelated.

C. Evaluation Questions

Some questions ask you to consider the validity, accuracy, or value of the author's ideas and/or the facts presented in the text. These heavily demand inference skills.

D. Application Questions

These questions challenge your higher cognitive skills through generalization of the concepts presented in the passage. Use the given information to solve new problems described in the questions.

Now let's dissect and understand each question type in the following sections.

3.3.1 Recall Questions

Literal types of questions commonly appear similar to any one of the following examples:

- Term: What is the most common form of cancer?

- Statistical Number: Which of the following shows the number of times that the city was hit by an earthquake?

- Location: At which of the following countries was surgery first recognized as a legitimate medical practice?

- Synonyms: A meteor is also known as...

- Characteristics: Which of the following clinical methods characterizes the treatment used by the doctor?

- Description: The law of conservation is stated in the passage as...

- Definition: As used in the passage, which of the following best defines "dentistry"?

Since these are primarily detail questions, most of them can be easily answered using "scan and locate" (SaL), as well as "skim for ideas" (SI) strategies.

Now let's do some exercises to ensure that you can successfully deal with these question types. Please take a piece of paper to cover the answers while you are responding to the questions. Notice that just as in the real exam, questions do not necessarily follow the chronological order of information discussed in the passage.

Read the following excerpts and promptly locate the details asked in the questions that follow.

PASSAGE 1

(1). As early as February 21, 1775, the Provincial Congress of Massachusetts appointed a committee to determine what medical supplies would be necessary should colonial troops be required to take the field. Three days later, the Congress voted to "make an inquiry where fifteen doctor's chests can be got, and on what terms"; and on March 7, it directed the committee of supplies "to make a draft in favor of Dr. Joseph Warren and Dr. Benjamin Church, for five hundred pounds, lawful money, to enable them to purchase such articles for the provincial chests of medicine as cannot be got on credit."

(2). A unique ledger of the Greenleaf apothecary shop of Boston reveals that this pharmacy on April 4, 1775, supplied at least 5 of the 15 chests of medicines. The account, in the amount of just over £247, is listed in the name of the Province of the Massachusetts Bay, and shows that £51 was paid in cash by Dr. Joseph Warren. The remaining £196 was not paid until August 10, after Warren had been killed in the Battle of Bunker Hill.

(3). The 15 medicine chests, including presumably the five supplied by Greenleaf, were distributed on April 18—three at Sudbury and two each at Concord, Groton, Mendon, Stow, Worcester, and Lancaster. No record has been found to indicate whether or not the British discovered the medical chests at Concord, but, inasmuch as the patriots were warned of the British movement, it is very likely that the chests were among the supplies that were carried off and hidden. The British destroyed as much of the remainder as they could locate.

1. What is the name of the pharmacy from which the committee purchased the medicine chests?

   Answer: _____

2. In whose account were the medical supplies listed?

   Answer: _____

3. What amount would approximately represent the price of one medicine chest?

   Answer: _____

4. Three of the medicine chests were distributed at which location?

   Answer: _____

5. The Provincial Congress of Massachusetts decided to canvass for 15 doctor's chests on which date?

   Answer: _____

PASSAGE 2

(1). The term bioinformatics was coined by Paulien Hogeweg and Ben Hesper in 1978 for the study of informatic processes in biotic systems. Its primary use since at least the late 1980s has been in genomics and genetics, particularly in those areas of genomics involving large-scale DNA sequencing. Over the past few decades rapid developments in genomic and other molecular research technologies and developments in information technologies have combined to produce a tremendous amount of information related to molecular biology.

(2). It is the name given to these mathematical and computing approaches used to glean understanding of biological processes that bioinformatics has become known as the application of computer science and information technology to the field of biology. Bioinformatics now entails the creation and advancement of databases, algorithms, computational and statistical techniques and theory to solve formal and practical problems arising from the management and analysis of biological data.

6. Bioinformatics can be defined as what?

   Answer: _____

Answers:

1. Greenleaf
   Strategy: Sal; P2 S1*
   (P stands for Paragraph, S stands for Sentence; the corresponding numbers point to the paragraph number and the sentence within that paragraph)

2. The Province of the Massachusetts Bay
   Strategy: Sal; P2 S2

3. £51
   Strategies: Sal and Si; P2 S2

4. Sudbury
   Strategies: Sal and Si; P3 S1

5. February 24, 1775
   Strategies: Sal and Si; P1 S2.
   The Provincial Congress of Massachusetts Congress voted to "make an inquiry where fifteen doctor's chests can be got, and on what terms" three days after it appointed a committee for the medical supplies on February 21, 1775. February 21 plus 3 days makes February 24.

7. Who coined the term "bioinformatics"?

   Answer: _____

8. What would characterize the main functions of bioinformatics?

   Answer: _____

9. In what year did bioinformatics become useful to genomics and genetics?

   Answer: _____

10. In which particular area of genomics is bioinformatics useful?

    Answer: _____

Answers:

6. Bioinformatics is the application of computer science and information technology to the field of biology.
   Strategy: Sal; P2 S1

7. Paulien Hogeweg and Ben Hesper
   Strategy: Sal; P1 S1

8. Use of mathematical and computing approaches to understand biological processes
   Strategy: Si; P2 S1

9. 1980s
   Strategy: Si; P1 S2

10. large-scale DNA sequencing
    Strategy: Sal; P1 S2

3.3.2 Exception or Negative Questions

The following are some of the most common examples of this question type:

Each of the following characteristics generally pertains to modern art EXCEPT one. Which one is the EXCEPTION?

Which of the following symptoms was NOT mentioned in the passage?

Which of the following statements is false?

In these questions, using the "process of elimination" technique would be ideal in choosing the best answer out of multiple choices. There will be a number of instances when a statement would sound valid in a real world situation but is not discussed in the passage. At other times, an option would be correct but points to another closely-related concept. Therefore, you should "never lose sight of the question" as well.

PASSAGE 3

(1). Resistance to antibiotics is one of the critical complications in the treatment of infectious diseases. Enterococcal resistance to gentamicin, which is the effective antibiotic in this case, highlights the importance and the priority of the matter. Enterococci are among the most common microorganisms responsible for nosocomial infections in the hospital intensive care units and also the causative infectious agent in urinary and bile tract systems, resulting in bacteremia in infants and acute endocarditis in adults, in addition to dental and gingival infections. Therefore, isolation and identification of different enterococcal species and determination of their resistance pattern and their prevalence as well as obtaining their genetic patterns are of utmost importance. Examples of these methods include antibiogram by disk diffusion agar for determination of gentamicin resistance, evaluation of the genetic pattern utilizing DNA isolation, and observation of formed bands using electrophoresis on agarose gel 0.8% by ultraviolet. A general and comprehensive method for obtaining an ideal outcome by these methods can also be tested.

(2). Enterococci are gram-positive cocci, usually detected in feces. These bacteria grow in blood agar or BHI containing 5% blood, and are often non-hemolytic but sometimes α- or β-hemolytic. They do not produce any gases and are PYR, LAP, and bile escolin positive. They grow in 6.5% NaCl medium and can bear the 10-45°C temperature range. The Moller Hinton medium is utilized for testing enterococcal resistance against gentamicin. In previous studies, the bacteria from diluted culture in 0.5 McFarland solution was cultured in Moller Hinton medium and the 100 µg gentamicin was placed on it and after 24 hours the resistance degree was reported by measuring the hallow around the disk. For determination of enterococcal resistance genetic pattern, the molecular and DNA derivation was used afterwards.

(3). For plasmid derivation in alkaline lysis method, plasmids are turned to deluxe rapidly. Generally, when the antibiotic concentration required for bacterial death or its growth inhibition is higher, the microorganism shows resistance to it. Plasmids are naturally circular chromosomes without any small proteins, and are seen in bacteria as well as the bacterial genome. Their genome is composed of double-stranded DNA and their replication is dependent on the host cells but independent of the bacterial genome. Most of them are replicated in bacterial reproduction cycles. Plasmids bear many genes that the bacterium usually needs their productions and for this, their high quantities are justifiable.

1. The following are methods used for testing enterococcal resistance against

gentamicin EXCEPT one. Which is the EXCEPTION?

A. Antibiogram by Disk Diffusion Agar Test
B. The Moller Hinton medium
C. Fecal Analysis
D. Plasmid derivation in Alkaline Lysis method

2. Enterococci cause the following infections EXCEPT:

A. nosocomial infection.
B. bacteremia.
C. acute endocarditis.
D. urinary tract infection.
E. gingivitis.

3. Which is NOT a characteristic of enterococci?

A. Detected in feces
B. Do not produce any gases
C. Gram-positive cocci
D. Naturally circular chromosomes

PASSAGE 4

(1). According to Linda Hutcheon, one of the main features that distinguishes postmodernism from modernism is the fact the it "takes the form of self-conscious, self-contradictory, self-undermining statement." One way of creating this double or contradictory stance on any statement is the use of parody: citing a convention only to make fun of it. As Hutcheon explains, "Parody—often called ironic quotation, pastiche, appropriation, or intertextuality—is usually considered central to postmodernism, both by its detractors and its defenders." Unlike Fredric Jameson, who considers such postmodern parody as a symptom of the age, one way in which we have lost our connection to the past and to effective political critique, Hutcheon argues that "through a double process of installing and ironizing, parody signals how present representations come from past ones and what ideological consequences derive from both continuity and difference."

4. Each of the following is another name for parody EXCEPT one. Which is the EXCEPTION?

A. Black Comedy
B. Ironic Quotation
C. Pastiche
D. Appropriation
E. Intertextuality

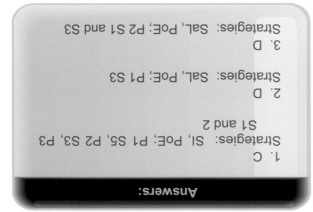

Answers:

1. C
Strategies: SI, PoE: P1 S5, P2 S3, P3 S1 and 2

2. D
Strategies: SaL, PoE: P1 S3

3. D
Strategies: SaL, PoE: P2 S1 and S3

5. Which of the following is NOT a form of a postmodern statement?

    A. Self-replicating
    B. Self-conscious
    C. Self-contradictory
    D. Self-undermining

Answers:

4. A
Strategy: Sal, PoE; P1 S3

5. A
Strategy: Sal, PoE; P1 S1

3.3.3 Math-related questions

These questions assess your comprehension of subtle mathematical relationships within a descriptive text. The following short exercises will give you an overview of how to deal with this question type.

PASSAGE 5

(1). All ordinary matter is made up of combinations of chemical elements, each with its own atomic number, indicating the number of protons in the atomic nucleus. Additionally, elements may exist in different isotopes, with each isotope of an element differing in the number of neutrons in the nucleus. A particular isotope of a particular element is called a nuclide. Some nuclides are inherently unstable. That is, at some point in time, an atom of such a nuclide will spontaneously transform into a different nuclide. This transformation may be accomplished in a number of different ways, including radioactive decay, either by emission of particles [usually electrons (beta decay), positrons or alpha particles] or by spontaneous fission, and electron capture.

(2). While the moment in time at which a particular nucleus decays is unpredictable, a collection of atoms of a radioactive nuclide decays exponentially at a rate described by a parameter known as the half-life, usually given in units of years when discussing dating techniques. After one half-life has elapsed, one half of the atoms of the nuclide in question will have decayed into a "daughter" nuclide or decay product. In many cases, the daughter nuclide itself is radioactive, resulting in a decay chain, eventually ending with the formation of a stable (nonradioactive) daughter nuclide; each step in such a chain is characterized by a distinct half-life. In these cases, usually the half-life of interest in radiometric dating is the longest one in the chain, which is the rate-limiting factor in the ultimate transformation of the radioactive nuclide into its stable daughter. Isotopic systems that have been exploited for radiometric dating have half-lives ranging from only about 10 years (e.g., tritium) to over 100 billion years.

(3). In general, the half-life of a nuclide depends solely on its nuclear properties; it is not affected by external factors such as temperature, pressure, chemical environment, or presence of a magnetic or electric field. (For some nuclides which decay by the process of electron capture, such as beryllium-7, strontium-85, and zirconium-89, the decay rate may be slightly affected by local electron density, therefore these isotopes may not be as suitable for radiometric dating.) But in general, the half-life of any nuclide is essentially a constant. Therefore, in any material containing a radioactive nuclide, the proportion of the original nuclide to its decay product(s) changes in a predictable way as the original nuclide decays over time. This predictability allows the relative abundances of related nuclides to be used as a clock to measure the time from the incorporation of the original nuclide(s) into a material to the present.

1. Based on information in the passage, how much would be left of a 5-gram radioactive nuclide parent that decays to a daughter nuclide after 3 half-lives?

Answer: _____

Answers:

1. 0.625 gram
Strategies: OA, quick calculation; P2
The passage indicates that one-half of the atoms of a parent nuclide will decay to a daughter nuclide. Thus if a parent nuclide starts out as having a value of 5 grams, it will be left with 2.5 grams after the passage of 1 half-life; 1.25 grams after the passage of two half-lives; and 0.625 after 3 half lives.

PASSAGE 6

(1). Piano music is divided by bar lines into small sections called measures. It also has numbers near the beginning of the music. These numbers are called the time signature. The time signature is related to the rhythm of the music. Each time signature contains 2 numbers: the top number tells you the number of beats or counts in each measure. The number at the bottom tells you which type of note gets the beat. A 4 at the bottom means that the QUARTER NOTE gets one beat. The 4/4 time signature is a very common time signature.

(2). The WHOLE NOTE is a white note with no stem. It receives 4 counts, or 4 beats (1-2-3-4). The HALF NOTE is a white note with a stem. It receives 2 counts (1-2). That means in the same time that you play one whole note, you could play two half notes. The QUARTER NOTE is a black note with a stem. It receives one count, or one beat. You can play 2 quarter notes in the time it takes to play a half note, or you could play 4 quarter notes in the time it takes to play a whole note.

(3). Now for the DOTTED NOTE. A dot can be slapped onto any note: whole notes, half notes, quarter notes, eighth notes, etc. Putting a dot behind a note changes the duration of the note by increasing it by half of its original value. For example: A whole note is worth 4 counts; A dotted whole note would increase the duration of the note by half of its original value (+2), so a dotted whole note would be worth 6 counts. A dotted half note would be worth 3 counts. A dotted quarter note would be worth 1 and a half counts.

2. In a 2/4 time signature, how many half notes can fit in a measure?

Answer: _____

3. Two quarter notes and one half note is equivalent to what note?

Answer: _____

4. Two dotted quarter notes would be worth how many counts?

Answer: _____

5. If an eighth note is worth half a count, how many eighth notes would it take a whole note?

Answer: _____

The "piano passage" on the actual DAT is regarded as the hardest passage, and candidates generally cringe upon encountering it. This is important to practice with - just in case.

Answers:

2. 1

    Strategy: SI; P1 and P2

    In the 2/4 time signature, the '2' tells us that there are 2 beats in every measure, and the '4' tells us that the quarter note gets one beat. Since a half note is worth 2 counts, this means that only 1 half note can fit a measure with 2/4 time signature.

3. Whole Note

    Strategies: SaL, quick calculation; P2

    One quarter note is equivalent to 1 beat, so two quarter notes equal 2 beats. One half note gets 2 beats. This means that combining two quarter notes and one half note yield 4 beats, which is equivalent to a whole note.

4. 3 quarter notes or 1 half note and 1 quarter note

    Strategies: SaL, quick calculation; P3, last sentence

    A dotted quarter note is worth 1 and a half counts. 1 and a half counts multiplied by 2 is 3 counts, which is either 3 quarter notes (1 beat each) or 1 half note (2 beats) and 1 quarter note (1 beat).

5. 8

    Strategies: SaL, quick calculation; P2

    Since a whole note is equivalent to 4 counts, this would be equivalent to 8 half counts or 8 eighth notes.

3.3.4 True or False Statements

These frequently require scanning (SaL), skimming (SI), and close attention to the surrounding details. Study the following short passages and validate the corresponding statements as any one of the following:

A. *Both statements are true.*

B. *Both statements are false.*

C. *The first statement is true. The second statement is false.*

D. *The first statement is false. The second statement is true.*

PASSAGE 7

(1). Thermodynamics is a 'phenomenal' science, in the sense that the variables of the science range over macroscopic parameters such as temperature and volume. Whether the microphysics underlying these variables are motive atoms in the void or an imponderable fluid is largely irrelevant to this science. The developers of the theory both prided themselves on this fact and at the same time worried about it. Clausius, for instance, was one of the first to speculate that heat consisted solely of the motion of particles (without an ether), for it made the equivalence of heat with mechanical work less surprising. However, as was common, he kept his "ontological" beliefs separate from his statement of the principles of thermodynamics because he didn't wish to (in his words) "taint" the latter with the speculative character of the former.

1. Macroscopic parameters refer to the philosophy underlying thermodynamics. Microphysics refers to empirical varia-bles, such as temperature and volume.

    Answer: _____

Answer:

1. B

Strategies: SI, Sal; P1 S1 and S2

Let's have a quick refresher with the RC strategies that we used here: SI stands for Skimming for Ideas. Sal stands for Scan and Locate. P refers to Paragraph and S to Sentence, which means that P1 S1 and S2 directs you to review Paragraph 1 Sentences 1 and 2 of the passage to find the correct answer.

PASSAGE 8

(1). Industrial noise is usually considered mainly from the point of view of environ-mental health and safety, rather than nuisance, as sustained exposure can cause permanent hearing damage. Tradi-tionally, workplace noise has been a hazard linked to heavy industries such as ship-building and associated only with noise induced hearing loss (NIHL). Modern thinking in occupational safety and health identifies noise as hazardous to worker safety and health in many places of employment and by a variety of means.

(2). Noise can not only cause hearing impairment (at long-term exposures of over 85 decibels (dB), known as an exposure action value, but it also acts as a causal factor for stress and raises systolic blood pressure. Additionally, it can be a causal factor in work accidents, both by masking hazards and warning signals, and by impeding concentration. Noise also acts synergistically with other hazards to increase the risk of harm to workers. In particular, noise and dangerous substances (e.g. some solvents) that have some tendencies towards ototoxicity may give rise to rapid ear damage.

2. Occupational noise is associated only with noise induced hearing loss and heavy industries such as ship-building. Aside from hearing impairment, noise can also cause stress and elevation of systolic blood pressure.

    Answer: _____

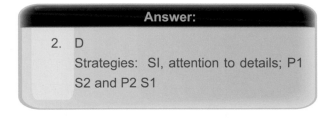

Answer:

2. D

Strategies: SI, attention to details; P1 S2 and P2 S1

PASSAGE 9

(1). A violin consists of a body or corpus, a neck, a bridge, a soundpost, four strings, and various fittings. The fittings are the tuning pegs, tailpiece and tailgut, endpin, possibly one or more fine tuners on the tailpiece, and perhaps a chinrest, either attached directly over the tailpiece or to the left of it.

(2). The body of the violin is made of two arched plates fastened to a "garland" of ribs with animal hide glue. The rib garland includes a top block, four corner blocks (sometimes omitted in cheap mass-produced instruments,) a bottom block, and narrow strips called linings, which help solidify the curves of the ribs, and provide extra gluing surface for the plates. The ribs are what is commonly seen as the "sides" of the box. From the top or back, the body shows an "hourglass" shape formed by an upper bout and a lower bout. Two concave C-bouts between each side's corners form the waist of this figure, providing clearance for the bow.

3. Four corner blocks in the rib garland may not be found in mass-produced violins.

A chinrest is normally provided in the violin.

Answer: _____

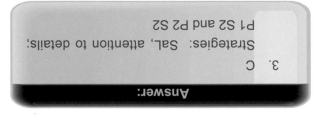

Answer:

3. C

Strategies: SaI, attention to details; P1 S2 and P2 S2

PASSAGE 10

(1). The study of bacteria practically began with the use of the microscope. It was toward the close of the seventeenth century that the Dutch microscopist, Leeuwenhoek, working with his simple lenses, first saw the organisms which we now know under this name, with sufficient clearness to describe them. Beyond mentioning their existence, however, his observations told little or nothing. Nor can much more be said of the studies which followed during the next one hundred and fifty years. During this long period many a microscope was turned to the observation of these minute organisms, but the majority of observers were contented with simply seeing them, marveling at their minuteness, and uttering many exclamations of astonishment at the wonders of Nature.

(2). A few men of more strictly scientific natures paid some attention to these little organisms. Among them we should perhaps mention Von Gleichen, Muller, Spallanzani, and Needham. Each of these, as well as others, made some contributions to our knowledge of microscopical life, and among other organisms studied those which we now call bacteria. Speculations were even made at these early dates of the possible causal connection of these organisms with diseases, and for a little the medical profession was interested in the suggestion. It was impossible then, however, to obtain any evidence for the truth of this speculation, and it was abandoned as unfounded, and even forgotten completely, until revived again about the middle of the 19th century. During this century of wonder a sufficiency of exactness was, however, introduced into the study of microscopic organisms to call for the use of names, and we find Muller using the names of Monas, Proteus, Vibrio, Bacillus, and Spirillum, names which still continue in use, although commonly with a different significance from that given them by Muller. Muller did indeed make a study sufficient to recognize the several distinct types, and attempted to classify these bodies. They were not regarded as of much importance, but simply as the most minute organisms known. It was Louis Pasteur who brought bacteria to the front, and it was by his labors that these organisms were rescued from the obscurity of scientific publications and made objects of general and crowning interest.

4. Louis Pasteur was the first to recognize the existence of microscopic organisms. Muller was the first to classify the different kinds of bacteria.

   Answer: _____

5. Speculations were made of the possible causal connection of microscopic organisms with diseases during the mid-18th century.
   Despite little interest in the significant role of microscopic organisms to diseases, some organisms were specifically named by the mid-19th century.

   Answer: _____

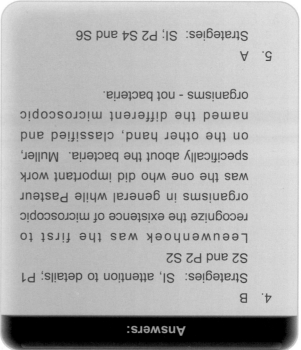

Answers:

4. B
Strategies: SI, attention to details; P1 S2 and P2 S2
Leeuwenhoek was the first to recognize the existence of microscopic organisms in general while Pasteur was the one who did important work specifically about the bacteria. Muller, on the other hand, classified and named the different microscopic organisms - not bacteria.

5. A
Strategies: SI; P2 S4 and S6

With questions that present a statement and a reason, careful attention to the specified details is necessary. A common decoy used is mixing up two different pieces of information from the passage, making the combination of the statement and its reason appear to be correct.

In the succeeding excerpts, let's test your acute observation of the written details. Assess the respective questions as any one of the following:

A. *Both the statement and reason are correct and related.*
B. *Both the statement and the reason are correct but NOT related.*
C. *The statement is correct but the reason is NOT.*
D. *The statement is NOT correct, but the reason is correct.*
E. *NEITHER the statement NOR the reason is correct.*

PASSAGE 11

(1). One of the boldest and most determined of all the early explorers was Ferdinand Magellan, a young Portuguese nobleman. He felt sure that somewhere on that long coast which so many explorers had reached he would find a strait through which he would be able to pass, and which would lead into the Indian Ocean; and so Magellan formed the idea of circumnavigating the globe.

(2). He applied to the King of Portugal for aid; but as the Portuguese king was not willing to help him, he went to Spain, where his plan found favor.

(3). The Spanish king gave him a fleet of five vessels, and on September 20, 1519, he set sail for the Canary Islands. Continuing the voyage toward Sierra Leone, the vessels were becalmed, and for a period of three weeks they advanced only nine miles. Then a terrific storm arose, and the sailors, who had grumbled and found fault with everything during the entire voyage, broke into open mutiny. This mutiny Magellan quickly quelled by causing the principal offender to be arrested and put in irons.

(4). The voyage was then continued, and land was at last sighted on the Brazilian coast, near Pernambuco.

(5). The fleet then proceeded down the coast as far as Patagonia, where the weather grew so very cold that it was decided to seek winter quarters and postpone the remainder of the journey until spring. This was done, Magellan finding a sheltered spot at Port St. Julian, where plenty of fish could be obtained and where the natives were friendly.

(6). These native Patagonians Magellan described as being very tall, like giants, with long, flowing hair, and dressed scantily in skins.

(7). Great hardships had been endured by the crew. Food and water had been scarce, the storms had been severe, and suffering from cold was intense. The sailors did not believe there was any strait, and they begged Magellan to sail for home. It was useless to try to influence this determined man. Danger made him only the more firm. Magellan told them that he would not return until he had found the opening for which he was looking.

(8). Then the mutiny broke out anew. But Magellan by his prompt and decisive action put it down in twenty-four hours. One offender was killed, and two others were put in irons and left to their fate on the shore when the ships sailed away.

(9). As soon as the weather grew warmer the ships started again southward. After nearly two months of sailing, most of the time through violent storms, a narrow channel was found, in which the water was salt. This the sailors knew must be the entrance to a strait.

6. Ferdinand Magellan sought the aid of the King of Portugal because the Spanish King did not support his plan of circumnavigating the globe.

Answer: _____

7. Mutiny broke out again because the sailors found fault with everything during the entire voyage.

Answer: _____

8. Magellan formed the idea of circum-navigating the globe because he felt sure that he would find a strait through which he would be able to pass, and which would lead into the Pacific Ocean.

Answer: _____

Answers:

6. E
Strategies: SaL, attention to details; P2
The statement and the reason are reversed.

7. B
Strategies: SI, attention to details; P3 S3, P7 and P8 S1
Details about the first mutiny was mixed up with the second mutiny.

8. C
Strategies: SaL, attention to details; P1 S2
The erroneous detail in the statement's reason is "Pacific Ocean," which should be "Indian Ocean."

PASSAGE 12

(1). Niels Henrik David Bohr was a Danish physicist who made fundamental contributions to understanding atomic structure and quantum mechanics, for which he received the Nobel Prize in Physics in 1922. Bohr mentored and collaborated with many of the top physicists of the century at his institute in Copenhagen. He was part of a team of physicists working on the Manhattan Project. Bohr married Margrethe Nørlund in 1912, and one of their sons, Aage Bohr, grew up to be an important physicist who in 1975 also received the Nobel Prize. Bohr has been described as one of the most influential scientists of the 20th century.

(2). Bohr's legacy to physics and its interpretation is a controversial one. He contributed decisively to the development of atomic and nuclear physics in many ways (especially to quantum theory from 1913 to 1925), and he is widely recognized as possessing remarkable insight into the nature of physical problems. Yet his theoretical approach and interpretive outlook sometimes have been questioned as vague, unclear, or inconsistent. Scholarship from 1970 to 2007 emphasized both the radical successes and some of the interpretive challenges of Bohr's work.

9. Bohr's legacy to physics and its interpretation is controversial because his theoretical approach and interpretive outlook have been questioned as vague, unclear, or inconsistent.

   Answer: _____

10. Niels Henrik David Bohr received the Nobel Prize in Physics in 1975 for his fundamental contributions to understanding atomic structure and quantum mechanics.

   Answer: _____

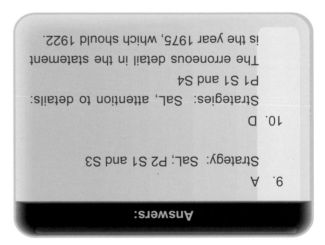

Answers:

9. A

Strategy: Sa1; P2 S1 and S3

10. D

Strategies: Sa1, attention to details: P1 S1 and S4

The erroneous detail in the statement is the year 1975, which should 1922.

3.3.5 Evaluation Questions

Evaluation Questions mainly ask you to identify key concepts and/or facts either directly taken from the text or inferred from it. This type of question can be further subcategorized into tone, implication, and main idea questions.

- **Tone Questions**

  These entail judging the attitude or opinion of the author towards the subject.

  What is the overall tone of the passage?

  With which statement would the author of the passage agree?

- **Implication Questions**

  Based on clues and evidences in the passage, you may be asked to draw conclusions about ideas such as what would follow if the author is correct in his/her argument or what a particular discovery might lead to.

  A court jester is most likely to equate which of the following modern-day jobs?

  Which of the following is the best description of a "rocket" locomotive?

From statements in the passage, it can be inferred that the author probably is a(n)...

Which of the following sentences could best be added to the specific paragraph x?

- **Main Idea Questions**

  These test your comprehension of the theme of the article. Questions may ask you for the main idea, central idea, purpose, a possible title for the passage, and so on. You may be asked to determine which statement best expresses the author's arguments or conclusions.

  What is the main idea of the passage?

  What would be the best title for this passage?

  Which of the following sentences best fits the passage?

  Which of the following sentences is the best conclusion for the closing paragraph?

  With which statement would the author of the passage agree? (This question may border between Tone and Main Idea Questions.)

An ideal strategy for these questions would be to outline and annotate (OA). Likewise, watch out for extreme words and mean statements among the answer options.

Constant practice should help develop these strategies for the slow reader. Again, remember that the most important part of any practice is to set aside enough time to single out your mistakes, try to understand why you keep getting the wrong answers, and if you have to, modify your strategies in order to optimize your results in the actual test.

In order to get a clear gauge of your possible challenges with these question types, consider the following short passages, answer the different guide questions, and study the explanations provided.

PASSAGE 13

(1). Freud wrote several important essays on literature, which he used to explore the psyche of authors and characters, to explain narrative mysteries, and to develop new concepts in psychoanalysis (for instance, *Delusion and Dream in Jensen's Gradiva* and his influential readings of the Oedipus myth and Shakespeare's **Hamlet** in **The Interpretation of Dreams**). The criticism has been made, however, that in his and his early followers' studies "what calls for elucidation are not the artistic and literary works themselves, but rather the psychopathology and biography of the artist, writer or fictional characters." Thus many psychoanalysts among Freud's earliest adherents did not resist the temptation to psychoanalyze poets and painters sometimes to Freud's chagrin. Later analysts would conclude that "clearly one cannot psychoanalyze a writer from his text; one can only appropriate him."

1. What would be the best title for this passage?

    A. Freudian Analysis of Literary Works
    B. The Interdisciplinary Work of Freud on Classical Literature
    C. Criticisms on the Psycho-analysis of Literature
    D. Pitfalls of Psychoanalysis in Art and Literature

2. With which statement would the author of the passage agree?

    A. Freud's work has been in-fluential both in psychology and literature.
    B. One cannot always conclude about a writer's psyche based on his literary work alone.
    C. Many psychoanalysts were wrong in their findings about art and literature.
    D. Psychology and Literature can never go hand in hand.

PASSAGE 14

(1). In 1831 we have Faraday at the climax of his intellectual strength, forty years of age, stored with knowledge and full of original power. Through reading, lecturing, and experimenting, he had become thoroughly familiar with electrical science: he saw where light was needed and expansion possible. The phenomena of ordinary electric induction belonged, as it were, to the alphabet of his knowledge: he knew that under ordinary circumstances the presence of an electrified body was sufficient to excite, by induction, an unelectrified body. He knew that the wire which carried an electric current was an electrified body, and still that all attempts had failed to make it excite in other wires a state similar to its own.

(2). What was the reason of this failure? Faraday never could work from the experiments of others, however clearly described. He knew well that from every experiment issues a kind of radiation, luminous, in different degrees to different minds, and he hardly trusted himself to reason upon an experiment that he had not seen. In the autumn of 1831, he began to repeat the experiments with electric currents, which, up to that time, had produced no positive result. And here, for the sake of younger inquirers, if not for the sake of us all, it is worthwhile to dwell for a moment on a power which Faraday possessed in an extraordinary degree. He

Answers:

1. C
Strategy: OA
A title generally embodies the content, i.e., the overall idea of a specific work. Hence this question calls for understanding of the excerpt's main idea. In this paragraph, the author introduces Freud's work in analyzing various literary works then moves on to discuss various criticisms in using psychoanalysis when appraising literature and art. The keywords are "criticisms" and "psychoanalysis."

2. B
Strategies: OA (paraphrasing); extreme statements
This question requires distinguishing the author's opinion on the subject from the passage's general topic. One effective way is to watch out for structure words. A few examples are "thus," "nevertheless," "needless to say," "moreover," "however," "therefore," "on the other hand," etc. Sentences that start with these cues usually signal the author's opinion. In this example, the structure word "thus" is found in the third sentence of the paragraph: "Thus, many psychoanalysts among Freud's earliest adherents did not resist the temptation to psychoanalyze poets and painters sometimes to Freud's chagrin.'" The author reinforces his/her view of the psychoanalysts' failure to provide faithful assessment of aesthetic works by immediately citing an example of other analysts' criticism: "Later analysts would conclude that 'clearly one cannot psychoanalyze a writer from his text; one can only appropriate him.'"

united vast strength with perfect flexibility. His momentum was that of a river, which combines weight and directness with the ability to yield to the flexures of its bed. The intentness of his vision in any direction did not apparently diminish his power of perception in other directions; and when he attacked a subject, expecting results, he had the faculty of keeping his mind alert, so that results different from those which he expected should not escape him through pre-occupation.

3. Which of the following sentences is the best conclusion for the closing paragraph?

   A. Faraday finally sought the advice of other scientists working on a similar experiment.

   B. Unfortunately, Faraday had to abandon his work.

   C. Luckily, Faraday found the missing element that would make his experiment successful.

   D. And so, Faraday persevered in conducting his experiments with electric currents.

4. Which of the following sentences best fits the passage?

   A. Faraday was a genius in electrical science.

   B. Faraday's failure was directly related to his refusal to colla-

borate with other scientists.

   C. Faraday was a man of great intellectual insights and determination.

   D. Faraday was a stubborn scientist.

Answers:

3. D
Strategy: OA or SI
The overall tone of the passage is that of optimism and admiration for Faraday's perseverance and intellectual independence. A and B are exact opposites of the statements in P2 S2 to S3 and P2 S7 respectively. C does not have enough clue or clear evidence as basis. D matches the characteristics described by the author about Faraday.

4. C
Strategy: OA or SI
This is a main idea question, which means that the best choice should be the statement that most represents the central point of the passage. Paragraph 1 discusses the extent of Faraday's knowledge especially about electrical science. Paragraph 2 illustrates Faraday's persistence despite failures in his experiments. Therefore, the most encompassing idea about the passage is that of Option C. A and B, although true, are only mentioned in specific parts of Paragraph 1 and Paragraph 2 respectively. D misinterprets the author's characterization of Faraday.

PASSAGE 15

(1). This project was inspired by a number of visits I made to various science and engineering museums in order to investigate the design of small electronic consumer devices. The research trips were unsuccessful, but only in the sense that my original expectations had not been met. I found that the objects on display in most cases looked exactly like the final product that would then be presented to the market. I had expected to see unfinished hotchpotches of machines, exposed working components and a cacophony of tangled cables. I was also hoping for a look beyond, or behind, the scenes of the design process and into a space manufacturers might ordinarily keep from public view. Instead, the objects that I came across were merely empty shells, made only to demonstrate the aesthetic of the product's design.

5. What is the overall tone of the passage?

    A. Disgust
    B. Disappointment
    C. Businesslike
    D. Curious

6. From statements in the passage, it can be inferred that the author probably is a(n):

    A. art critic.
    B. tourist.
    C. auctioneer.
    D. engineer.

Answers:

5. B

Strategy: SI; P1 S2 and S6

6. A

Strategy: SI; P1 S1 and last sentence
In both sentences, the author referred to "design" and "aesthetic of the product's design." A tourist would not be too critical; an auctioneer would have mentioned something about a bid; and, an engineer would not keep considering the "aesthetics of a product's design."

3.3.6 Application Questions

These are questions involving concepts that were introduced in the passage and how they would apply to general or real world situations. Usually, a situation or function is given, and you will be made to identify which particular theory, process, or instrument would best fit the description or offer a solution. You should use the information presented in the passage to solve new problems described in the questions; reevaluate the passage based on new facts associated with the questions.

Possible effective strategies could include "scan and locate" (SaL), "skim for ideas" (SI), "outline and annotate" (OA) or sketch the described apparatus or process in order to concretize the concepts.

PASSAGE 16

(1). There still exists among ourselves an activity, which on the technical plane gives us quite a good understanding of what a science we prefer to call 'prior' rather than 'primitive,' could have been on the plane of speculation. This is what is commonly called 'bricolage' in French. In its old sense the verb 'bricoler' applied to ball games and billiards, to hunting, shooting and riding. It was however always used with reference to some extraneous movement: a ball rebounding, a dog straying or a horse swerving from its direct course to avoid an obstacle. And in our own time the 'bricoleur' is still someone who works with his hands and uses devious means compared to those of a craftsman.

(2). The 'bricoleur' is adept at performing a large number of diverse tasks; but, unlike the engineer, he does not subordinate each of them to the availability of raw materials and tools conceived and procured for the purpose of the project. His universe of instruments is closed and the rules of his game are always to make do with 'whatever is at hand', that is to say with a set of tools and materials which is always finite and is also heterogeneous because what it contains bears no relation to the current project, or indeed to any particular project, but is the contingent result of all the occasions there have been to renew or enrich the stock or to maintain it with the remains of previous constructions or destructions.

(3). The set of the bricoleur's means cannot therefore be defined in terms of a project (which would presuppose besides, that, as in the case of the engineer, there were, at least in theory, as many sets of tools and materials or 'instrumental sets', as there are different kinds of projects). It is to be defined only by its potential use or, putting this another way and in the language of the 'bricoleur' himself, because the elements are collected or retained on the principle that 'they may always come in handy'. Such elements are specialized up to a point, sufficiently for the 'bricoleur' not to need the equipment and knowledge of all trades and professions, but not enough for each of them to have only one definite and determinate use. They each represent a set of actual and possible relations; they are 'operators' but they can be used for any operations of the same type.

1. Which of the following constructions below would NOT be an example of "bricolage"?

    A. Scrapbooking
    B. Surrealistic Poetry
    C. Junk Art
    D. A Land Survey
    E. Decorative Food Servings

2. Which activity would NOT be an illustration of "bricolage"?

    A. Stage sets made up of scrap metal for a theatrical performance
    B. A birdhouse constructed from toothpicks and various wood scraps
    C. A well-designed deck with pre-cut lumber
    D. A quilt sewn together with various leftover fabrics
    E. A maze constructed from the various hedges and shrubs in the garden

3. The Digital Era and Computer Apps have given bricolage a refreshing outlook due to advanced manipulation of popular media. Which entries BEST represent a type of digital "bricolage"?

    A. Using digital audio loops (cut and paste) for recording mixes and remixes
    B. GPS used in other contexts such as cruise ships, restaurants, etc.
    C. Photoshopped pictures, which distort the original to something humorous
    D. Constructing a website

Answers:

1. D
   Strategy: SI; P1 last sentence, P2 S1, P3 S1
   Scrapbooking, surrealistic poetry, junk art, and decorative food servings all entail "working with hands" and using "devious means." On the other hand, land surveying would require using instruments, calculations and some engineering background.

2. C
   Strategy: SaL or OA; P1 and P2
   Descriptions in the passage suggest that bricolage would involve making do with "whatever is at hand." Only a well-designed deck with lumber cut to a specific shape or size would not fit this description.

3. A
   Strategy: SaL; P2 last sentence
   "His universe of instruments is closed and the rules of his game are always to make do with 'whatever is at hand', that is to say with a set of tools and materials which is always finite and is also heterogeneous because what it contains bears no relation to the current project, or indeed to any particular project, but is the contingent result of all the occasions there have been to renew or enrich the stock or to maintain it with the remains of previous constructions or destructions."

3.4 Reading Comprehension (RC) Mini Tests with Answer Key, Explanations and Strategies

Now that we have outlined the structure of the DAT Reading Comprehension section, the types of questions, and most importantly, the approach and strategies that will help you excel, you can proceed to test yourself with our GS RC mini tests.

As described earlier, the DAT RC is comprised of three passages. A mini test presents only one passage at a time. The objective is to get you started in applying the techniques discussed in sections 3.1 to 3.3, and allow you to assess your current level of competence. We strongly suggest that you ALWAYS time yourself for every practice test. Otherwise, you would be eliminating one of the major components of your preparation making it more difficult to get a top DAT RC score.

At the end of each mini test, you should work through the answers and explanations. The answer key specifies the **Question Type** and the **Strategies** that are appropriate for the question. Keep notes of your wrong answers and then go back to the specific section(s) in this chapter, reviewing and analyzing how you can still improve on your next attempts. Only when you feel ready, you can try to get an initial run of the whole RC exam by taking the full-length GS RC Practice Test at the end of the Reading Comprehension chapters. As you progress with your review, you should also consider full-length practice tests (i.e. NS, PAT, RC and QR in one sitting) including those from the ADA, Gold Standard and TopScore.

Before you proceed, let's reiterate some important abbreviations and references in our answer keys:

OA	Outline and Annotate	Discussed in Section 3.3
SaL	Scan and Locate	Discussed in Section 3.3
SI	Skim for Ideas	Discussed in Section 3.3
PoE	Process of Elimination	Discussed in Section 3.2
Attention to details		Discussed in Section 3.2
Never lose sight of the question		Discussed in Section 3.2
P	Paragraph	P1 would mean Paragraph 1 and so forth
S	Sentence	S1 would mean Sentence 1 and so forth

*A note on "Recall Questions": Most recall questions do not need detailed explanations and only require you to re-read a specific paragraph and sentence. Hence only the paragraph and sentence numbers are provided in the answer key explanations of some of these questions.

From this point, advance to the next pages ONLY when you are ready. Please give each attempt your best shot. Good luck!

RC Mini Test 1

The following is a sample mini test which is comparable to the level of difficulty required for the Reading Comprehension Test of the DAT. Please note that this sample would roughly be 1/3 of the actual Reading Comprehension Test portion of the DAT.

You have 20 minutes to complete this portion of the DAT Mini Test; the actual test is 60 minutes. Please time yourself accordingly.

> BEGIN ONLY WHEN YOUR TIMER IS READY.

Passage 1

NASA Science Balloons

(1). Balloons may seem like an old-fashioned technology to most of the public, but they are very much alive and well. Weather balloons have been commonplace for decades, and the military still makes considerable use of them. The public is very familiar with hot-air sport ballooning, as well as with the exciting record-breaking flights across continents and oceans, using very high-tech balloon technologies. While the "great age" of manned balloon flights into the stratosphere is history, balloons continue to be important tools for scientific research. Unmanned stratospheric balloons are used for astronomy and climate studies, and balloons are also potentially an important tool for exploring other planets.

(2). The US National Science Foundation set up a scientific balloon program in 1961, originally based in Boulder, Colorado. In 1963, the balloon program was moved to Palestine, Texas, halfway between Dallas and Houston, since at the time the area was largely unpopulated and balloon payloads falling out of the sky were unlikely to land on a house. The US National Aeronautics & Space Administration (NASA) picked up the balloon program in 1982. The Palestine operation is now designated the "Columbia Scientific Balloon Facility (CSBF)" – the name having been changed from the "National Scientific Balloon Facility" in 2005 in honor of the crew of the space shuttle Columbia, which burned up on reentry in 2003.

(3). The CSBF is directed by the Physical

Sciences Laboratory of New Mexico State University at Las Cruces. However, population growth near Palestine has forced the CSBF to perform more launches at remote sites. Launches are regularly performed at Fort Sumner, New Mexico; Lynn Lake, Manitoba, Canada; McMurdo Station, Antarctica; Fairbanks, Alaska; and Alice Springs, Australia. Special launches have also been performed from a number of other locales. The CSBF has performed over 2,000 balloon flights since its inception. At its peak, in the 1970s, the CSBF was performing up to 80 missions a year, but the organization's launch rate is now much lower, a few dozen missions a year. Partly this is because the feasible missions have mostly been done, but it is also due to funding limitations. However, the CSBF is not in danger of extinction, since researchers know that it is much easier, quicker, and cheaper to use a balloon than a spacecraft to fly a payload into near-space conditions. The fact that balloon payloads, unlike satellite payloads, are usually recovered intact for re-use is another plus.

(4). The modern "zero-pressure balloon" vehicle used by the CSBF is generally similar to the SKYHOOK balloons originally invented by Otto Winzen. It is made from special polyethylene film, typically 0.8 mil thick, fabricated from longitudinal panels sealed with tapes. A scientific balloon typically has a volume of 1.08 million cubic meters (38 million cubic feet) and can carry 1,700 kilograms (3,750 pounds) of suspended load to 39 kilometers (128,000 feet). At this altitude, the scientific payload is above 99.7% of the atmosphere's mass. The "flight train" consists of the balloon and a scientific instrument package hitched to the balloon through a parachute pack. A NASA zero-pressure science balloon is inflated through the traditional roller system, with enough lifting gas provided for 10% lift over the load and balloon mass, and the gas expanding as the balloon rises.

(5). Data from the payload and balloon are telemetered directly to ground stations or through satellite links. Occasionally they are also recorded on board via film, magnetic tape, or solid-state digital storage media. Radio commands are used for instrument and balloon control. Balloon position is obtained by direct visual tracking, airplane tracking, or use of Global Position System (GPS) navigation receivers. The flight ends when the parachute and payload are separated via radio command, usually from a tracking aircraft. During separation, the balloon is destroyed by tearing open a set of rip panels, permitting the payload to parachute to the ground. With recent improvements in design, materials, and quality control, the large zero-pressure balloon has become an extremely reliable vehicle, with very high mission success rates. One drawback, however, is its limited mission endurance. While long-standing studies on cosmic rays, atmospheric circulation, and weather continue, much recent effort has been devoted to the atmospheric chemistry, and to astronomy at wavelengths – such as the infrared, ultraviolet, and X-ray bands – that are blocked by the atmosphere.

(6). An alternative approach, the "constant volume" or "superpressure" balloon, features a relatively unyielding plastic envelope filled at relatively high pressure, ensuring retention of a constant volume. A superpressure balloon does not need ballast, or at least not as much as a zero-pressure balloon, and can float at high altitudes for many months. The CSBF is now working on a superpressure "Ultra-Long Duration Balloon (ULDB)" that can stay at altitude for several months, orbiting the Earth several times. Raven Industries conducted a flight of a prototype ULDB in October 1999, but the balloon ruptured when it reached altitude. A second prototype, a tenth the size of a full-scale ULDB, was launched in June 2000 and was a success, remaining aloft for 27 hours. The full-scale ULDB design features an envelope with an inflated diameter of 59 meters (193 feet) and a height of 35 meters (115 feet). It is intended to remain aloft with 900 kilograms (a ton) of payload at altitudes of 35 kilometers (115,000 feet) for up to 100 days. The first full-scale ULDB test flight took place in late February 2001 from an Alice Springs, Australia launch site, but sprung a leak and was destroyed a few hours after launch. Subsequent launches took place roughly once a year, with mixed results. NASA still plans to begin operational ULDB launches in 2010.

(7). The superpressure balloon concept is not entirely new, going back at least to the US Air Force's "Global Horizontal Sounding Technique (GHOST)" balloon program, with eighty-eight GHOST balloons about 3 meters (10 feet) in diameter released over a period of ten years beginning in 1966. They all carried a small payload, the primary goal of the mission being to simply track the balloons to map high-altitude winds. In 1966, A GHOST balloon was the first balloon to circle the Earth, taking ten days to make the journey. Some of the GHOST balloons were said to have remained aloft for a year. Later in the program, they relayed their data through satellites. This project provided new results on the seasonal variations of global air currents.

(8). Balloons have proven very useful for scientific research on Earth; there are those who believe they are potentially very useful for exploring other planets as well. Robot "rovers" have been sent to the Moon and Mars since the 1960s, but such machines tend to be expensive and have limited range, and due to the long communications time-lag over interplanetary distances, they have to be smart enough to navigate without running into obstacles or falling off cliffs. If a planet has an atmosphere, however, a balloon would have many advantages over a rover. A robot balloon, or "aerobot", would be much cheaper and lighter than a rover, with the light weight reducing booster launch costs. An aerobot could cover a great deal of ground, and its view from a height would give them the ability to examine wide swathes of terrain with far more detail than would be obtained by an orbiting satellite. For exploratory missions, the aerobot's relative lack of directional control would not be a big concern, since there would be generally no need to direct it to a specific location. While the French were working on planetary aerobots, NASA's Jet Propulsion Laboratory (JPL) had become interested in the idea as well, with a JPL team performing several balloon flights in the Earth's atmosphere during the 1990s to validate technology. The JPL team envisioned a simple "Mars weather balloon" to validate the technology operationally; to be followed by a large superpressure balloon flight; and finally a solar-powered Mars blimp. NASA hasn't committed to an aerobot mission yet, but the agency has collaborated with the Centre National d'Études Spatiales (CNES) on the development of a series of low-cost "Scout" missions to Mars, and a Mars aerobot is on the list of options. A company named Global Aerospace Corporation performed an investigation of a Mars aerobot for NASA, with the aerobot envisioned as carrying both a science gondola and a set of small drop probes that could be released to provide detailed inspection of a number of sites.

- Adapted from "NASA Science Balloons" (http://www.vectorsite.net/avbloon_5.html#m1) Thanks to Greg Goebel.

1. Of the regular balloon launch sites, which of the following is NOT listed in the article?

   A. Fort Sumner
   B. Lynn Lake
   C. Columbia
   D. Alice Springs
   E. Fairbanks

2. The US National Science Foundation set up a scientific balloon program in 1961. NASA set up a similar program in 1963.

   A. Both statements are true.
   B. Both statements are false.
   C. The first sentence is true. The second sentence is false.
   D. The first sentence is false. The second sentence is true.
   E. The passage does not contain enough information to make a judgment.

3. Of the balloons discussed in the passage, which is NOT mentioned? Which is the EXCEPTION?

   A. Zero-pressure balloons
   B. Hot air balloons
   C. Superpressure balloons
   D. Weather balloons
   E. Anisotropic balloons

4. Which balloon provided new results on the seasonal variations of global air currents?

   A. Ultra-Long Duration balloon
   B. GHOST balloons
   C. Anisotropic balloons
   D. Zero-pressure balloons
   E. Aerobot balloons

5. Which of the following is NOT true about the modern zero-pressure balloons used by CSBF?

A. It can remain aloft for 27 hours.
B. It has a typical volume of 1.08 million cubic meters.
C. It is typically 0.8 mil thick, made of special polyethylene film.
D. It can typically carry 3750 pounds of suspended load.
E. None of the above

6. Which of the following acronyms is NOT correct?

A. JPL - Jet Propulsion Laboratory
B. GHOST - Global Horizontal Sounding Technique
C. ULDB - Ultra-Long Duration Balloon
D. CSBF - Columbia Super Balloon Facility
E. NASA - National Aeronautics & Space Administration

7. In the 1970s, CSBF was performing up to:

A. 80 missions a year.
B. 88 missions a year.
C. 70 missions a year.
D. 800 missions a year.
E. 90 missions a year.

8. The space shuttle Columbia burned up on reentry in which of the following years?

A. 2005
B. 1982
C. 1962
D. 2003
E. 2000

9. Based on statements in the passage, it can be inferred that a "payload" is:

A. a tracking device.
B. a communication device.
C. a data collection device.
D. the total weight of all of the balloons.
E. total balloon contents.

10. Which of the following is NOT true concerning the latest ULDBs? Which is the EXCEPTION?

A. It has an inflated diameter of 193 feet.
B. It has an inflated height of 115 feet.
C. It can carry up to a ton of payload.
D. It can carry a ton of payload for 100 days.
E. It can carry a ton of payload at altitudes over 200,000 feet.

11. Which of the following was the first balloon to circle the Earth?

    A. ULDB
    B. Aerobot
    C. GHOST
    D. SKYHOOK
    E. Solar-powered blimp

12. The primary goal of a GHOST balloon was:

    A. to interlink with satellites.
    B. to map high-altitude winds.
    C. to understand atmospheric chemistry.
    D. to study cosmic rays.
    E. to provide geographical surveillance.

13. Balloon payloads are usually recovered intact.
    Satellite payloads, on the other hand, are much cheaper to use.

    A. Both statements are true.
    B. Both statements are false.
    C. The first statement is true, the second statement is false.
    D. The first statement is false, the second statement is true.

14. The first full-scale ULDB test flight took place in late February 2001 from which of the following locations?

    A. Fort Sumner
    B. Lynn Lakes
    C. Fairbanks
    D. Alice Springs
    E. Palestine

15. From the following list of popular narratives, which would be the most relevant to the article?

    A. Moby Dick
    B. Hamlet
    C. Ulysses
    D. 20,000 Leagues Under the Sea
    E. Around the World in 80 days

16. Which of the following would NOT be an advantage of a Mars Aerobot over a Mars Rover? Which is the EXCEPTION?

    A. Cost
    B. Range
    C. Predictability of direction
    D. Weight
    E. Details of view

17. The improved large zero-pressure balloon has very low mission success rates.
Yet, this version has very high mission endurance.

    A.   Both statements are true.

    B.   Both statements are false.

    C.   The first statement is true, while the second statement is false.

    D.   The first statement is false, while the second statement is true.

> If time remains, you may review your work. If your allotted time (20 minutes) is complete, please proceed to the Answer Key.

RC Mini Test 1 Answer Key

1. C	7. A	13. C
2. C	8. D	14. D
3. E	9. C	15. E
4. B	10. E	16. C
5. A	11. C	17. B
6. D	12. B	

RC Mini Test 1 Explanations and Strategies

1. Question Type: *Exception/Negative Question*
    Strategies: *SaL, PoE; P3 S3, P2 last sentence*

    (A) Fort Sumner, (B) Lynn Lake, (D) Alice Springs and (E) Fairbanks are all mentioned in Paragraph 3. On the other hand, Columbia was the name of the space shuttle that burned up in 2003 as indicated in the last sentence of Paragraph 2.

2. Question Type: *True False Statement (Two Statements)*
    Strategies: *SaL, attention to details; P2 S1 to S3*

    The third sentence of Paragraph 2 states that NASA picked up the balloon program in 1982, not 1963.

3. Question Type: *Exception/Negative Question*
    Strategies: *SaL, PoE*

    Paragraph 4 discusses (A) zero-pressure balloons and Paragraph 6 (C) superpressure balloons. (D) Weather balloons is mentioned in P1 S2 and (B) hot air balloons in P1 S3. Only (E) anisotropic balloons are not mentioned anywhere in the passage.

4. Question Type: *Recall*
    Strategy: *SaL; P7 last sentence*

5. Question Type: *Exception/Negative Question*
    Strategies: *SaL, PoE, attention to details*

    The modern zero-pressure balloons are discussed in Paragraph 4, specifically Statement B in S3, Statement C in S2, and Statement

D in S3. On the other hand, Statement A is mixed up with the information in P6 S5, which supposedly pertains to the ULDB superpressure balloon – not the zero-pressure balloons used by CSBF.

6. Question Type: *Exception/Negative Question*
   Strategies: *SaL, PoE, attention to details*

   JPL is mentioned in P8 S7, GHOST in P7 S1, ULDB in P6 S3, and NASA in P2 S3. CSBF is indeed mentioned in P2 S4 but as Columbia Scientific Balloon Facility – not Columbia Super Balloon Facility.

7. Question Type: *Recall*
   Strategy: *SaL; P3 S6*

8. Question Type: *Recall*
   Strategy: *SaL; P2 last sentence*

9. Question Type: *Evaluation Question*
   Strategies: *SI, attention to details; P5 S1 to S5*

   Several contextual cue words in the first 5 sentences of Paragraph 5 hint that a payload functions as a data collection device: "Data from the payload and balloon are telemetered," "recorded on board via film, magnetic tape, or solid-state digital storage media," "direct visual tracking, airplane tracking, or use of Global Position System (GPS) navigation receivers."

10. Question Type: *Exception/Negative Question*
    Strategies: *SaL, PoE; P6*

    Each answer choice is mentioned in the following specific sentences in Paragraph 6: A and B inS6; C and D in S7. Only the data in E cannot be found in the paragraph or anywhere in the passage.

11. Question Type: *Recall*
    Strategies: *SaL; P7 S3*

12. Question Type: *Recall*
    Strategy: *SaL; P7 S2*

13. Question Type: *True False Statement (Two Statements)*
    Strategies: *SaL, PoE, attention to details; P3 S8 and last sentence*

    The first statement is true as indicated in P3 last sentence. However, the second statement is false: balloon payloads - NOT satellite payloads - are cheaper.

14. Question Type: *Recall*
    Strategy: *SaL; P6 S7*

15. Question Type: *Evaluation Question (Main Idea)*
    Strategies: *SI, prior knowledge*

    This question can be easily answered with simple inference and familiarity with the titles presented in the different choices. Understanding that the passage is about air balloons or balloon flights, the narrative that has this same theme should match as the correct answer.

16. Question Type: *Exception/Negative Question*
    Strategies: *SI, PoE, attention to details; P8 S4 to S6*

    Answering this question may require more attention to details because the answer choices are paraphrased from lines in the passage. (A) Cost would equate "aerobot would be much cheaper"; (B) Range would be "could cover a great deal of ground"; (C) Predictability of direction would be "lack of directional control," which is not considered as an aerobot's advantage over a rover – therefore, the correct answer; (D) weight is "lighter than a rover"; and (E) Details of view is "the ability to examine wide swathes of terrain with far more detail."

17. Question Type: *True False Statement (Two statements)*
    Strategies: *SaL, attention to details; P5 S7 and S8*

    The information in the two statements are reversed.

Would you like to discuss any of the answers or strategies in this section? Go to www.dat-prep.com/forum to share and learn.

RC Mini Test 2

The following is a sample mini test which is comparable to the level of difficulty required for the Reading Comprehension Test of the DAT. Please note that this sample would roughly be 1/3 of the actual Reading Comprehension Test portion of the DAT.

You have 20 minutes to complete this portion of the DAT Mini Test; the actual test is 60 minutes. Please time yourself accordingly.

BEGIN ONLY WHEN YOUR TIMER IS READY.

Passage 2

Symbiosis

(1). Symbiosis (from Ancient Greek sýn "with" and bíōsis "living") is a close and often long-term interaction between different biological species. In 1877, Bennett used the word symbiosis (which previously had been used for people living together in community) to describe the mutualistic relationship in lichens. In 1879, the German mycologist Heinrich Anton de Bary defined it as "the living together of unlike organisms." The definition of symbiosis is controversial among scientists. Some believe symbiosis should only refer to persistent mutualisms, while others believe it should apply to all types of persistent biological interactions (i.e., mutualistic, commensalistic, or parasitic).

(2). Some symbiotic relationships are obligate, meaning that both symbionts entirely depend on each other for survival. For example, many lichens consist of fungal and photosynthetic symbionts that cannot live on their own. Others are facultative, meaning that they can but do not have to live with the other organism. Symbiotic relationships include those associations in which one organism lives on another (ectosymbiosis, such as mistletoe), or where one partner lives inside the other (endosymbiosis, such as lactobacilli and other bacteria in humans or zooxanthelles in corals).

(3). Endosymbiosis is any symbiotic relationship in which one symbiont lives within the tissues of the other, either in the intracellular or extracellular space. Examples are rhizobia, nitrogen-fixing bacteria that live in root nodules on legume roots; actinomycete nitrogen-fixing bacteria called Frankia, which live in alder tree root nodules; single-celled algae inside reef-building corals; and bacterial endosymbionts that provide essential nutrients to about 10%–15% of insects. Ectosymbiosis, also referred to as exosymbiosis, is any symbiotic relationship in which the symbiont lives on the body surface of the host, including the inner surface of the digestive tract or the ducts of exocrine glands. Examples of this include ectoparasites such as lice, commensal ectosymbionts such as the barnacles that attach themselves to the jaw of baleen whales, and mutualist ectosymbionts such as cleaner fish.

(4). Mutualism is any relationship between individuals of different species where both individuals derive a benefit. Generally, only lifelong interactions involving close physical and biochemical contact can properly be considered symbiotic. Mutualistic relationships may be either obligate for both species, obligate for one but facultative for the other, or facultative for both. Many biologists restrict the definition of symbiosis to close mutualist relationships. A large percentage of herbivores have mutualistic gut fauna that help them digest plant matter, which is more difficult to digest than animal prey. Coral reefs are the result of mutualisms between coral organisms and various types of algae that live inside them. Most land plants and land ecosystems rely on mutualisms between the plants, which fix carbon from the air, and mycorrhizal fungi, which help in extracting minerals from the ground.

(5). An example of mutual symbiosis is the relationship between the ocellaris clownfish that dwell among the tentacles of Ritteri sea anemones. The territorial fish protects the anemone from anemone-eating fish, and in turn the stinging tentacles of the anemone protect the clownfish from its predators. A special mucus on the clownfish protects it from the stinging tentacles. Another example is the goby fish, which sometimes lives together with a shrimp. The shrimp digs and cleans up a burrow in the sand in which both the shrimp and the goby fish live. The shrimp is almost blind, leaving it vulnerable to predators when above ground. In case of danger the goby fish touches the shrimp with its tail to warn it. When that happens, both the shrimp and goby fish quickly retract into the burrow.

(6). One of the most spectacular examples of obligate mutualism is between the siboglinid tube worms and symbiotic bacteria that live at hydrothermal vents and cold seeps. The worm has no digestive tract and is wholly reliant on its internal symbionts for nutrition. The bacteria oxidize either hydrogen sulfide or methane, which the host supplies to them. These worms were discovered in the late 1980s at the hydrothermal vents near the Galapagos Islands and have since been found at deep-sea hydrothermal vents and cold seeps in all of the world's oceans. There are also many types of tropical and sub-tropical ants that have evolved very complex relationships with certain tree species.

(7). Commensalism describes a relationship between two living organisms where one benefits and the other is not significantly harmed or helped. It is derived from the English word commensal, used for human social interaction. The word derives from the medieval Latin word, formed from "com" and "mensa," meaning "sharing a table." Commensal relationships may involve one organism using another for transportation (phoresy) or for housing (inquilinism), or it may also involve one organism using something that another created after its death (metabiosis). Examples of metabiosis are maggots, which feast and develop on corpses, and hermit crabs using gastropod shells to protect their bodies.

(8). A parasitic relationship is one in which one member of the association benefits while the other is harmed. Parasitic symbioses take many forms, from endoparasites that live within the host's body to ectoparasites that live on its surface. In addition, parasites may be necrotrophic, which is to say they kill their host, or biotrophic, meaning they rely on their host's surviving. Biotrophic parasitism is an extremely successful mode of life. Depending on the definition used, as many as half of all animals have at least one parasitic phase in their life cycles, and it is also frequent in plants and fungi. Moreover, almost all free-living animals are host to one or more parasite taxa. An example of a biotrophic relationship would be a tick feeding on the blood of its host.

(9). Amensalism is the type of symbiotic relationship that exists where one species is inhibited or completely obliterated and one is unaffected. This type of symbiosis is relatively uncommon in rudimentary reference texts, but is omnipresent in the natural world. An example is a sapling growing under the shadow of a mature tree. The mature tree can begin to rob the sapling of necessary sunlight and, if the mature tree is very large, it can take up rainwater and deplete soil nutrients. Throughout the process the mature tree is unaffected. Indeed, if the sapling dies, the mature tree gains nutrients from the decaying sapling. Note that these nutrients become available because of the sapling's decomposition, rather than from the living sapling, which would be a case of parasitism.

(10). While historically, symbiosis has received less attention than other interactions such as predation or competition, it is increasingly recognized as an important selective force behind evolution, with many species having a long history of interdependent co-evolution. In fact, the evolution of all eukaryotes (plants, animals, fungi, and protists) is believed under the endosymbiotic theory to have resulted from a symbiosis between various sorts of bacteria. Up to 80% of vascular plants worldwide form symbiotic relationships with fungi, for example, in arbuscular mycorrhiza.

(11). The biologist Lynn Margulis, famous for her work on endosymbiosis, contends that symbiosis is a major driving force behind evolution. She considers Darwin's notion of evolution, driven by competition, to be incomplete and claims that evolution is strongly based on co-operation, interaction, and mutual dependence among organisms. According to Margulis and Dorion Sagan, "Life did not take over the globe by combat, but by networking."

(12). Symbiosis played a major role in the co-evolution of flowering plants and the animals that pollinate them. Many plants that are pollinated by insects, bats, or birds have highly specialized flowers modified to promote pollination by a specific pollinator that is also correspondingly adapted. The first flowering plants in the fossil record had relatively simple flowers. Adaptive speciation quickly gave rise to many diverse groups of plants, and, at the same time, corresponding speciation occurred in certain insect groups. Some groups of plants developed nectar and large sticky pollen, while insects evolved more specialized morphologies to access and collect these rich food sources. In some taxa of plants and insects the relationship has become dependent, where the plant species can only be pollinated by one species of insect.

1. Understory vegetation grows beneath the breeding colonies of herons. As the heron's population becomes dense, the trees on which they build their nests eventually die down due to the bird's heavy toxic excrements. The herons may suffer from the loss of their nesting trees, but they do not necessarily get hurt or benefit from the damaged vegetation. This type of symbiotic relationship is described to be:

A. commensalism.
B. parasitism.
C. amensalism.
D. ectosymbiosis.

2. In the example of mutual symbiosis between the shrimp and the goby fish, what is the primary benefit of their relationship?

A. Protection
B. Shelter
C. Nutrition
D. Transportation
E. Propagation

3. Each of the following are considered mutually beneficial symbionts EXCEPT one. Which one is the EXCEPTION?

    A. Rhizobia
    B. Bacterial endosymbionts
    C. Lice
    D. Frankia
    E. Lactobacilli

4. Which of the following best describes symbiosis?

    A. The ability of unlike organisms to live together
    B. Close relationship between two different species
    C. Lifelong close physical and biochemical contact of different species
    D. Persistent biological interactions in a community of diverse species
    E. Long-term mutually beneficial relationships of different biological species

5. Termites can chew and ingest wood, but they rely on their intestinal flagellates trichonympha to break down their food for them and chemically digest cellulose into sugars. The termite, in turn, provides food, shelter and constant internal environment to the trichonympha. Both cannot survive in the absence of the other. This type of relationship is an example of:

    A. inquilinism.
    B. necrotrophic parasitism.
    C. biotrophic parasitism.
    D. obligate mutualism.
    E. facultative mutualism.

6. Most orchids are plants that depend on their hosts for physical support and not nutrition. To which of the following symbiotic interaction would orchids belong?

    A. Ectoparasitism
    B. Biotrophic parasitism
    C. Facultative mutualism
    D. Metabiosis
    E. Inquilinism

7. Historically, symbiosis has received less attention than predation and competition. Yet, it is believed as an important selective force behind the evolution of eukaryotes.

   A. Both statements are true.
   B. Both statements are false.
   C. The first sentence is true while the second sentence is false.
   D. The first sentence is false while the second sentence is true.

8. Ectosymbiosis is the same as:

   A. ectoparasitism.
   B. endosymbiosis.
   C. mistletoe.
   D. exosymbiosis.
   E. phoresy.

9. Bennett first used the word "symbiosis" to describe the mutualistic relationship of:

   A. lichens.
   B. coral reefs.
   C. unlike organisms.
   D. lactobacilli

10. A parasite is said to be biotrophic when:

   A. it survives on a dead host.
   B. it relies on the host's survival.
   C. it lives within the host's body.
   D. it feeds on the host's blood.

11. The biologist Lynn Margulis contradicts Darwin's notion of evolution because the latter assumes co-operation, interaction, and mutual dependence among organisms.

   A. Both the statement and reason are correct and related.
   B. Both the statement and the reason are correct but NOT related.
   C. The statement is correct, but the reason is NOT.
   D. The statement is NOT correct, but the reason is correct.
   E. NEITHER the statement NOR the reason is correct.

12. Adaptive speciation caused the flowering plants and their pollinators to undergo the following developments EXCEPT one. Which one is the EXCEPTION?

   A. Specialized morphology of pollinators
   B. Diversity of the plant species
   C. Pollination by insects, bats, or birds
   D. Obligate relationship of some plants and insects

13. Eukaryotes include the following EXCEPT:

   A. plants.
   B. animals.
   C. fungi.
   D. bacteria.
   E. protists.

14. An obligate symbiotic relationship is described to be that:

   A. both symbionts cannot live on their own.
   B. both symbionts can but do not have to live with the other organism.
   C. one of the two symbionts can live on its own.
   D. one of the symbionts lives on the other.
   E. both symbionts are protective of the other.

15. The definition of symbiosis is controversial among scientists because some believe that symbiosis should refer to all types of persistent biological interactions.

   A. Both the statement and reason are correct and related.
   B. Both the statement and the reason are correct but NOT related.
   C. The statement is correct, but the reason is NOT.
   D. The statement is NOT correct, but the reason is correct.
   E. NEITHER the statement NOR the reason is correct.

16. Who is the first scientist to provide a definition for symbiosis?

   A. Lynn Margulis
   B. Bennett
   C. Charles Darwin
   D. Heinrich Anton de Bary
   E. Dorion Sagan

17. Parasitic symbioses involve only relationships in which one member of the association lives within the host's body.

Half of all animals have at least one parasitic phase in their life cycles.

A. Both statements are true.
B. Both statements are false.
C. The first sentence is true while the second sentence is false.
D. The first sentence is false while the second sentence is true.

18. Any symbiotic relationship in which one symbiont lives within the tissues of the other, either in the intracellular or extracellular space is known as:

A. phoresy.
B. inquilinism.
C. metabiosis.
D. endosymbiosis.
E. endoparasitism

If time remains, you may review your work. If your allotted time (20 minutes) is complete, please proceed to the Answer Key.

RC Mini Test 2 Answer Key

1. C	7. A	13. D
2. A	8. D	14. A
3. C	9. A	15. A
4. C	10. B	16. D
5. D	11. C	17. D
6. E	12. C	18. D

RC Mini Test 2 Explanations and Strategies

1. Question Type: *Application Question*
   Strategies: *SI, OA; P9*

   The first sentence in Paragraph 9 defines "amensalism" as the type of symbiotic relationship where one species is inhibited or completely destroyed while the other one is unaffected. The example given in this question closely matches the situation of the sapling and the mature tree, cited in Paragraph 9. Although the herons' existence eventually caused damage to the understory vegetation, the herons in return neither benefited nor got harmed from the lost vegetation. Therefore, the correct answer is C.

   (A) Commensalism is roughly the opposite of this, i.e., one species benefits and the other is not significantly harmed or helped. This is also unlike (B) parasitism, where one member in the relationship benefits from either the existence or annihilation of another. On the other hand, (D) ectosymbiosis refers to a symbiotic relationship in which the symbiont feeds on the body surface of the host. This cannot be the correct answer because the herons do not live or feed on the vegetation.

2. Question Type: *Evaluation Question*
   Strategy: *SaL; P5 last 2 sentences*

   Cue words in the statements such as the shrimp being "vulnerable to predators" and the goby fish touches the shrimp with its tail "to warn" strongly suggest that their relationship is based on protection. The context of the paragraph likewise alludes to symbiotic relationships that work around protection.

3. Question Type: *Evaluation Question*
    Strategies: *OA, prior knowledge; P3 S2 and last sentence*

    Contextual clues in Paragraph 3 suggest that rhizobia, Frankia, bacterial endosymbionts provide nutrients (benefits) to their hosts while lactobacilli are generally known as "good" (in the biological context, "mutually beneficial") bacteria. Lice, on the other hand, are parasites and considered as pests – therefore, NOT "good."

4. Question Type: *Evaluation Question (Implication)*
    Strategies: *SaL or OA, PoE, attention to details; P1 S1*

    What makes this question tricky is that the passage offers several definitions of the term "symbiosis." However, A is a definition merely given by Heinrich Anton de Bary as indicated in P1 S3; D is only one of the opinions about symbiosis by some scientists, according to P1 last sentence; and E is loosely a definition from Bennett in P1 S2. This narrows down the choice between B and C. One easy way to determine the best option is to quickly and smartly locate the most conclusive statement that describes "symbiosis." This can be found in P4 S2, "Generally, only lifelong interactions involving close physical and biochemical contact can properly be considered symbiotic." This closely points to C. B, on the other hand, offers a very general definition.

    Another strategy would be to infer how symbiosis mainly works in the various rela-

tionships described in the different paragraphs and then choose the most inclusive definition among the answer choices: C.

5. Question Type: *Application*
    Strategies: *OA/paraphrasing; P6*

    The example in this question is similar to the case of the siboglinid tube worms and symbiotic bacteria discussed in Paragraph 6. The relationship illustrated refers to obligate mutualism: both symbionts entirely depend on each other for survival (P2 S1).

    The other answers are wrong based on each of their definitions:
    (A) Inquilinism pertains to a relationship between two living organisms where one benefits through housing without causing harm or profiting the other either.
    (B) Necrotrophic parasitism is a kind of parasitism that eventually kills the host.
    (C) Biotrophic parasitism only benefits the parasite for as long as the host is alive.
    (E) Facultative mutualism means that both members of the relationship can but do not have to live with the other.

6. Question Type: *Application Question*
    Strategy: *SI or OA; P2, P7, P8*

    Inquilinism is a form of commensalism described as a relationship between two living organisms where one benefits through physical shelter (housing) while the other is not significantly harmed or helped. This type of symbiotic interaction fits the description of an orchid to its host. (A) Ectoparasitism is a close choice. However, ectoparasites live on the surface of their host primarily for nourishment and in the process, cause harm. The other options are off-tangent.

7. Question Type: *True False Statement (Two Statements)*
   Strategies: *SaL, attention to details; P10*

   The first statement is almost verbatim of the first half of P10 S1: "While historically, symbiosis has received less attention than other interactions such as predation or competition. . ." The second statement is a paraphrase of the second half of P10 S2 and S3.

8. Question Type: *Recall*
   Strategy: *SaL; P3 S3*

9. Question Type: *Recall*
   Strategy: *SaL; P1 S2*

10. Question Type: *Recall*
    Strategy: *SaL; P8 S3*

11. Question Type: *True False Statements (Statement and Reason)*
    Strategies: *SI, attention to details; P11 S2*

    The information provided in the reason is reversed.

12. Question Type: *Exception/Negative Question*
    Strategies: *SI, PoE, never lose sight of the question; P12*

    Options A, B, and D are simple paraphrase of the information found in P12 S4 and S5. Pollination by insects, bats, or birds, on the other hand, is not an offshoot of adaptive speciation but rather, a "standard" activity or function of pollinators. The question is specifically asking for the developments, which arose from adaptive speciation, in the flowering plants and their pollinators – not what each already does. Therefore, the answer is C.

13. Question Type: *Exception/Negative Question*
    Strategies: *SaL, PoE; P10 S2*

    In P10 S2, the eukaryotes are specifically identified in a parenthesis to include plants, animals, fungi, and protists. Nowhere in the passage indicates bacteria as a eukaryote.

14. Question Type: *Recall*
    Strategy: *SaL; P2 S1*

15. Question Type: *True False Statement (Statement and Reason)*
    Strategy: *SaL; P1 last 2 sentences*

16. Question Type: *Recall*
    Strategies: *SaL, PoE; P1 S3*

    Bennett was the first to use the term "symbiosis," not define it. Dorion Sagan and Lynn Margulis are the ones who said that "life did not take over the globe by combat, but by networking." Charles Darwin was only mentioned in the passage in relation to Margulis' contention about the theory of evolution.

17. Question Type: *True False Statements (Two Statements)*
    Strategies: *SaL, PoE, attention to details; P8 S2 and S5*

The first statement presents an incomplete definition of parasitic symbioses, which should include endoparasitism (living within a host's body), ectoparasitism (living on the surface of a host), necrotrophic parasitism (killing the host) and biotrophic parasitism (relying on the host's survival).

18. Question Type: *Recall*
    Strategy: *SaL, P3 S1*

Would you like to discuss any of the answers or strategies in this section? Go to www.dat-prep.com/forum to share and learn.

RC Mini Test 3

The following is a sample mini test which is comparable to the level of difficulty required for the Reading Comprehension Test of the DAT. Please note that this sample would roughly be 1/3 of the actual Reading Comprehension Test portion of the DAT.

You have 20 minutes to complete this portion of the DAT Mini Test; the actual test is 60 minutes. Please time yourself accordingly.

BEGIN ONLY WHEN YOUR TIMER IS READY.

Passage 3

Empirical Science

(1). A scientist, whether theorist or experimenter, puts forward statements, or systems of statements, and tests them step by step. In the field of the empirical sciences, more particularly, he constructs hypotheses, or systems of theories, and tests them against experience by observation and experiment. I suggest that it is the task of the logic of scientific discovery, or the logic of knowledge, to give a logical analysis of this procedure; that is, to analyze the method of the empirical sciences.

(2). But what are these "methods of the empirical sciences"? And what do we call "empirical science"?

(3). According to a widely accepted view — to be opposed in this book — the empirical sciences can be characterized by the fact that they use "inductive methods," as they are called. According to this view, the logic of scientific discovery would be identical with inductive logic, i.e. with the logical analysis of these inductive methods.

(4). It is usual to call an inference "inductive" if it passes from singular statements (sometimes also called "particular" statements), such as accounts of the results of observations or experiments, to universal statements, such as hypotheses or theories.

(5). Now it is far from obvious, from a logical point of view, that we are justified in inferring universal statements from singular ones, no matter how numerous; for any conclusion drawn in this way may always turn out to be false: no matter how many instances of white swans we may have observed, this does not justify the conclusion that all swans are white.

(6). The question whether inductive inferences are justified, or under what conditions, is known as the problem of induction. The problem of induction may also be formulated as the question of the validity or the truth of universal statements which are based on experience, such as the hypotheses and theoretical systems of the empirical sciences. For many people believe that the truth of these universal statements is "known by experience"; yet it is clear that an account of an experience — of an observation or the result of an experiment — can in the first place be only a singular statement and not a universal one. Accordingly, people who say of a universal statement that we know its truth from experience usually mean that the truth of this universal statement can somehow be reduced to the truth of singular ones, and that these singular ones are known by experience to be true; which amounts to saying that the universal statement is based on inductive inference. Thus to ask whether there are natural laws known to be true appears to be only another way of asking whether inductive inferences are logically justified.

(7). Yet if we want to find a way of justifying inductive inferences, we must first of all try to establish a principle of induction. A principle of induction would be a statement with the help of which we could put inductive inferences into a logically acceptable form. In the eyes of the upholders of inductive logic, a principle of induction is of supreme importance for scientific method: ". . . this principle," says Reichenbach, "determines the truth of scientific theories. To eliminate it from science would mean nothing less than to deprive science of the power to decide the truth or falsity of its theories. Without it, clearly, science would no longer have the right to distinguish its theories from the fanciful and arbitrary creations of the poet's mind."

(8). Now this principle of induction cannot be a purely logical truth like a tautology or an analytic statement. Indeed, if there were such a thing as a purely logical principle of induction, there would be no problem of induction; for in this case, all inductive inferences would have to be regarded as purely logical or tautological transformations, just like inferences in deductive logic. Thus the principle of induction must be a synthetic statement; that is, a statement whose negation is not self-contradictory but logically possible. So the question arises why such a principle should be accepted at all, and how we can justify its acceptance on rational grounds.

(9). Some who believe in inductive logic are anxious to point out, with Reichenbach, that "the principle of induction is unreservedly accepted by the whole of science and that no man can seriously doubt this principle in everyday life either." Yet even supposing this were the case — for after all, "the whole of science" might err — I should still contend that a principle of induction is superfluous, and that it must lead to logical inconsistencies.

(10). That inconsistencies may easily arise in connection with the principle of induction should have been clear from the work of Hume, also, that they can be avoided, if at all, only with difficulty. For the principle of induction must be a universal statement in its turn. Thus if we try to regard its truth as known from experience, then the very same problems which occasioned its introduction will arise all over again. To justify it, we should have to employ inductive inferences; and to justify these we should have to assume an inductive principle of a higher order; and so on. Thus the attempt to base the principle of induction on experience breaks down, since it must lead to an infinite regress.

(11). Kant tried to force his way out of this difficulty by taking the principle of induction (which he formulated as the "principle of universal causation") to be "a priori valid." But I do not think that his ingenious attempt to provide an a priori justification for synthetic statements was successful.

(12). My own view is that the various difficulties of inductive logic here sketched are insurmountable. So also, I fear, are those inherent in the doctrine, so widely current today, that inductive inference, although not "strictly valid," can attain some degree of "reliability" or of "probability." According to this doctrine, inductive inferences are "probable inferences." "We have described," says Reichenbach, "the principle of induction as the means whereby science decides upon truth. To be more exact, we should say that it serves to decide upon probability. For it is not given to science to reach either truth or falsity . . . but scientific statements can only attain continuous degrees of probability whose unattainable upper and lower limits are truth and falsity." At this stage I can disregard the fact that the believers in inductive logic entertain an idea of probability that I shall later reject as highly unsuitable for their own purposes. I can do so because the difficulties mentioned are not even touched by an appeal to probability. For if a certain degree of probability is to be assigned to statements based on inductive inference, then this will have to be justified by invoking a new principle of induction, appropriately modified. And this new principle in its turn will have to be justified, and so on. Nothing is gained, moreover, if the principle of induction, in its turn, is taken not as "true" but only as "probable." In short, like every other form of inductive logic, the logic of probable inference, or "probability logic," leads either to an infinite regress, or to the doctrine of apriorism.

(13). The theory to be developed in the following pages stands directly opposed to all attempts to operate with the ideas of inductive logic. It might be described as the theory of the deductive method of testing, or as the view that a hypothesis can only be empirically tested — and only after it has been advanced.

(14). Before I can elaborate this view (which might be called "deductivism," in contrast to "inductivism") I must first make clear the distinction between the psychology of knowledge which deals with empirical facts, and the logic of knowledge which is concerned only with logical relations. For the belief in inductive logic is largely due to a confusion of psychological problems with epistemological ones. It may be worth noticing, by the way, that this confusion spells trouble not only for the logic of knowledge but for its psychology as well.

- from Karl Popper's *Logic of Scientific Discovery*

1. The problem of induction is best represented by which of the following equations?

   A. X = Z always
   B. X = Z many times, so X must be the same as Z
   C. X never equals Z, so X is unique and apart from Z
   D. X is sometimes Z, but only in certain situations
   E. X is derived from Z on the basis of logic

2. Of the following, which is tested by a scientist against experience with observation and experiment?

   A. Inductive logic
   B. Deductive logic
   C. Empirical sciences
   D. Hypotheses and theories
   E. None of the above

3. The idea of an "infinite regress" results from the idea that a theory is:

   A. after experience.
   B. before experience.
   C. deductively sound.
   D. inductively inferred.
   E. a priori.

4. With which of the following statements would the author of the passage agree?

   A. Deductive logic should be preferred over inductive logic.
   B. The methods of empirical science are marked by circular reasoning.
   C. Inductive logic is questionable and suspect.
   D. Tautological statements support observation and hypotheses.
   E. Scientists need to justify inductive inferences.

5. Based on usage in this passage, which of the following best defines "empirical"?

A. Arbitrary
B. Inferable
C. Falsifiable
D. Observable
E. More than one of the above

6. Which of the following analogies best represents the idea of infinite regress?

A. A bridge connected to another bridge
B. A circle within another circle
C. A snake eating its own tail (uberous)
D. A mirror turned towards another mirror
E. A vessel with many interconnected chambers

7. Inductive logic, by its nature, supposedly passes from the "singular event" to:

A. the hypothetical derived.
B. the a priori established.
C. the universally true.
D. the testable observation.
E. the experimental deduced.

8. The author's tone and type of audience are which of the following terms?

A. Critical - Scientific Community
B. Arcane - General Populace
C. Careful - Students
D. Witty - Academic
E. Profound - Logicians

9. The principle of induction serves to decide upon probability in science because it is given to science to reach either truth or falsity.

A. Both the statement and reason are correct and related.
B. Both the statement and the reason are correct but NOT related.
C. The statement is correct but the reason is NOT.
D. The statement is NOT correct, but the reason is correct.
E. NEITHER the statement NOR the reason is correct.

10. Reichenbach organizes a principle of induction around:

    A. the establishment of logical inferences.

    B. social consensus of the scientific community.

    C. logically derived a priori formulations.

    D. other inductive tautologies.

    E. None of the above

11. Of the following, which according to the passage are the functions of the principle of induction?

    1. Characterizes empirical science as tautological

    2. Justifies inductive inferences as a logical form

    3. Determines the truth of scientific theories

    4. Distinguishes science from creative art

    A. All of the above

    B. 2, 3 and 4 only

    C. 2 and 3 only

    D. 3 only

    E. 4 only

12. The problem of induction is basically:

    A. how to refine this logical process.

    B. how to avoid this process in favor of deduction.

    C. whether its applications are logically faulty.

    D. whether inductive inferences are justified or under what conditions.

    E. how there is an inherent contradiction in inductive inferences.

13. In the last paragraph, the statement to "make clear the distinction between the psychology of knowledge which deals with empirical facts, and the logic of knowledge which is concerned only with logical relations" can be inferred to be the author's juxtaposition between:

    A. what is observable and what is testable.

    B. what is hypothetical and what is logically sound.

    C. what is testable and what is inductive.

    D. what is observable and what is logically sound.

    E. what is inductive and what is universally true.

14. What is the task of the logic of scientific discovery?

    A. To analyze the method of empirical sciences

    B. To put forward statements and test them step by step

    C. To test scientific theories against experience by observation and experiment

    D. To employ inductive logic

    E. All of the above

15. Which of the following is the best description of a synthetic statement?

    A. A statement based on experience

    B. A universal statement based on inductive inference

    C. The power to decide the truth or falsity of a theory

    D. A statement whose negation is not self-contradictory but logically possible

    E. A purely logical or tautological transformation

> If time remains, you may review your work. If your allotted time (20 minutes) is complete, please proceed to the Answer Key.

RC Mini Test 3 Answer Key

1. B	6. D	11. B
2. D	7. C	12. D
3. D	8. A	13. D
4. C	9. C	14. A
5. D	10. B	15. D

RC Mini Test 3 Explanations and Strategies

1. Question Type: *Evaluation Question (Main Idea)*
   Strategy: *OA*

   The whole passage is about how inductive logic compiles on examples in order to move from the singular examples to the universal. A is incorrect because that would posit the problem of induction as an exact correspondence between entities or phenomena. C is also incorrect because this equation suggests an inequality, subtraction or difference of phenomena or entities. This is closer to deduction, not induction. D is incorrect because it gives X a contextually determined essence. E is a made up phrase, simply made to distract the test taker.

2. Question Type: *Recall*
   Strategy: *SaL; P1 S2*

3. Question Type: *Evaluation Question (Implication)*
   Strategy: *SaL or OA, P10 last 2 sentences, P12 last sentence*

   The idea of infinite regress can be inferred based on the author's discussion in Paragraph 10: a theory supported through induction must be inductively inferred as well, resulting to an endless chain of induction. After Experience or A Posteriori, as well as Before Experience or A Priori, are related but not as specific to the idea of infinite regress. C is quite the contrary, and can be ruled out.

4. Question Type: *Evaluation Question (Tone and Main Idea)*
   Strategies: *OA, attention to details in P3*

Early in the passage, the author expresses his opposition to the inductive method: "According to a widely accepted view — to be opposed in this book — the empirical sciences can be characterized by the fact that they use 'inductive methods'." This statement would readily give a clear hint of the author's tone – that of contradiction, which is closest to viewing inductive logic as "questionable and suspect."

Another strategy is to paraphrase the main idea of each significant paragraph in order to have a clear outline of the author's overall point.

(1). I suggest that it is the task of the logic of scientific discovery, or the logic of knowledge, to give a logical analysis of this procedure; that is, to analyze the method of the empirical sciences.

(3). The author explicitly contradicts the inductive method.

(4). Induction starts with the specific "particular" or "singular" to the general or "universal."

(5). This method is not justified because "any conclusion drawn in this way may always turn out to be false."

(6). The problem of the inductive method is that the truth of the universal statements is questionable and cannot be justified because they are based on a particular observation or a singular result of an experiment. In other words, a universal statement cannot be justified by a singular experience or event.

(7). In order to justify the inductive method, a principle of induction must first be established. (A principle of induction would be a statement with the help of which we could put inductive inferences into a logically acceptable form.)

(8). Ideally, a principle of induction must present a synthetic statement - a statement whose negation is not self-contradictory but logically possible.

(9). The author believes that a principle of induction is superfluous (unnecessary), and that it must lead to logical inconsistencies. On the other hand, Reichenbach asserts that "the principle of induction is unreservedly accepted by the whole of science and that no man can seriously doubt this principle in everyday life either."

(10). The principle of induction is prone to infinite regress.

(11). Kant fails to provide an a priori justification for synthetic statements.

(12). Inductive logic is problematic in several ways: inductive inference, although not "strictly valid," can attain some degree of "reliability" or of "probability"; "probability logic," leads either to an infinite regress, or to the doctrine of apriorism.

(13). The author introduces the idea of deductivism.

(14). The author distinguishes his idea of "the psychology of knowledge which deals with empirical facts (from) the logic of knowledge which is concerned only with logical relations.

The preceding brief notes clearly indicate that the author's concern in this excerpt is questioning the validity of inductive logic. Therefore, the most reasonable answer to this question would be C.

The author does mention his preference to deductivism over inductivism. However, this is not elaborated in the passage. A, then, would not be an accurate answer. (B) Circular reasoning in empirical science is not asserted in the passage either.

Although tautology in relation to logic is mentioned, the idea that (D) tautological statements support observation and hypotheses is off-tangent in the context of the passage. Lastly, the author does not seek that (E) "scientists need to justify inductive inferences." Rather, he dismisses the use of such method as resulting to infinite regress.

5. Question Type: *Evaluation Question (Implication)*
    Strategies: *OA, PoE; P1, P3, P4, P6*

    (A) Arbitrary is the term used by the author to describe poetic creations. This can be readily eliminated then. On the other hand, inferring from paragraphs that refer to "empirical" or

"empirical science" often suggests the following key ideas: "experience by observation and experiment" (P1 S2); "the empirical sciences can be characterized by the fact that they use 'inductive methods'" (P3 S1), correlating to the notion in Paragraph 4 that induction entails "observations or experiments." These lead to D (observable) as the best choice.

Although (B) inference is repeatedly mentioned in the passage, this is used in reference to the inductive method per se, not empirical science. (C) Falsifiable is an element of theory, which limits scope, i.e., the theory does not include everything, thus this is prescriptive evaluation and reservations of a given theory, not a definition in itself. E can thus be eliminated as well.

6. Question Type: *Application Question*
    Strategies: *OA/paraphrasing, PoE; P10 and P12*

    Since "infinite regress" is the idea that inductive logic which is inferred is based on an inference, and that inference is based on another inference and so on, the best analogy would be (D) of a mirror turned towards a mirror reproducing its own representation. The notion of (C) a snake eating its own tail, comes close to representing the tautological reasoning sometimes used to support inductive modes of logic: Premise = CLAIM = Premise. However, the idea of something eating up its own self suggests an end, therefore not "infinite."

The analogy of (A) a bridge connected to another bridge is also close but is only limited to one extension – not one after another. (B)

A circle within a circle suggests related but separate inferences – not a continuation. This is the same with the idea in E. These make all the other options incorrect.

7. Question Type: *Evaluation Question (Implication); Recall*
   Strategies: *Paraphrasing, SaL; P4*

   This question is merely a paraphrase of the general idea found in Paragraph 4, which states induction starts with the specific – "particular" or "singular" – to the general or "universal."

8. Question Type: *Evaluation Question (Tone)*
   Strategy: *SI*

   The author makes clear from the beginning that he is opposed to the idea of inductive logic. He then devotes a majority of his succeeding discussions in pointing out the problems of induction. He is therefore, critical. In addition, constant references to empirical science and experiments make this passage generally suited for the scientific community, which can include students or the academic audience and logicians as well.

   However, (D) witty does not characterize the tone of the author. (C) Careful and (E) profound may be reasonable descriptions of the quality of the author's writing, but they are not as encompassing and specific.

   (B) Arcane connotes ambiguous or difficult to understand, which is illogical to have something written in this language to be meant

for the general populace. Thus B is wrong.

9. Question Type: *True False Statements (Statement and Reason)*
   Strategy: *SaL; P12 S4 to S6*

10. Question Type: *Recall*
    Strategies: *SaL, attention to details; P9 S1*

    As the passage states in a quote from Reichenbach, " the principle of induction is unreservedly accepted by the whole of science and that no man can seriously doubt this principle in everyday life." This amounts to a social consensus of the inductive method. Answer A is nonsense. E (None of the Above) can be ruled out. D may be true, in the idea of infinite regress, but the question states "the principle of induction." C is more or less philoso-babble constructed in the answers to distract the test taker.

11. Question Type: *Recall; Evaluation (Implication)*
    Strategies: *SI, paraphrasing; P7 and P8 S1*

    This question pertains to the discussion of establishing a principle of induction found in Paragraph 7. According to the author, "a principle of induction would be a statement with the help of which we could put inductive inferences into a logically acceptable form" (Statement 2). For Reichenbach, this principle "determines the truth of scientific theories" (Statement 3) and "distinguish(es) (scientific) theories from the fanciful and arbitrary creations of the poet's mind" (Statement 4).

P8 S1 would eliminate Statement 1: "Now this principle of induction cannot be a purely logical truth like a tautology or an analytic statement." Therefore, the best answer is B.

12. Question Type: *Recall*
    Strategy: *SaL; P6 S1*

13. Question Type: *Evaluation (Implication)*
    Strategies: *OA/paraphrasing, inference*

    This question requires clearly understanding what "empirical" mainly connotes in the passage. As already determined and explained in Question No. 5, empirical or empirical facts would indicate something "observable." Additionally, the author makes a significant remark in Paragraph 8 that for a method, such as that of induction, to work, a synthetic statement must result: one that is logically valid or possible. Hence, the correct answer is D: the author juxtaposes "what is observable (empirical facts) and what is logically sound (logical relations)."

    A is incorrect because logical relations is not indicated in the passage as "testable." B is also wrong because hypothetical does not directly characterize an "empirical fact." Hypothesis is only part of this process. C is primarily incorrect because of the term "induction" being correlated to logic. The author explicitly opposes this view. E sounds correct; however, it must be noted that the author has not established the concept of logic to be "universally true." Therefore, E is an erroneous statement.

14. Question Type: *Recall*
    Strategy: *SaL; P1 last sentence*

    The two key phrases here are "empirical facts" and "logical relations" - meaning "observations" and "logic as a system of itself." Therefore, an analysis of the method of empirical sciences – as explicitly stated in the last sentence of Paragraph 1 – is the best answer. B and C are corollaries or peripheral statements that simply relate to the passage in general while D goes against the main idea of the author.

15. Question Type: *Recall*
    Strategy: *SaL; P8 S3*

Would you like to discuss any of the answers or strategies in this section? Go to www.dat-prep.com/forum to share and learn.

GOLD STANDARD DAT
RC PRACTICE TEST

Reading Comprehension Test

Time Limit: 60 Minutes

Passage 1

Scientific Analysis and Reasoning

(1). Unlike some other classical figures (Auguste Comte and Émile Durkheim, for example) Max Weber did not attempt, consciously, to create any specific set of rules governing social sciences in general, or sociology in particular. Compared to Durkheim and Marx, Weber was more focused on individuals and culture and this is clear in his methodology. Whereas Durkheim focused on the society, Weber concentrated on the individuals and their actions; and whereas Marx argued for the primacy of the material world over the world of ideas, Weber valued ideas as motivating actions of individuals, at least in the big picture.

(2). Weber was concerned with the question of objectivity and subjectivity. Weber distinguished social action from social behavior, noting that social action must be understood through how individuals subjectively relate to one another. Study of social action through interpretive means must be based upon understanding the subjective meaning and purpose that the individual attaches to their actions. Social actions may have easily identifiable and objective means, but much more subjective ends and the understanding of those ends by a scientist is subject to yet another layer of subjective understanding (that of the scientist). Weber noted that the importance of subjectiv-

ity in social sciences makes creation of full-proof, universal laws much more difficult than in natural sciences and that the amount of objective knowledge that social sciences may achieve is precariously limited. Overall, Weber supported the goal of objective science, but he noted that it is an unreachable goal – although one definitely worth striving for.

> *There is no absolutely "objective" scientific analysis of culture . . . All knowledge of cultural reality . . . is always knowledge from particular points of view . . . An "objective" analysis of cultural events, which proceeds according to the thesis that the ideal of science is the reduction of empirical reality to "laws," is meaningless. . . [because]. . . the knowledge of social laws is not knowledge of social reality but is rather one of the various aids used by our minds for attaining this end.*
>
> - Max Weber, "Objectivity" in *Social Science,* 1897

(3). The principle of "methodological individualism," which holds that social scientists should seek to understand collectivities (such as nations, cultures, governments, churches, corporations, etc.) solely as the result and the context of the actions of individual persons, can be traced to Weber, particularly to the first chapter of **Economy and Society**, in which he argues that only individuals "can be treated as agents in a course of subjectively understandable action." In other words, Weber argued that social phenomena can be understood scientifically only to the extent that they are captured by models of the behavior of purposeful individuals, models which Weber called "ideal types," from which actual historical events will necessarily deviate due to accidental and irrational factors. The analytical constructs of an ideal type never exist in reality, but provide objective benchmarks against which real-life constructs can be measured.

> *We know of no scientifically ascertainable ideals. To be sure, that makes our efforts more arduous than in the past, since we are expected to create our ideals from within our breast in the very age of subjectivist culture.*

> - Max Weber, 1909

(4). Weber's methodology was developed in the context of a wider debate about methodology of social sciences, the *Methodenstreit* (debate over methods). Weber's position was close to historicism, as he understood social actions as being heavily tied to particular historical contexts and its analysis required the understanding of subjective motivations of individuals (social actors). Thus Weber's methodology emphasizes the use of comparative historical analysis. Therefore, Weber was more interested in explaining how a certain outcome was the result of various historical processes rather than predicting an outcome of those processes in the future.

(5). Such views by Max Weber find their parallel in the field of twentieth-century scientific thoughts. Jacob Bronowski, writer of the book and the 1973 BBC television documentary series, **The Ascent of Man**, was a mathematician, biologist, historian of science, theatre author, poet and inventor. In the 1950s, he wrote an essay entitled *The Nature of Scientific Reasoning*, which similarly discusses subjectivity, this time among scientific theories, as the following excerpt would show:

(6). "No scientific theory is a collection of facts. It will not even do to call a theory true or false in the simple sense in which every fact is either so or not so. The Epicureans held that matter is made of atoms 2000 years ago and we are now tempted to say that their theory was true. But if we do so we confuse their notion of matter with our own. John Dalton in 1808 first saw the structure of matter as we do today, and what he took from the ancients was not their theory but something richer - their image: the atom. Much of what was in Dalton's mind was as vague as the Greek notion, and quite as mistaken. But he suddenly gave life to the new facts of chemistry and the ancient theory together, by fusing them to give what neither had: a coherent picture of how matter is linked and built up from different kinds of atoms. The act of fusion is the creative act.

(7). All science is the search for unity in hidden likenesses. The search may be on a grand scale, as in the modern theories which try to link the fields of gravitation and electromagnetism. But we do not need to be browbeaten by the scale of science. There are discoveries to be made by snatching a small likeness from the air too, if it is bold enough. In 1935, the Japanese physicist Hideki Yukawa wrote a paper which can still give heart to a young scientist. He took as his starting point the known fact that waves of light can sometimes behave as if they were separate pellets. From this he reasoned that the forces which hold the nucleus of an atom together might sometimes also be observed as if they were solid pellets. A schoolboy can see how thin Yukawa's analogy is, and his teacher would be severe with it. Yet Yukawa, without a blush, calculated the mass of the pellet he expected to see, and waited. He was right; his meson was found, and a range of other mesons, neither the existence nor the nature of which had been suspected before. The likeness had borne fruit.

(8). The scientist looks for order in the appearances of nature by exploring such likenesses. For order does not display itself of itself, if it can be said to be there at all, it is not there for the mere looking. There is no way of pointing a finger or camera at it; order must be discovered and, in a deep sense, it must be created. What we see, as we see it, is mere disorder.

(9). This point has been put trenchantly in a fable by Karl Popper. Suppose that someone wishes to give his whole life to science.

Suppose that he therefore sat down, pencil in hand, and for the next twenty, thirty, forty years recorded in notebook after notebook everything that he could observe. He may be supposed to leave out nothing: today's humidity, the racing results, the level of cosmic radiation and the stock market prices and the look of Mars, all would be there. He would have compiled the most careful record of nature that has ever been made; and, dying in the calm certainty of a life well-spent, he would of course leave his notebooks to the Royal Society. Would the Royal Society thank him for the treasure of a lifetime of observation? It would not. The Royal Society would treat his notebooks exactly as the English bishops have treated Joanna Southcott's box. It would refuse to open them at all, because it would know without looking that the notebooks contain only a jumble of disorderly and meaningless items."

- Part of this passage is adapted from J. Bronowski, *The Nature of Scientific Reasoning*

1. In the excerpt from Jacob Bronowski's essay, the author starts with "No scientific theory is a collection of facts." Which of the following reasons can NOT be inferred to be applicable to this statement?

   A. Theories are sometimes developed from other earlier theories.

   B. Facts from one era of history may differ from facts of later histories.

   C. Scientific theory can be a creative act through fusion of theories.

   D. Facts are immutable throughout time, while theories are not.

2. Weber's concept of methodological individualism is BEST exemplified by how one:

   A. conceives collective institutions as the product of individual actions.

   B. focuses on how social action can be understood through subjective interpretation.

   C. interprets "ideal types" on the basis of debate over methods.

   D. stands in stark contrast to social realities interpreted by Marx and Durkheim.

   E. represents as an agent in subjective social actions.

3. Jacob Bronowski is identified as all of the following EXCEPT a(n):

   A. mathematician.

   B. biologist.

   C. author.

   D. poet.

   E. philosopher.

4. The fable by Karl Popper can be inferred to express the idea that in scientific study:

   A. order must be discovered and created.

   B. a clear focus is needed to sort out the mess of variables.

   C. indiscriminate research findings will not be applauded by the scientific community.

   D. what we see, as we see it, is mere disorder.

   E. the Royal Society, in reality, regard scientific theories to be meaningless.

5. "Methodenstreit" means:

   A. methodology of social sciences.

   B. methodological individualism.

   C. debate over methods.

   D. scientific analysis and reasoning.

   E. social action.

6. According to Bronowski, science is characterized by a number of ideas. Which of the following is NOT an idea advanced in his essay?

   A. Science looks for order in the appearance of Nature.
   B. Science looks for unity in hidden likenesses.
   C. Science proceeds to build theory through testing and observation.
   D. Science is selective in its searches for order and likeness.

7. All knowledge of cultural reality is always knowledge from certain points of view.

   Social phenomena can be understood scientifically only to the extent that they are captured by "ideal types."

   A. Both statements are true.
   B. Both statements are false.
   C. The first statement is true. The second statement is false.
   D. The first statement is false. The second statement is true.

8. Hideki Yukawa discovered:

   A. that light waves could behave like pellets.
   B. the meson.
   C. that the nucleus of an atom was not held together similar to pellets.
   D. the link between gravitation and electromagnetism.
   E. that scientific theory is creative.

9. The notion of an objective scientific analysis of culture is unattainable because it will always be marked by subjective perspectives.

   A. Both the statement and reason are correct and related.
   B. Both the statement and the reason are correct but NOT related.
   C. The statement is correct but the reason is NOT.
   D. The statement is NOT correct, but the reason is correct.
   E. NEITHER the statement NOR the reason is correct.

10. Weber's opinion toward objectivity in the social sciences is that:

    A. it is practically non-existent.

    B. it is nothing more than an ideal.

    C. it is masked by our very own subjectivity.

    D. objective knowledge is limited.

    E. it is more focused on individuals and culture.

11. Weber's "ideal types" are:

    A. striving for objectivity through subjective means.

    B. ideal methodologies for understanding social action.

    C. socially-constructed realities based on subjective interpretation.

    D. models of social behavior.

    E. deviations due to accidental and irrational factors.

12. It can be inferred from the passage that "Methodenstreit" was:

    A. a concern of how to properly define social action.

    B. an argument of how to proceed theoretically in the study of social sciences.

    C. a theoretical quagmire of evaluating objectivity.

    D. a postulation of proof concerning subjectivity.

13. Which of the following concepts DOES NOT point out a difference of Weber from other classical figures in the social sciences?

    A. Weber focused on individuals and their social actions.

    B. Weber valued the ideas that drive individual actions.

    C. Weber created standards albeit subjective for understanding society.

    D. Weber was concerned with the question of objectivity and subjectivity.

    E. Weber noted that social action must be understood through how individuals subjectively relate to one another.

14. Which of the following sociological studies would be reasonably expected to interest Weber?

    A. A report on repercussions of President Bush's "War on Terrorism" policy

    B. A subjective study of social behavior among victims of domestic violence

    C. An analysis of Napoleon Bonaparte's motivation for waging the Napoleonic Wars

    D. A research report on culture presenting the different findings and impressions of the researchers

15. According to Bronowski, the order of Nature must be:

    A. discovered.
    B. understood.
    C. fused.
    D. deduced.
    E. debated.

16. Weber wrote the first chapter of *Economy and Society* in:

    A. 1808.
    B. 1897.
    C. 1909.
    D. 1935.
    E. 1973.

17. The view that matter has primacy over ideas was promoted by:

    A. Dalton.
    B. the Epicureans.
    C. Comte.
    D. Marx.
    E. Durkheim.

Passage 2

Drifting Rocks

(1). Another one of the devious little mysteries of science are the strange stones of Death Valley in California. These stones sit on sun-baked, flat, cracked earth, but for some baf-fling reason, they have moved across the wasteland. They have, in fact, left trails of their movement.

(2). The home of these mysterious stones is known, logically, as the "Racetrack Playa", a dry lakebed occasionally dampened by flash storms. The Racetrack measures 4.5 kilometers by 2.1 kilometers (2.8 by 1.3 miles), and is only about 5 centimeters (2 inches) higher at one end than the other.

(3). The trails left by the stones vary from a few meters to almost a kilometer in length. Some of the trails are straight; some are zig-zagged; some go in circles. In some cases, the trails vary in width, meaning the stones must have rotated as they moved. One hundred sixty two of the Racetrack's moving stones have been documented, and many of them have names, always female. They range from fist-sized to the size of an ice chest.

(4). In 1948, two US Geological Survey geologists suggested that the little desert whirlwinds known as "dust devils" might be responsible for moving the stones around. Then George Stanley, a geologist of Fresno State College in California, suggested the stones might have become frozen in ice sheets during the winter and slid around with the sheets on an underlying slick of water.

(5). Between 1968 and 1975, two geologists, Robert Sharp of the California Institute of Technology and Dwight Carey of the University of California at Los Angeles, made careful measurements of the positions of 30 rocks in an attempt to answer the mystery of the drifting rocks once and for all. They tried to pound stakes around some of the rocks, on the principle that if the motion were caused by floating ice, the stakes would hold the ice in place. The mystery only seemed to deepen. In one case, a rock drifted out of the stakes while another remained where it was, and in other cases rocks moved near other rocks that remained stationary.

(6). Sharp and Carey never really managed to link the movement of a rock to any event and finally gave up. By this time, research has become somewhat restricted by the fact that the Racetrack is now a protected Wilderness area. The US National Park Service was trying to protect the Racetrack, which was suffering from increasing numbers of intruders who were not always considerate of the special nature of the place. Sometimes park rangers find citizens dancing naked on the dried mud, apparently obtaining inspiration from the place's cosmic energies. Drug runners also occasionally use it as a landing strip, though ranger vigilance has largely eliminated this practice. Rangers had to dig a trench to keep four-wheel drive vehicles out and kept the place tidied up.

(7). Meanwhile, researchers continue to puzzle over the drifting rocks. One early suggestion was that the rocks were driven by gravity, sliding down a gradual slope over a long period of time. But this theory was discounted when it was revealed that the northern end of the playa is actually several centimeters higher than the southern end and that most of the rocks were in fact traveling uphill.

(8). Nonetheless, John B. Reid, Jr. of Hampshire College in Amherst, Massachusetts, is a partisan of the ice floe theory while Paula Messina, assistant professor of geology at San Jose State University in California, thinks they move in the wind over a slick of mud when the Racetrack is wet. Reid does not buy the wind theory, basing his objections on studies performed by him and his students in the late 1980s and early 1990s, when they measured the force required to move some of the Racetrack's bigger rocks and determined that wind speeds of hundreds of kilometers per hour would be required to budge them – though it has been pointed out that Reid's measurements, taken in dry conditions, may not have accurately reflected what would happen when the Racetrack was wet.

(9). Though no one has yet been able to conclusively identify just what makes the rocks move, for the past ten years, Dr. Paula Messina has made it her quest to understand what has bewildered geologists for decades. "It's interesting that no one has seen them move, so I am kind of sleuthing to see what's really going on here," says Dr. Messina.

(10). Many scientists had dedicated much of their careers to the racing rocks, but the remoteness of the area kept their research limited in scope. No one had been able to map the complete set of trails before the advent of a quick, portable method known as global positioning. Dr. Messina was the first to have the luxury of this high technology at her fingertips.

(11). In 1996, armed with a hand-held GPS unit, she digitally mapped the location of each of the 162 rocks scattered over the playa. "I'm very fortunate that this technology was available at about the same time the Racetrack captured my interest," she says. "It took only ten days to map the entire network – a total of about 60 miles." Since then, she has continued to chart the movements of each rock within a centimeter of accuracy. Walking the length of a trail, she collects the longitude and latitude points of each, which snap into a line. She then takes her data back to the lab where she is able to analyze changes in the rocks' positions since her last visit.

(12). She has found that two components are essential to their movement: wind and water. The fierce winter storms that sweep down from the surrounding mountains carry plenty of both. The playa surface is made up of very fine clay sediments that become extremely slick when wet. "When you have pliable, wet, frictionless sediments and intense winds blowing through," offers Dr. Messina, "I think you have the elements to make the rocks move."

(13). At an elevation of 3,700 feet, strong winds can rake the playa at 70 miles per hour. But Dr. Messina is quick to point out that sometimes even smaller gusts can set the rocks in motion. The explanation for this lies in her theory, which links wind and water with yet another element: bacteria.

(14). After periods of rain, bacteria lying dormant on the playa begin to "come to." As they grow, long, hairlike filaments develop and cause a slippery film to form on the surface. "Very rough surfaces would require great forces to move the lightest-weight rocks," she says. "But if the surface is exceptionally smooth, as would be expected from a bio-geologic film, even the heaviest rocks could be propelled by a small shove of the wind. I think of the Racetrack as being coated by Teflon, under those special conditions."

(15). In science, hypotheses are often based on logic. But over the years, Dr. Messina has discovered that on the Racetrack, logic itself must often be tossed to the wind. "Some of the rocks have done some very unusual things," she says. In her initial analysis, she hypothesized that given their weight, larger rocks would travel shorter distances and smaller, lighter rocks would sail on further, producing longer trails. It also seemed reasonable that the heavier, angular rocks would leave straighter trails and rounder rocks would move more erratically.

(16). What she discovered surprised her. "I was crunching numbers and found that there was absolutely no correlation between the size and shape of the rocks and their trails. There was no smoking gun, so this was one of the big mysteries to me." What appears as a very flat, uniform terrain is in fact a mosaic of microclimates. In the southeastern part of the playa, wind is channeled through a low pass in the mountains, forming a natural wind tunnel. This is where the longest, straightest trails are concentrated. In the central part of the playa, two natural wind tunnels converge from different directions, creating turbulence. It is in this area that the rock trails are the most convoluted. "What I think is happening," proposes Dr. Messina, "is that the surrounding topography is actually what is guiding the rocks and telling them where to go."

(17). Some people have suggested attaching radio transmitters to the rocks or erecting cameras to catch them "in the act" in order to put an end to the speculation. But as Death Valley National Park is 95 percent designated wilderness, all research in the park must be noninvasive. It is forbidden to erect any permanent structures or instrumentation. Further, no one is permitted on the playa when it is wet because each footprint would leave an indelible scar.

(18). As for Dr. Messina, she is content in the sleuthing. "People frequently ask me if I want to see the rocks in action and I can honestly answer that I do not," she says. "Science is all about the quest for knowledge, and not necessarily knowing all the answers. Part of the lure of this place is its mystery. It's fine with me if it remains that way."

- Adapted from "Drifting Rocks" (http://www.vectorsite.net/tamyst.html) Thanks to Greg Goebel.

18. The Racetrack Playa has an elevation of:

A.   5 centimeters.
B.   60 miles.
C.   10000 meters.
D.   3,700 feet.
E.   31,00 feet.

19. John B. Reid, Jr. believed in the same theory that George Stanley suggested in the late 1940s.

Robert Sharp and Dwight Carey disproved that the movement of the rocks was caused by floating ice.

A.   Both statements are true.
B.   Both statements are false.
C.   The first sentence is true while the second sentence is false.
D.   The first sentence is false while the second sentence is true.

20. In Messina's final hypothesis, she attributed the explanation behind the drifting rocks to be caused by:

A.   bacteria-based slippery clay.
B.   wind tunnels.
C.   the terrain's topography.
D.   ice floe.
E.   mysterious forces.

21. The approximate sizes of the rocks have been described to range:

    A. from a few centimeters to 200 centimeters.

    B. from fist-sized to the size of an ice chest.

    C. from 100 centimeters up to a meter in size.

    D. from 200 centimeters up to 500 centimeters.

    E. The passage does not contain any description of size besides varied.

22. Suppose that Reid and his students were able to conduct their measurements in wet conditions with successful results. This would undermine another assertion made in the passage that:

    A. floating ice causes the movements of the rocks.

    B. the "dust devils" are causing the rocks to move.

    C. the stones, frozen in ice sheets during the winter, slide around with the sheets on an underlying slick of water.

    D. the wind is responsible for moving the stones over a slick of mud whenever the Racetrack is wet.

23. Winter storm winds come into the playa of up to:

    A. 80 mph gusts.

    B. 70 mph gusts.

    C. 90 mph gusts.

    D. 60 mph gusts.

    E. This information is not within the passage.

24. Dr. Messina's GPS unit has an x and y co-ordinate accuracy of:

    A. one centimeter.

    B. ten centimeters.

    C. five centimeters.

    D. twenty centimeters.

    E. This information is not contained in the passage.

25. How many drifting rocks are there in total?

    A. 126

    B. 30

    C. 162

    D. 261

    E. 612

26. The theory that the rocks were sliding down a gradual slope over a long period of time was proven to be true when it was revealed that wind speeds of hundreds of kilometers per hour would be required to budge them.

    A. Both the statement and reason are correct and related.

    B. Both the statement and the reason are correct but NOT related.

    C. The statement is correct but the reason is NOT.

    D. The statement is NOT correct, but the reason is correct.

    E. NEITHER the statement NOR the reason is correct.

27. Many of the moving stones in the Racetrack Playa have names which are:

    A. mythological.
    B. scientific.
    C. Native American.
    D. female.
    E. male.

28. Which of the following is the BEST reason that makes Dr. Messina's theory relatively strong?

    A. Limited variables
    B. Multiple causes
    C. Use of GPS
    D. Singular effects
    E. More accurate measurements

29. Reid's main contention with Messina concerning the drifting rocks concerns:

    A. ice.
    B. mud.
    C. direction.
    D. wind speed.
    E. trails.

30. Attaching radio transmitters to the rocks is not permitted on the Racetrack because rain or snow would negate any data collected from radios.

    A. Both the statement and reason are correct and related.

    B. Both the statement and the reason are correct but NOT related.

    C. The statement is correct but the reason is NOT.

    D. The statement is NOT correct, but the reason is correct.

    E. NEITHER the statement NOR the reason is correct.

31. Which of the following statements concerning Sharp and Carey is NOT true? Which is the EXCEPTION?

    A. They made careful measurements of 30 rocks on the Playa.

    B. They used stakes to try to hold the rocks in place.

    C. Both had insignificant and contradictory results.

    D. Both are part of the US Geological Survey.

    E. Both gave up in their research.

32. What Messina found from her GPS analysis was that:

    A. wind tunnels of variable strength move the rocks around the slippery mud in a random pattern.

    B. a combination of mud, slipperiness, wind, wet clay and bacteria account for the random distributions.

    C. there was absolutely no correlation between the size and shape of the rocks and their trails.

    D. the icefloe and dust devil theories could be ruled out based on trail positioning.

    E. all prior theories lack the necessary GPS and computer analysis, therefore theoretically dubious.

33. Each of the following describes the rock trails EXCEPT one. Which one is the EXCEPTION?

    A. Straight

    B. Back and forth

    C. Circling

    D. Zigzagged

    E. Varying in width

Passage 3

Forensic Dentistry

(1). Bite marks are an important and sometimes controversial aspect of forensic odontology. Forensic odontology is the study of dental applications in legal proceedings. The subject covers a wide variety of topics including individual identification, mass identification, and bite mark analysis. The study of odontology in a legal case can be a piece of incriminating evidence or an aspect of wide controversy. There have been many cases throughout history, which have made use of bite marks as evidence.

(2). Bite marks are usually seen in cases involving sexual assault, murder, and child abuse and can be a major factor in leading to a conviction. Biting is often a sign of the perpetrator seeking to degrade the victim while also achieving complete domination. Bite marks can be found anywhere on a body, particularly on soft, fleshy tissue such as the stomach or buttocks. In addition, bite marks can be found on objects present at the scene of a crime. Bite marks are commonly found on a suspect when a victim attempts to defend him or herself.

(3). Even though using bite mark evidence began around 1870, the first published account involving a conviction based on bite marks as evidence was in the case of Doyle v. State, which occurred in Texas in 1954. The bite mark in this case was on a piece of cheese found at the crime scene of a burglary. The defendant was later asked to bite another piece of cheese for comparison. A firearms examiner and a dentist evaluated the bite marks independently and both concluded that the marks were made by the same set of teeth. The conviction in this case set the stage for bite marks found on objects and skin to be used as evidence in future cases.

(4). Another landmark case was People v. Marx, which occurred in California in 1975. A woman was murdered by strangulation after being sexually assaulted. She was bitten several times on her nose. Walter Marx was identified as a suspect and dental impressions were made of his teeth. Impressions and photographs were also taken of the woman's injured nose. These samples along with other models and casts were evaluated using a variety of techniques, including two-dimensional and three-dimensional comparisons, and acetate overlays. Three experts testified that the bite marks on the woman's nose were indeed made by Marx, and he was convicted of voluntary manslaughter.

(5). Although there are many cases in which bite mark evidence has been critical to the conviction or exoneration of criminal defendants, there is continuing dispute over its interpretation and analysis.

(6). Factors that may affect the accuracy of bite mark identification include time-dependent changes of the bite mark on living bodies, effects of where the bite mark was found, damage on soft tissue, and similarities in dentition among individuals. Other factors include poor photography, impressions, or measurement of dentition characteristics.

(7). For bites on human skin, a potential bite injury must be recognized early, as the clarity and shape of the mark may change in a relatively short time in both living and dead victims. Bite marks most often appear as elliptical or round areas of contusion or abrasion, occasionally with associated indentations.

(8). Once the mark is initially evaluated, it should be examined by a forensic odontologist to determine if the dimensions and configuration are within human ranges. Since a large proportion of individuals (80-90%) secrete the ABO blood groups in their saliva, swabbing the area and a control area elsewhere on the body should be completed before the body is washed. Although there have been descriptions of using fingerprint dusting methods, photography is the primary means of recording and preserving the bite mark and is critically important in documenting the evidence. When there are indentations in the skin, or to preserve the three-dimensional nature of the bitten area, impressions should be taken to fabricate stone models. This is done by fabricating custom impression trays and taking an impression of the mark and surrounding skin with standard dental impression material. These impressions are then poured in dental stone to produce models. After the initial analysis is complete, there may be a need to preserve the actual skin bearing the mark. A ring of custom tray material can be made to fit like a hoop, closely approximating the skin, which can then be attached to the skin with cyanoacrylate adhesive and stabilized with sutures. When the pathologist completes the autopsy, the bite mark can be excised with the supporting framework in place.

(9). Studies have also been performed in an attempt to find the simplest, most efficient, and most reliable way of analyzing bite marks. Most bite mark analysis studies use porcine skin (pigskin), because it is comparable to the skin of a human, and it is considered unethical to bite a human for study in the United States. Limitations to the bite mark studies include differences in properties of pigskin compared to human skin and the technique of using simulated pressures to create bite marks. Although similar histologically, pigskin and human skin behave in dynamically different ways due to differences in elasticity. Furthermore, postmortem bites on nonhuman skin, such as those used in the experiments of Martin-de-las-Heras et al., display different patterns to those seen in antemortem bite injuries. In recognition of the limitations of their study, Kouble and Craig suggest using a G-clamp on an articulator in future studies to standardize the amount

of pressure used to produce experimental bite marks instead of applying manual pressure to models on pigskin. Future research and technological developments may help reduce the occurrence of such limitations.

(10). Kouble and Craig compared direct methods and indirect methods of bite mark analysis. In the past, the direct method compared a model of the suspect's teeth to a life-size photograph of the actual bite mark. In these experiments, direct comparisons were made between dental models and either photographs or "fingerprint powder lift-models." The "fingerprint powder lift" technique involves dusting the bitten skin with black fingerprint powder and using fingerprint tape to transfer the bite marks onto a sheet of acetate. Indirect methods involve the use of transparent overlays to record a suspect's biting edges. Transparent overlays are made by free-hand tracing the occlusal surfaces of a dental model onto an acetate sheet. When comparing the "fingerprint powder lift" technique against the photographs, the use of photographs resulted in higher scores determined by a modified version of the ABFO scoring guidelines. The use of transparent overlays is considered subjective and irreproducible because the tracing can be easily manipulated. On the other hand, photocopier-generated overlays where no tracing is used is considered to be the best method in matching the correct bite mark to the correct set of models without the use of computer imaging.

(11). While the photocopier-generated technique is sensitive, reliable, and inexpensive, new methods involving digital overlays have proven to be more accurate. Two recent technological developments include the 2D polyline method and the painting method. Both methods use Adobe Photoshop. Use of the 2D polyline method entails drawing straight lines between two fixed points in the arch and between incisal edges to indicate the tooth width. Use of the painting method entails coating the incisal edges of a dental model with red glossy paint and then photographing the model. Adobe Photoshop is then used to make measurements on the image. A total of 13 variables were used in analysis. Identification for both methods were based on canine-to-canine distance (1 variable), incisor width (4 variables), and rotational angles of the incisors (8 variables). The 2D polyline method relies heavily on accurate measurements, while the painting method depends on precise overlaying of the images. Although both methods were reliable, the 2D polyline method gave efficient and more objective results.

(12). Nevertheless, bite mark analysis is not without its critics. Recently, the scientific foundation of forensic odontology, and especially bite mark comparison, has been called into question. A 1999 study, frequently referenced in news stories but difficult to actually locate, by a member of the American Board of Forensic Odontology found a 63 percent rate of false identifications. However, the study was based on an informal workshop during an ABFO meeting, which many members did not consider a valid scientific setting.

(13). An investigative series by the Chicago Tribune entitled "Forensics under the Microscope" examined many forensic science disciplines to see if they truly deserve the air of infallibility that has come to surround them. The investigators concluded that bite mark comparison is always subjective and no standards for comparison have been accepted across the field. The journalists discovered that no rigorous experimentation has been conducted to determine error rates for bite mark comparison, a key part of the scientific method. Critics of bite mark comparison cite the case of Ray Krone, an Arizona man convicted of murder on bite mark evidence left on a woman's breast. DNA evidence later implicated another man and Krone was released from prison. Similarly, Roy Brown was convicted of murder due in part to bite mark evidence, and freed after DNA testing of the saliva left in the bite wounds matched someone else.

- Portions of this passage are adapted from "Experimental Studies of Forensic Odontology to Aid in the Identification Process" by Susmita Saxena, Preeti Sharma, and Nitin Gupta. *Journal of Forensic Dental Sciences*, 2010 Jul-Dec; 2(2): 69–76.

34. Recent investigation into bite mark analysis shows that this procedure suffers from:

    A.   a shortage of methods to actually quantify the identification of a person's teeth.

    B.   a lack of rigorous experimentation to determine error rates.

    C.   failure to follow the scientific method at a paradigmatic level.

    D.   a lack of willing research associates, concerned with such analysis.

    E.   a shortage of replication studies, to help confirm analysis results.

35. A 1999 study claims a bite mark false identification rate of:

    A.   36%.
    B.   33%.
    C.   63%.
    D.   66%.
    E.   The passage does not indicate this information.

36. Which of the following is NOT a factor that may affect the accuracy of bite mark identification? Which is the EXCEPTION?

    A.   Time-dependent changes of the bite mark on living bodies

    B.   Effects of where the bite mark was found

    C.   Damage on soft tissue

    D.   Jaw alignment ratios in proportion to dental symmetry

    E.   Poor photography, impressions, or measurement of dentition characteristics

37. Which of the following sentences would be the best conclusion for the closing paragraph?

   A. When reporting on bite mark evidence, dentists should be transparent about the inherent obstacles to accurate analysis.

   B. Despite issues on the accu-racy of bite mark analysis proce-dures, several legal precedents allow for the admissibility of such evidence.

   C. Indeed, an opinion is worth no-thing unless the evidence is clear-ly describable and accurate when presented in court.

   D. After all, bite mark analysis has almost non-existent valid rules, regulations, or processes for accreditation to standardize the evidence they provide in court.

   E. Despite dentistry being a scien-tific field, forensic odontology remains a subjective science prone to errors.

38. Of the 2D polyline method of identi-fication, which of the following set of variables used in analysis is correct?

   A. Canine-to-canine distance (2 variables), incisor width (3 variables), and rotational angles of the incisors (8 variables)

   B. Canine-to-canine distance (1 variable), incisor width (4 variables), and rotational angles of the incisors (8 variables)

   C. Canine-to-canine distance (1 variable), incisor width (8 variables), and rotational angles of the incisors (4 variables)

   D. Canine-to-canine distance (4 variables), incisor width (1 variable), and rotational angles of the incisors (8 variables)

   E. Canine-to-canine distance (8 variables), incisor width (1 variable), and rotational angles of the incisors (4 variables)

39. A direct method of identification would be the "fingerprint powder lift" technique.

An indirect method of identification would be the use of transparent overlays.

   A. Both statements are true.
   B. Both statements are false.
   C. The first statement is true.
       The second statement is false.
   D. The first statement is false.
       The second statement is true.

40. Which of the following methods do Kouble and Craig suggest to address the problems posed with the use of pigskin in bite mark analysis?

    A. Experimenting with other animal forms such as cows or horses to determine error rates

    B. Using a G-clamp manipulator to increase the standard intensity of pressure used

    C. Using a comparison of both direct and indirect methods in relation to pressure used

    D. Using a G-clamp on an articulator to standardize the amount of pressure used

    E. Keeping the pigskin at the same temperature as the victim kept in the forensic lab

41. Forensic odontology was first publicly recognized in:

    A. 1780.
    B. 1954.
    C. 1975.
    D. 1945.
    E. 1870.

42. Which legal proceedings context concerning bite mark identification is NOT mentioned in the passage? Which is the EXCEPTION?

    A. Manslaughter
    B. Kidnapping
    C. Child Abuse
    D. Sexual Abuse
    E. Burglary

43. Suppose an investigator is skeptical over the bite mark evidence presented against a murder suspect. How would a forensic odontoligst BEST convince the investigator that the procedure performed is reliable?

    A. Bite marks found on the victim's body were deep, indicating that the act was deliberate and premeditated.

    B. A second set of dental impressions was obtained from the suspect himself.

    C. The autopsy was performed 24 hours after the crime was committed.

    D. The marked area was swabbed for traces of saliva and submitted for DNA testing.

    E. Photocopier-generated overlays were employed to match the murderer's correct bite mark.

44. Which of the following persons was convicted of burglary based on bite mark evidence left on a piece of cheese?

    A. Marx
    B. Krone
    C. Doyle
    D. Brown
    E. Martin-de-las-Heras

45. The use of transparent overlays is considered subjective and irreproducible because there are differences between pigskin and human skin.

    A. Both the statement and reason are correct and related.
    B. Both the statement and the reason are correct but NOT related.
    C. The statement is correct but the reason is NOT.
    D. The statement is NOT correct, but the reason is correct.
    E. NEITHER the statement NOR the reason is correct.

46. What is The BEST method for bite mark analysis to date?

    A. Transparent overlays
    B. Photography
    C. Fingerprint dusting
    D. 2D polyline method
    E. Painting method

47. The 2D polyline method employs Adobe Photoshop in bite mark analysis identification.

The painting method uses AUTOCAD in bite mark analysis identification.

    A. The first statement is true, while the second statement is false.
    B. The first statement is false, while the second statement is true.
    C. Both statements are true.
    D. Both statements are false.
    E. There is not enough information within the passage to make a judgment.

48. ABFO stands for:

    A. American Board of Forensic Odontologists.
    B. American Board of Forensic Odontology.
    C. Associated Board for Forensic Odontology.
    D. Associated Board of Forensic Odontologists.
    E. American Board for Forensic Odontology.

49. Which of the following bite mark analysis techniques were NOT used in the case of the People vs. Marx? Which is the EXCEPTION?

    A. Acetate overlays
    B. Two dimensional comparisons
    C. The "fingerprint lift method"
    D. Three dimensional comparisons
    E. Other models and casts

50. The experiments of Martin-de-las-Heras et al., found that:

    A. the use of G-Clamp on an articulator standardized the amount of pressure in bite mark analysis.
    B. postmortem bites on nonhuman skin displayed the same patterns as antemortem bites.
    C. transparent overlays and tracing could easily be sketched in error.
    D. postmortem bites on nonhuman skin displayed different patterns from antemortem bites.
    E. the 2D polyline method without tracing is the most efficient method to date.

Practice Test 1 Answer Key

1. D	18. D	35. C
2. A	19. C	36. D
3. E	20. C	37. B
4. A	21. B	38. B
5. C	22. B	39. A
6. C	23. B	40. D
7. A	24. A	41. B
8. B	25. C	42. B
9. A	26. E	43. D
10. B	27. D	44. C
11. D	28. B	45. B
12. B	29. D	46. D
13. C	30. C	47. A
14. C	31. D	48. B
15. A	32. C	49. C
16. C	33. B	50. D
17. D	34. B	

Practice Test 1 Explanations and Strategies

1. Answer: D
    Question Type: *Exception/Negative Question;
    Evaluation Question (Main Idea)*
    Strategies: *SI, PoE; P6*

    This question requires a careful inference of
    the basic premises of an author's view. By
    using the process of elimination, the correct
    statements can be inferred and are mentioned
    in Paragraph 6. D, being the exception, is the

    correct answer, which is supported by the
    phrase "which every fact is either so or not so"
    in Sentence 2 of Paragraph 6.

2. Answer: A
    Question Type: *Evaluation Question (Impli-
    cation)*
    Strategies: *SI, paraphrasing, never lose sight
    of the question; P3 S1*

This is another inference question that requires you to carefully understand the essence of a theoretical concept. All options are mentioned in the passage at one point or another. Thus you need to remain focused on what the question is truly asking, which can be found in the first sentence of Paragraph 3: "The principle of 'methodological individualism,' which holds that social scientists should seek to understand collectivities (such as nations, cultures, governments, churches, corporations, etc.) solely as the result and the context of the actions of individual persons. . ."

3.   Answer: E
     Question Type: *Exception/Negative Question*
     Strategy: *SaL; P5 S2*

4.   Answer: A
     Question Type: *Evaluation Question (Main Idea)*
     Strategies: *SI, inference; P8*

Although D is close and a direct quote in the passage, it is the preceding quote in that penultimate paragraph which provides the best answer (A) stating, "The scientist looks for order in the appearances of nature by exploring such likenesses. For order does not display itself of itself, if it can be said to be there at all, it is not there for the mere looking. There is no way of pointing a finger or camera at it; order must be discovered and, in a deep sense, it must be created". We cannot just infer D and leave it at that, but infer that the answer to this disorder is through discovery and creation of order, from the jumble of appearance. The fable is supposed to illustrate this preceding

idea.

The other answers are also partially correct but lack the overall explanatory power of A.

5.   Answer: C
     Question Type: *Recall*
     Strategy: *SaL; P4 S1*

6.   Answer: C
     Question Type: *Exception/Negative Question*
     Strategies: *SaL, inference; P7, P8*

A, B and D are ideas advanced by Bronowski as can be found in the following, respectively: P8 S1, P7 S1, and P8 S2. He never mentions theory-building through testing and observation, even though one could infer that this method underlies "science."

7.   Answer: A
     Question Type: *True or False Statements*
     Strategy: *SaL; P2 S2 of quoted paragraph; P3 S2*

8.   Answer: B
     Question Type: *Evaluation (Implication)*
     Strategies: *SI, inference, prior knowledge; P7 S10*

The answer to this question can be tricky unless you are familiar with the subject from prior knowledge. This is because Yukawa's discovery is presented in the passage in narrative form rather than as a straightforward description. Hence you need to be careful in reading the paragraph where this is discussed (P7) in order to infer the correct answer.

"Yukawa, without a blush, calculated the mass of the pellet he expected to see, and waited. He was right; his meson was found, and a range of other mesons, neither the existence nor the nature of which had been suspected before."
The other statements are corollaries, hypotheses, or distractions.

9. Answer: A
    Question Type: *True or False Statements (Statement and Reason)*
    Strategy: *SI; P2 quoted paragraph*

    The answer is supported by Weber's own quote:

    "There is no absolutely 'objective' scientific analysis of culture... All knowledge of cultural reality... is always knowledge from particular points of view."

    Here, "particular points of view" expresses "perspective."

10. Answer: B
    Question Type: *Evaluation Question (Main idea)*
    Strategies: *SI, inference; P2 last sentence and quoted paragraph*

    This question requires a keen understanding of the gist of Weber's view on objectivity in the social sciences. This can be best inferred in Paragraph 2 as follows:

    "Overall, Weber supported the goal of objective science, but he noted that it is an unreachable goal – although one definitely worth striving for. . . An 'objective' analysis of cultural events,

which proceeds according to the thesis that the ideal of science is the reduction of empirical reality to 'laws,' is meaningless. . . [because]. . . the knowledge of social laws is not knowledge of social reality but is rather one of the various aids used by our minds for attaining this end."

11. Answer: D
    Question Type: *Recall*
    Strategy: *SI; P3 S2*

    "In other words, Weber argued that social phenomena can be understood scientifically only to the extent that they are captured by models of the behavior of purposeful individuals, models which Weber called 'ideal types.'"

12. Answer: B
    Question Type: *Evaluation Question (Main Idea)*
    Strategies: *SI, inference; P4 S1*

    This question requires you to deduce the meaning of the term in question in its paraphrased form. A, C, and D are partially correct, but only to the extent that they can be included in B, meaning any debate about methodology used in a given discipline or science, is one that sets up standards for the proper theoretical approach – or how to proceed theoretically, in adopting a methodology for the study.

13. Answer: C
    Question type: *Recall*
    Strategy: *SI; P1 and P2*

    C is the opposite of the idea expressed in Sentence 1 of Paragraph 1. The rest are either verbatim or can be inferred from Paragraphs 1 and 2.

14. Answer: C
    Question Type: *Application Question*
    Strategies: *SI, inference; P4 S3*

    The answer to this question cannot be found in an exact statement in the passage. However, you are required to use the information provided in the passage as basis for evaluating the given options.

    Paragraph 4 of the passage makes clear that Weber is more concerned in studying the motivating factors of individual actions, rather than in determining the effect of such actions: "Weber's methodology emphasizes the use of comparative historical analysis. Therefore, Weber was more interested in explaining how a certain outcome was the result of various historical processes rather than predicting an outcome of those processes in the future."
    Option C obviously complements Weber's methodology.

15. Answer: A
    Question Type: *Recall*
    Strategy: *SaL; P8 S3*

16. Answer: C
    Question Type: *Recall*
    Strategy: *SaL; P3 S1 and quoted paragraph*

17. Answer: D
    Question Type: *Recall*
    Strategy: *SaL; P1 last sentence*

18. Answer: D
    Question Type: *Recall*
    Strategy: *SaL; P13 S1*

19. Answer: C
    Question Type: *True or False Statements (Two Statements)*
    Strategies: *SI, attention to details; P4 S2*

    The statements given in this question are paraphrased from different parts of the passage. This requires locating the relevant paragraphs and then inferring the main ideas.

    The first statement is derived from information contained in Paragraph 4 Sentence 2 and Paragraph 8 Sentence 1. Essentially, both George Stanley in the late 1940s and John B. Reid, Jr. in the 80s and 90s attributed the movement of the rocks to the floating ice sheets.

    The second statement is derived from the last two sentences of Paragraph 5 and Sentence 1 of Paragraph 6. Although Sharp and Carey were not able to prove anything, nothing was also conclusive in the measurements they conducted.

20. Answer: C
    Question Type: *Recall*
    Strategy: *SaL; P16 S1*

21. Answer: B
    Question Type: *Recall*
    Strategy: *SaL; P3 last sentence*

22. Answer: B
    Question Type: *Application Question*
    Strategies: *OA, inference; P8 S2, P13 S1*

    This question requires that you infer the implications behind the theories brought forward in the passage.

    In Paragraph 8, although Reid was able to discount the factor of the wind in the rocks' movements, results of his study were only based on dry conditions. This still leaves the possibility of the wind being a factor in the drifting rocks phenomenon during the wet weather.

    On the other hand, had Reid's findings been proven consistent on wet conditions, this might even give more credit to the floating ice theory as the wind would be eliminated as a contributing factor in the rocks' movements in ANY condition. This eliminates option A.

    B cannot be the best answer because "dust devils" only occur on dry conditions. Results derived from dry conditions are already enough to discount the "dust devils" as the driving force behind the drifting rocks.

C is also wrong. The statement in this option has nothing to do with the contention about the wind as a factor in the rocks' movements.

This leaves D as the most possible answer. According to Reid's study, "wind speeds of hundreds of kilometers per hour would be required to budge (the rocks)." In Paragraph 13, strong winds are measured to yield a force of only 70 miles per hour.

23. Answer: B
    Question Type: *Recall*
    Strategy: *SaL; P13 S1*

24. Answer: A
    Question Type: *Recall*
    Strategy: *SI; P11 S4*

25. Answer: C
    Question Type:*Recall*
    Strategy: *SaL; P3 S3*

26. Answer: E
    Question Type: *True or False Statements (Statement and Reason)*
    Strategies: *SaL, inference; P7 S2 and S3, P8 S2*

    The information given in this question is almost verbatim of certain parts in the passage. What is tricky here is that the first statement is obviously wrong. Paragraph 7 indeed explains that the theory of the rocks sliding down a gradual slope due to gravity was discounted when it was discovered that the rocks were in fact traveling uphill. On the other hand, the second statement is true as indicated in

Paragraph 8. However, Reid's conclusion about the wind speeds has more to do with the wind and the "dust devil" theories and does not have a direct link to the rock's sliding movement. Hence, this bit of information is still an incorrect reason in relation to the gravity theory. This makes (E) neither the statement NOR the reason correct.

27. Answer: D
Question Type: *Recall*
Strategy: *SaL; P3 S3*

28. Answer: B
Question Type: *Evaluation Question (Implication)*
Strategies: *OA, inference; P6 S1, P8, P10 to P16*

It must be noted that the other researchers who conducted measurements in the Playa either failed to prove anything or focused on only one possible cause of the rocks' movements.

Sharp and Carey never really managed to link the movement of a rock to any event and finally gave up.

John Reid was able to disprove the wind theory but ironically did not come up with a proof to support the ice floe theory.

On the other hand, Messina conducted several observations for a span of ten years to trace the cause behind the "drifting rocks" mystery. Rightfully so for a subject as complex and variable as the rocks in the Playa, Dr. Messina came up with a number of plausible explanations as denoted in Paragraphs 12, 13, and 16.

29. Answer: D
Question Type: *Recall*
Strategy: *SaL; P8 S1*

30. Answer: C
Question Type: *True or False Statement (Statement and Reason)*
Strategy: *SaL; P17*

31. Answer: D
Question Type: *Exception/Negative Question*
Strategy: *SaL; P4 S1, P5, P6 S1*

Option A is supported by Sentence 1 of Paragraph 5, Option B by Sentence 2, and Option C by the last two sentences. Option E is also supported by Sentence 1 of Paragraph 6. On the other hand, the two geologists from US Geological Survey were never named in Sentence 1 of Paragraph 4 while Sharp and Carey were clearly identified with California Institute of Technology and University of California at Los Angeles, respectively.

32. Answer: C
Question Type: *Recall*
Strategy: *SaL; P16 S1*

33. Answer: B
Question Type: *Recall*
Strategy: *SaL; P3 S2 S3*

34. Answer: B
Question Type: *Recall*
Strategies: *SI, attention to details; P13 S3*

35. Answer: C
    Question Type: *Recall*
    Strategy: *SaL; P12 S3*

36. Answer: D
    Question Type: *Exception/Negative Question*
    Strategy: *SaL; P6*

    "Jaw alignment ratios in proportion to dental symmetry" does not constitute "similarities in dentition among individuals."

37. Answer: B
    Question Type: *Evaluation Question (Main Idea)*
    Strategy: *OA; P1, P3, P4, P10, P11, P12*

    This question requires your overall understanding of the passage's main message. By looking at significant clues in the different paragraphs, you will realize that the main purpose of the author is to illustrate that despite the various contentions on the methods used in bite mark analysis, they all boil down to the fact that the evidence they bring about is after all, admissible in court.

    This is clearly conveyed from the beginning of the passage (P1 last two sentences): "The study of odontology in a legal case can be a piece of incriminating evidence or an aspect of wide controversy. There have been many cases throughout history, which have made use of bite marks as evidence." The last sentence of Paragraph 3 further supports this view stating, "The conviction in this case set the stage for bite marks found on objects and skin to be used as evidence in future cases."

While the statement in A sounds ideal, no specific part in the passage indicates the author advocating this view.

C is obviously off on a tangent.

Option D is countered by Paragraph 10 Sentence 7 in defense of standardization of the bite marks analysis procedure: "the use of photographs resulted in higher scores determined by a modified version of the ABFO scoring gui-delines."

Option E can likewise be contended by the fact that the passage presented scientific methods used in bite mark evidence and oppositions were made mostly by journalists (non-scientific). The 1999 study cited in Sentence 3 of Paragraph 12 also casts doubt to the real persona (and hence credibility) of the member of the American Board of Forensic Odontology who was "frequently referenced in news stories but difficult to actually locate."

38. Answer: B
    Question Type: *Recall*
    Strategy: *SaL; P11 S7*

39. Answer: A
    Question Type: *Recall*
    Strategy: *SaL; P10 S3, S5*

40. Answer: D
    Question Type: *Recall*
    Strategies: *SaL, attention to details; P9 S6*

41. Answer: B
    Question Type: *Recall*
    Strategies: *SaL, never lose sight of the question;*
    P3 S1

    This question can be tricky, and you have to be careful in identifying that what is being asked is the date when forensic odontology (dental applications in legal proceedings) was first publicly recognized. This could have only been possible with the publication of the case of Doyle v. State in 1954.

42. Answer: B
    Question Type: *Recall*
    Strategies: *SaL, attention to details; P2 S1, P3 S2, P4 last sentence*

43. Answer: D
    Question Type: *Application Question*
    Strategies: *SI or OA, attention to details; P8 S2, P13*

    This question can be easily answered if you have been paying close attention to the information presented in the last paragraph of the passage. It should be noted that the significant evidence that reversed the court's sentences to Krone and Brown was DNA testing. Swabbing of the saliva specimen, which is essential in DNA testing, in bite mark analysis procedure is further supported by Sentence 2 of Paragraph 8.

    Option A is quite subjective and therefore, not convincing. Option B is a plausible method to confirm a dental match of a suspect; so is E. However, a DNA match still qualifies

as stronger evidence. C describes one of the factors affecting the accuracy of bite mark analysis. The best answer is D.

44. Answer: C
    Question Type: *Recall*
    Strategy: *SaL; P3*

45. Answer: B
    Question Type: *True or False Statements (Statement and Reason)*
    Strategies: *SI, inference; P9 S4, P10 S8*

    A quick review of Paragraphs 9 and 10 would prove that both the statement and reason in this question convey correct information. However, the reason for the use of transparent overlays being subjective and irreproducible is because the tracing can be easily manipulated. Thus, the reason given in the question is not related.

46. Answer: D
    Question Type: *Recall*
    Strategies: *SaL, PoE, attention to details; P11 last sentence*

    Reviewing the last sentence of Paragraph 11 would help eliminate option E. Sentence 8 of Paragraph 10 likewise negates option A as the correct answer. Sentence 3 Paragraph 8 indicates (C) Fingerprint dusting as merely one of the methods and (B) photography as the primary means - not the best method - of recording and preserving bite marks. This leaves D as the best answer.

47. Answer: A
    Question Type: *True or False Statements (Two Statements)*
    Strategy: *SaL; P11 S3*

48. Answer: B
    Question Type: *Recall*
    Strategies: *SaL, attention to details; P12 S3*

49. Answer: C
    Question Type: *Recall*
    Strategies: *SaL, attention to details; P4*

50. Answer: D
    Question Type: *Recall*
    Strategies: *SI, inference; P9 S5*

Would you like to discuss any of the answers or strategies in this test? Go to www.dat-prep.com/forum to share and learn.